"Kim Henry takes us on a journey through the fruit of the Spirit. Pack your bags, let your heart be lifted, and join her as she leads the way. God is smiling down on each traveler."

—Debbie Macomber

#1 *New York Times* best-selling author

"You'll love this engaging devotional."

—Jerry Jenkins

21-time *New York Times* best-selling author

"Kim Henry's encouraging daily guide paints a beautiful roadmap for a Spirit-led life blessed with spiritual hope, practical helps, and Christlike character that will inspire our hearts, give us joy, and make God smile."

—Patricia Raybon

Award-winning author of
The One Year® God's Great Blessings Devotional

"Kim Henry inspires and teaches without lecturing or preaching. Her devotions are conversational, uplifting, and reader-friendly. Open this book and enjoy moments of inspiration and wisdom."

—Dr. Dennis E. Hensley

Author of *Jesus in All Four Seasons*

"In bite-sized lessons, Kim Henry shows us how to live fruitful lives that make God smile."

—Debbie W. Wilson

Author of *Little Women, Big God*

Making
GOD
Smile

Living the Fruit of the Spirit
One Day at a Time

Kim Taylor Henry

WORTHY®
Inspired

Making God Smile
Copyright © 2018 by Kim Henry

Published by Worthy Inspired, an imprint of Worthy Publishing Group, a division
of Worthy Media, Inc., One Franklin Park, 6100 Tower Circle, Suite 210,
Franklin, TN 37067.

WORTHY is a registered trademark of Worthy Media, Inc.

HELPING PEOPLE EXPERIENCE THE HEART OF GOD

eBook available wherever digital books are sold.

Cataloging-in-Publication Data is on file with the Library of Congress.

Unless otherwise noted, Scripture quotations are taken from the *Holy Bible,* New Living
Translation, Copyright © 1996, 2004, 2007. Used by permission of Tyndale House Publishers,
Inc., Wheaton, Illinois 60189. All rights reserved. | Scripture quotations marked AMP are
taken from the Amplified® Bible, Copyright © 1954, 1958, 1962, 1964, 1965, 1987 by
The Lockman Foundation. Used by permission. (www.Lockman.org). | Scripture quotations
marked CEV are from the Contemporary English Version Copyright © 1991, 1992, 1995 by
American Bible Society, Used by Permission. | Scripture quotations marked KJV are taken from
the King James Version of the Bible. Public domain. | Scripture quotations marked NIV84 are
from the Holy Bible, *New International Version®, NIV®.* Copyright © 1973, 1978, 1984 by
Biblica, Inc.™ Used by permission of Zondervan. All rights reserved worldwide. | Scripture
quotations marked MSG are taken from *THE MESSAGE,* copyright © 1993, 1994, 1995,
1996, 2000, 2001, 2002 by Eugene H. Peterson. Used by permission of NavPress. All rights
reserved. Represented by Tyndale House Publishers, Inc. | Scripture quotations marked TLB
are taken from The Living Bible copyright © 1971 by Tyndale House Foundation. Used by
permission of Tyndale House Publishers Inc., Carol Stream, Illinois 60188. All rights reserved.
The Living Bible, TLB, and The Living Bible logo are registered trademarks of Tyndale House
Publishers. | Scripture quotations marked GNT are from the Good News Translation in Today's
English Version—Second Edition Copyright © 1992 by American Bible Society. Used by
Permission.

Unless otherwise noted, biblical terms defined according to W. E. Vine, *Vine's Expository
Dictionary* (Nashville, TN: Thomas Nelson, 1997).

For foreign and subsidiary rights, contact rights@worthypublishing.com

ISBN: 978-1-68397-263-1

Cover Design by Jeff Jansen | AestheticSoup.net
Page Layout by Bart Dawson

Printed in the United States of America
18 19 20 21 22 LBM 8 7 6 5 4 3 2 1

CONTENTS

CAN I REALLY MAKE GOD SMILE?

*I chose you and appointed you so that you might go
and bear fruit—fruit that will last.*

John 15:16 niv84

My fifteen-month-old granddaughter sat on the floor and picked up her sock. "Can you put it on?" her mother asked. Maddie attempted to stretch the material over her foot. She tugged to no avail, then switched feet.

"You're doing such a good job!" her mother said, even though the sock's opening still wasn't welcoming Maddie's toes. Maddie picked up her shoe, fiddled with its laces, and struggled unsuccessfully to put it on. Then she tried again.

"You're doing great," her father said.

My granddaughter never did get her socks or shoes on that day, but her parents smiled as they watched, because although Maddie didn't achieve her goal, they knew she had tried. She wanted to please them; her heart was with them; she gave it her best.

That is what God asks of us. When we try to live as he calls us to live, we won't always succeed. But if we want to please him, if our heart is with him, and we do our best, God—our heavenly Father—will smile. Eventually, we'll likely get it right. And God will smile even more.

"But," you may say, "I'm an adult, and I still haven't gotten it right. How can my life make God smile?"

God's concept of time is different from ours (2 Peter 3:8).

He loves us as a parent loves their child (1 John 3:1). He looks at our hearts (1 Samuel 16:7). He knows living his way is hard, even impossible, for us. That's why he sent Jesus to pay for our sins and the Holy Spirit to help us live a life filled with his fruit of love, joy, peace, patience, kindness, goodness, faithfulness, gentleness, and self-control (Galatians 5:22–23). God knows it's a journey. He's ready to walk with us every step of the way. And as he does, he'll smile.

Fruit here means the manner in which we live our lives. Everyone produces fruit of some kind, bad or good. Jesus tell us we're recognized by our fruit (Luke 6:44). By it, we demonstrate whether we're truly following Jesus or not.

After Jesus left this earth he sent God's Spirit to live in us who believe, to teach us and remind us of everything Jesus said (John 14:26; Romans 8:9–11). Through his Spirit also, we are given the ability to live his fruit. As Christians, we're to produce that fruit—to make it abundant in our lives. But, in our humanness, we're too weak to do that. We can do it only through the power given to us by God's Spirit.

For God's fruit is fruit of the *Spirit*, not fruit of the *believer*. To live it consistently, we need to follow the Spirit's leading in every part of our lives (Galatians 5:16). When we do, we will produce his fruit; we'll live the way he wants us to. When we ignore him and try to produce it alone, we'll still produce fruit, but it won't be the Spirit's fruit. It will be its opposite— lack of love, absence of joy, discord, impatience, unkindness and self-centeredness, deficiency of goodness, unfaithfulness, harshness, and little self-control.

After trying so long to produce an entire fruit orchard all at once and through sheer willpower, I finally realized I needed to let the Holy Spirit lead me. Since I didn't yet seem capable of letting him lead me in all of them all at once, I decided to begin focusing on one fruit at a time.

I felt led to begin with *faithfulness* and firmly establish my commitment to stay the course. From there, I'd focus on *self-control* for, without that, my sinful nature prevails. The journey would take time; I'd need *patience*. With *faithfulness, self-control*, and *patience* improving, I'd become gentler. *Gentleness* would lead to greater *kindness*. With that solid foundation, I'd be better equipped to *love* consistently. *Goodness* would come more readily. From all these, *peace* would flow, and finally, abundant *joy*. I had my plan, and from it came my journey . . . and this book. I pray that what I experienced will help you with your struggles to match your actions to your intention to honor God with your life.

Making God Smile focuses on each fruit of God's Spirit for forty days so they establish deep, strong roots and become a permanent part of who we are. The number forty appears repeatedly in the Bible. It generally represents a time of testing, followed by renewal, restoration, or a momentous change.

- It rained for forty days and forty nights as God cleansed the earth and started afresh (Genesis 7:12). . . . *We can be cleansed of our sin and start afresh.*
- Twice Moses spent forty days and forty nights on Mount Sinai communicating with God and receiving the Ten Commandments (Exodus 24:18; 34:28–29). When Moses completed those forty days and nights, his face was radiant. . . . *Our lives can be radiant with the joy of the Lord.*
- Moses sent men to explore God's Promised Land. After forty days they returned with some of its fruit!

(Numbers 13:1–27) . . . *We can carry the fruit of God's Spirit daily into our lives and the lives of others.*

- The Israelites wandered in the wilderness for forty years before coming to the Promised Land (Exodus 16:35). . . . *We can experience the fulfillment of God's promises.*
- The Philistine giant Goliath taunted the Israelite army for forty days before being slain by David (1 Samuel 17:16). . . . *We can slay the giants that keep us from living as God intended.*
- Jesus fasted forty days and forty nights during his wilderness temptation by Satan, and he emerged victorious (Matthew 4:1–2). . . . *We can emerge victorious over Satan's attempts to keep us from a fruit-filled life.*

My journey has had its up and downs. I still fall short of who I want to be, but I'm closer. I still make mistakes, but fewer. I feel more calm, less buffeted by circumstance, and not as controlled by my emotions. I'm more patient, less reactive, and gentler. I choose kindness more often. I more freely express the love and joy that fill my heart. Most important, I know the Holy Spirit better. He's now my constant Companion and Friend.

For better or worse, my journey continues. Perhaps that is the point. If I had it all down pat, I might forget how much I need God. We all need him, every moment. When we're aware of this truth and choose to walk with him, we'll experience a peace, joy, richness, depth, and purpose to life that no one and nothing else can provide or take away. We will also know we're making God smile.

Thank you for joining me.

THE JOURNEY BEGINS . . .

Let the Holy Spirit guide your lives.
Then you won't be doing what your sinful nature craves.
The sinful nature wants to do evil,
which is just the opposite of what the Spirit wants. . . .
The Holy Spirit produces this kind of fruit in our lives:
love, joy, peace, patience, kindness, goodness,
faithfulness, gentleness, and self-control.

GALATIANS 5:16–17, 22–23

DAY 1

I will give you a new heart,
and I will put a new spirit in you.
EZEKIEL 36:26

I love new years. Not *New Year's*. New . . . years. A new year offers a fresh start, a chance to get it right this time. Sure, we have that chance every day, but there's something about an untouched year that brings greater motivation and hope of success.

Each January I chuckle as I walk into my favorite big-box store and right away see all the exercise equipment, vitamins, and workout clothes. But it's not my physical muscles I'm most concerned about right now. It's my self-discipline muscles. They've been saggy for too long. I want to know the abundant life Jesus has for me. And I want to make God smile. If you feel that way, too, we can start our new year together right now. Whatever the date, this can be our day one, the beginning of our journey to be the best we can be . . . for him.

The New Testament word *newness*, from the Greek *kainotes*, means "life of a new quality." Our new year is an opportunity to live a higher quality life. No matter our past, with God's help, we can improve, change, and learn to consistently let the Spirit lead us to live his fruit. As the prophet Ezekiel put it, "Put all your rebellion behind you, and find yourselves a new heart and a new spirit" (Ezekiel 18:31).

Let's stop focusing on what was and embrace God's gift of newness.

Thank you, Lord, for this new year of mine.
Teach me to live each day relying on your Spirit.

[Jesus] asked him, "Do you want to get well?"
JOHN 5:6 NIV84

The man Jesus was talking to had been unable to walk for thirty-eight years. Rather than responding to the question with a direct yes or no, he explained why healing hadn't been possible. Jesus simply said, "Get up! Pick up your mat and walk" (v. 8). The man did.

No matter how long we've been producing our own rotten fruit, we can stop making excuses, pick up our mat, and walk. We can—as Nike says—"Just do it."

People are known by their actions. I don't want to be thought of as unloving, down, anxious, impatient, unkind, lacking goodness, unfaithful, harsh, or having poor self-control. So why, when I love God, do I let my life offer up *any* spoiled fruit? I think because it's easy. It takes no effort to let words or actions occur without considering them, or reviewing them with God first.

Whatever we do enough times becomes a habit. Bad habits can be difficult to break. To break them we need to: 1) be aware of them, 2) desire and make a conscious decision to change them, and 3) replace them with new behavior. Most important, we need to ask God for the insight and strength to do this.

Yes, Jesus, I want to "get well" and get rid of my bad habits.
Help me replace them with habits that reveal
the fruit of your presence in my life.

Stay alert! Watch out for your great enemy, the devil.
He prowls around like a roaring lion,
looking for someone to devour.

1 PETER 5:8

I was out with my husband when I accidentally pocket-dialed our home phone. Later, when I was listening to the conversation our answering machine had recorded, I was surprised by the impatience in my voice. I hadn't felt disagreeable, but I sounded that way.

I'm often oblivious to my behavior as well as to my tone of voice. So much of what I do and say is reactive, automatic, given little or no advance thought. I'm very aware of how others impact me and sound to me. Seldom do I consider how I impact and sound to them.

The enemy wants us to run on the autopilot of our sinful nature and follow wherever our emotions lead. God wants us to make the deliberate choice, over and over again, to follow him, to hold his mighty hand, and let his Spirit lead us. If we do this often enough, it will become automatic.

To live the fruit of God's Spirit, I need to stay alert to what I'm thinking, saying, and doing as well as how I'm sounding. I need to continually focus on Jesus and what he desires. No matter what my feelings prod me to do or say, I can ask God for direction . . . and the strength to obey.

Father, keep me alert and aware.
Help me think before I act or speak.
Give me the strength to choose your way every time.

FAITHFULNESS

Now fear the Lord and serve him with all faithfulness.
JOSHUA 24:14 NIV84

Dear Lord,
Thank you that you are faithful and that you never change.
Thank you that I can count on you to be with me, hear me, guide
me. You have blessed me richly. You've given and given without
asking anything in return, save that I believe in you, love you,
and follow you.

I believe in you Lord, and I love you. It's in following you
that I so often fall short.

Thank you for never giving up on me. You know my heart:
you know I want to obey you. You also know how frequently
I've forgotten to turn to you first and instead followed my sinful
nature. As a result, I've created messes and then turned to you to
clean them up. I want to stop doing that. Help me learn to fol-
low you not just sometimes, but at all times. I'm tired of failing,
because it means I'm failing you—and I love you too much to
do that.

Help me to be faithful. Faithful to you, faithful in every-
thing. May faithfulness become part of who I am. I want to live
the fruit of your Spirit, and I acknowledge I can't do that without
your help. I am weak. You are strong. Thank you that I can be
strong through you.

Please empower me to stay faithful to you. Refocus me when
I wander. Help me remember to seek you first in all I do. Rid
me of the rotten fruit I produce and replace it with a continuous
harvest of your life-giving fruit. Help me to follow you, obey you,
serve you, and glorify you with my life.

Amen.

My power works best in weakness.

2 CORINTHIANS 12:9

Looking into the year ahead, I'm excited, but I'm also dreading failure. Why would I get it right this time when I've gotten it wrong so many times before?

I'm realizing it all depends on the fruit of faithfulness—or lack of it. God is eternally faithful (Psalm 117:2). Through his always-available power, I *can* continuously live the fruit of his Spirit. I can't do it without him. He won't do it without me.

Instead of surging ahead, vowing we'll never err again, we can accept we'll make mistakes. Fruit can thrive even if we sometimes forget to water it. Fruit doesn't grow overnight. But when its buds do appear, our neglect can cause them to wither. They need faithful care.

That's why our journey begins with the fruit of faithfulness. It's essential to all the other fruits. Like me, you may at first have difficulty remembering to let God's Spirit lead you in every one, all at once. So, let's start with faithfulness. This time—this year—can be different.

Lord, help me keep my commitment and stay the course.
Remind me that remembering to turn to you
takes time and effort, but through that faithfulness,
I can live a life filled with your good fruit.

The Lord! The God of compassion and mercy!
I am . . . filled with unfailing love and faithfulness.

Exodus 34:6

Being faithful means sticking with someone or something no matter what.

Faithfulness is part of God's character: He doesn't change (Malachi 3:6). He keeps his promises (Hebrews 10:23). In fact, the Bible is the story of God's faithfulness to humankind. He sticks to his Word no matter what.

It's easy to be faithful when fulfilling a promise takes little effort or is enjoyable. True faithfulness is when we are unswervingly dedicated, even when the circumstances are unpleasant, challenging, or even painful.

Faithfulness is remaining loyal to our spouse when their behavior or appearance becomes unattractive; to our children when they exhaust or disappoint us; to our parents when they become frail or dependent upon us; to our family and friends when they annoy, disappoint, or hurt us; to our jobs when they frustrate or bore us; to our fitness program when we'd rather do other things; to our promises when it would be easier to break them; to our values when others are urging us to ignore them; and to our commitments when we have competing demands upon our time.

Living the fruit of faithfulness means choosing dedication, devotion, and loyalty . . . no matter what.

Lord, I want to be faithful.
When I make a commitment, large or small,
help me see it through no matter what.

FAITHFULNESS

God is not a man, so he does not lie.
He is not human, so he does not change his mind.
Has he ever spoken and failed to act?
Has he ever promised and not carried it through?

NUMBERS 23:19

I've had more than my share of experiences where my initial enthusiasm for a commitment I made petered out, replaced by "I wish I'd never agreed to this." Sometimes I've given in and given up. The result? Disappointment. For me, for others, for God.

There's no requirement we commit to anything. We can promise to try. We can offer to do our best. But if we commit, faithfulness means following through—and asking God to help us. Living the fruit of faithfulness can be made easier by giving careful thought, and even prayer, before agreeing to anything. The hard truth is, if someone is unfaithful to any commitment, others may wonder if that person can ever be fully trusted.

God gives us his example to follow: He's faithful all the time, in all things. We can rely on him and trust his promises. Through the fruit of faithfulness, he's offering us the ability to stick to what we commit . . . no matter what.

Lord, I want my faithfulness to give you glory:
I want people to know that when
I commit to something, I'll do it.

*Those who live according to the flesh have their minds set
on what the flesh desires; but those who live in accordance with
the Spirit have their minds set on what the Spirit desires.*

ROMANS 8:5 NIV84

I have a recurring dream. I'm at school, about to take a test. But I've never gone to the class, never done the assignments. I'm not prepared. I inevitably fail.

Just as our knowledge is tested in school, our faithfulness is tested in life. Will we follow through on our commitments? Will we be faithful to do what God wants us to do? Satan doesn't want us to prepare. He wants us to fail. He loves unfaithfulness. To be prepared, we need to study God's Word. When we commit to something that aligns with God's will, we must understand we're saying, "No matter what, I'll do it."

Beth Moore, in *Get Out of That Pit*, stresses the importance of that mind-set: "We've got to make up our minds. A made-up mind means that certain questions are already answered before life asks them. . . . Until you finally make up your mind that you're cleaving to God and calling upon His power from now until Hades freezes over, your feet are set upon a banana peel."

That's the secret. Choose faithfulness before the temptation to take an easier path arrives. Resolve ahead of time. Waiting to decide is a recipe for failure.

---

*Lord, I want to be as faithful to you
and to my commitments as you are to me.
I want to produce your fruit in my life.
I've made up my mind*

DAY 8

Now it is required that those who have been given
a trust must prove faithful.

1 CORINTHIANS 4:2 NIV84

A man in his eighties never missed a day of visiting his Alzheimer's-stricken wife at her nursing home. An attendant asked him if his wife still recognized him. He said she hadn't for the last five years. "And you still visit her every day?"

The man smiled. "She doesn't know me anymore, but I still know her."

To whom or what have you committed to be faithful? Spouse, family, friends, job, schedule, diet, a fitness program, promises, bedtime, country, values, hobbies, or certain obligations? On a scale of 1–10, with 1 being "Not at all" and 10 being "Completely," how faithful are you to each? To what or whom are you most faithful? Least faithful? To whom or what would you like to become more faithful?

Is God on your list? How faithful are you to him? Are you as faithful as you want to be? As faithful as God wants you to be? If you're not sure, ask him.

Lord, enable me to be faithful in every area of my life.

Faith is the confidence that what we hope for
will actually happen; it gives us assurance
about things we cannot see.

HEBREWS 11:1

We put our faith in what and whom we know we can rely on. Our faith in God exists because he's demonstrated he can be trusted. Faithfulness creates faith.

Having faith in someone creates a desire to be faithful to them in return. Because God is faithful to me, I want to be faithful to him. When someone trusts in me, I want to deserve that faith by being faithful to them. When I am faithful to them, their trust in and faithfulness to me grows. Faith and faithfulness impact each other in a circular manner.

How does our character become one of faithfulness? When we put our faith in Jesus, God gives us his Spirit, who enables us to be faithful. "The LORD—who is the Spirit—makes us more and more like him as we are changed into his glorious image" (2 Corinthians 3:18).

Jesus, I have faith in you. I'm grateful that because of that,
faithfulness can become part of who I am.

I am the vine; you are the branches.
Those who remain in me, and I in them,
will produce much fruit.

JOHN 15:5

Not being sure what the branch of a vine looks like, I went online and discovered it's a tiny thing, completely dependent on the vine for its nourishment. In the New Testament, *branch* is from the Greek *klema*, meaning "a tender, flexible shoot, a sprout." I love the image of me as a little sprout, attached to Jesus, my powerful, life-giving Vine.

Fruit is part of the reproductive body of a plant we can eat. Fruit nourishes. Fruit begets fruit. It multiplies. When others see the fruit of the Holy Spirit displayed in our lives, they may be inspired and encouraged to become a follower of Jesus.

Fruit also means outcome. The fruit of God's Spirit is the outcome of our remaining in Jesus the Vine. When we abide in him, we receive God's nourishment for our soul, enabling us to bear his fruit. The bonus is, it brings glory to God (John15:8).

Lord, thank you for caring for me, your sprout,
so that I can produce your fruit.
May I abide in you always.

DAY 11

Remain in me, and I will remain in you.
For a branch cannot produce fruit if it is severed from the vine,
and you cannot be fruitful unless you remain in me.

JOHN 15:4

Remaining in Jesus means being faithful to him. It means not allowing myself to dishonor him with my thoughts, words, or actions. It doesn't mean turning to him in praise when times are good but doubting his promises or withdrawing from him when things get tough. Nor does it mean seeking him when times are bad but forgetting him when life is going well.

Remaining in Jesus is an unceasing awareness of his presence and a daily, personal relationship with him by openly, honestly, and consistently talking with him and listening to him. It's not merely professing belief in him, showing up at church, saying grace, and occasionally praying. For me to produce God's fruit, Jesus must be a constant in my life, an essential part of who I am.

Have our failures to live his fruit been when we, as branches, have broken off from Jesus, our Vine, and done our own thing, not turning to or listening to the Holy Spirit, but only to our own thoughts, impulses, and desires?

Jesus, my Vine, I long to remain in you.
When I become detached, please graft me back in
and nourish me with your love.

Whoever has will be given more,
and they will have an abundance. Whoever does not have,
even what they have will be taken from them.
MATTHEW 25:29 NIV84

I felt pretty good about my faithfulness . . . until I became more watchful and aware of my actions. Things I'd never thought of in terms of faithfulness began to pop up all around, each one wearing an "I'm not impressed with your faithfulness" sign.

I'd made a bet with my husband, agreeing that if I lost I'd do the dishes (his job) for five nights. I lost—but complained so much that he offered to let me off the hook. Then I remembered . . . *faithfulness.* Realizing more than a bet was at stake, I did the dishes.

Another evening, I didn't feel like going to my church small-group meeting. I was about to plop down with a book instead when I remembered . . . *faithfulness.* I went.

I'd committed to cutting out sweets if my weight rose above a certain point. But dark chocolate beckoned. My weight went up. I kept eating dessert. *Certainly this one time wouldn't hurt.* Reaching for the ice cream, I remembered . . . *faithfulness.* I put the carton back.

Lord, when I'm tempted to be "just a little bit" unfaithful,
remind me that faithfulness matters, even in seemingly
little things. Help me choose to be faithful.

Now I can walk in your presence,
O God, in your life-giving light.
PSALM 56:13

I spent a lot of time talking with Jesus today. Not concentrated prayer time so much as an ongoing conversation. I thanked him often. I sought his guidance. I worshipped him in my heart. I tried to do everything I felt he was telling me to do.

Otherwise, today was just a normal day. But focusing on Jesus made it so much more. I felt peaceful, content, and filled with a quiet joy—not because of anything that happened, but because I was walking with him.

Too often I wait until something goes wrong to turn to God. But turning to him only when I don't know where else to turn isn't faithfulness.

Jesus said, "Now you are my friends, since I have told you everything the Father told me" (John 15:15). Suppose a friend said, "I want to spend some time with you. Let's take a walk together every day." You show up faithfully. But your friend only shows up when they're going through a crisis. Or even if they show up each day, they ignore you. Are they a faithful friend?

God shows up every day to walk with us, talk with us (Matthew 28:20). We need only take his outstretched hand and follow.

Lord, I'm going to try to show up every day and walk
and talk with you. If I forget, remind me you're waiting.

I am the true grapevine, and my Father is the gardener.
He cuts off every branch of mine that doesn't produce fruit,
and he prunes the branches that do bear fruit
so they will produce even more.

JOHN 15:1–2

When I was young, I was appalled when my father lopped off stacks of branches from our trees and cut our bushes down to nothing. I thought he was being destructive—and heartless. I felt sad for the skeletal trunks that now looked barren and forlorn. "Just wait," my father said.

Sure enough, when spring came, the plants he had pruned grew back fuller, stronger, and more beautiful. My father understood the benefits of pruning. So does our heavenly Father.

Jesus said, "Here on earth you will have many trials and sorrows" (John 16:33). Just when we feel we're flourishing, something difficult or painful may occur. But always, if we remain faithful to God, he will restore us. Our character will become more resilient and beautiful, our trust deeper, our faith stronger.

As the author of Hebrews wrote, "No discipline is enjoyable while it is happening—it's painful! But afterward there will be a peaceful harvest of right living for those who are trained in this way" (Hebrews 12:11).

Lord, may I remember that your pruning grows
my faithfulness in a way a trouble-free life wouldn't.

His faithful promises are your armor and protection.

PSALM 91:4

Imagine a world with no faithfulness, no one and nothing we can count on. We'd never be sure if employees would come to work, stores would open, planes would fly as scheduled, or teachers would show up for class. Think about everyone and everything you rely on. What if you could no longer count on them for anything? How important is faithfulness?

Unfaithfulness exists. Is any okay? If so, where do we draw the line? We're created to need and expect faithfulness. Unfaithfulness brings disappointment and unpredictability at best, heartache and chaos at worst. We respect and love those who are faithful. We dislike and avoid those who aren't. How faithful are we to God? Can he count on us to always turn to him, listen to him, follow him, put him first? If it's not okay for those we care about to be unfaithful to us, is it okay for us to be less than faithful to God?

God knows we need faithfulness to have the life he wants for us. He understands how difficult faithfulness can be. He's ready to give us the strength we need if we're faithful in turning to him.

Lord, may I never forget how vital faithfulness is:
to me, to others, and to you.
Open my eyes to any unfaithfulness in me.

FAITHFULNESS

Help, O Lord, for the godly are fast disappearing!
The faithful have vanished from the earth!

PSALM 12:1

Faithlessness is nothing new. Since the garden of Eden, people have broken promises, let each other down, failed to fulfill commitments, and quit when the going got rough. When people break promises, they might make excuses, or might not even bother. Worst of all, people get so wrapped up in their own little worlds that they either turn their back on God or completely forget about him. Unfaithfulness is part of mankind's sinful nature.

Faithfulness is part of God's nature (Deuteronomy 7:9). The Bible is filled with accounts of his unwavering devotion and reliability. Though Scripture also contains impressive examples of human faithfulness, the Bible is primarily the story of man's unfaithfulness to God and God's plan for bringing us back into relationship with him.

The temptation to be unfaithful can be huge. But God "will not allow the temptation to be more than you can stand. . . . He will show you a way out so that you can endure" (1 Corinthians 10:13). With God's help, we can remain faithful in a world that abounds with unfaithfulness. With God as our example and strength, we can become an example and strength for others, staying faithful, producing much fruit, and bringing glory to God (John 15:5, 8).

How grateful I am, Lord, that you have overcome
the world and that through you, I can too.

He keeps every promise forever.

PSALM 146:6

Faithfulness is easy when things are good. But untested, easy faithfulness may not be true faithfulness.

God remains faithful to us humans even though throughout history we've been stubborn, rebellious, and unfaithful. As one of the psalmists said, "Undependable as a crooked bow . . . they rebelled against him . . . and grieved his heart. . . . [Yet] he cared for them with a true heart" (Psalm 78:57, 40, 72). Have we been faithful to God—obeying him and trusting him—even when challenges come?

Think of how God has been faithful to you, the many times he has stood by you no matter what, provided for you, answered your prayers, been your guide, strength, and refuge.

Now think of ways you've been faithful to God.

What if God were to say, "I'll be as faithful to you as you are in living according to my Word"?

And what would it be like if we were as faithful to God as he is to us? Wow! So why aren't we?

Lord, you know everything about me.
Yet, you're faithful to me anyway.
Your faithfulness humbles me.
Help me grow in my faithfulness to you.

FAITHFULNESS

If you look for me wholeheartedly, you will find me.

JEREMIAH 29:13

About a half hour into a relaxing massage, I noticed music playing. When I commented on it, the masseuse chuckled. It had been on the entire time I'd been there. Off in my own little world of enjoyment, I hadn't heard it.

That's what I too often do with God's voice. I get so involved in whatever I'm doing—or in telling God what I want—I don't hear him speak. If I'm to hear him, I need to pay attention. I have the propensity to zone out. But if I focus and listen, I can hear.

Sarah Young, author of *Jesus Calling*, tells of how she realized that writing in her prayer journals was "one-way communication." She says, "I did all the talking. . . . I yearned for more. . . . I decided to listen to God. . . . I felt awkward the first time I tried this, but I received a message. . . . My journaling . . . changed from monologue to dialogue. Soon, messages began to flow."

Sarah Young heard God when she listened for him. He'd been there all the time. She just hadn't been paying attention.

Speak to me, Lord, and help me be faithful in listening.

*The one who enters through the gate is the shepherd
of the sheep. . . . The sheep recognize his voice
and come to him. . . . He walks ahead of them,
and they follow him because they know his voice.*

JOHN 10:2–4

How do we know when it's God and not just our own thoughts?

When someone we've never met phones us, do we know who they are just by hearing their voice? If an acquaintance calls, does their voice readily identify them? What about a good friend we talk to frequently? Certainly, spouses don't have to identify themselves to each other. The more time we spend with someone, the more readily we recognize their voice.

It's the same with God. The more we read his Word and talk with him, the easier it will become for us to recognize his voice. Unless we're the next Moses, it probably won't be audible. As J. I. Packer wrote in *Your Father Loves You*, "God . . . guides our minds as we think things out in His presence." Charles Stanley, in *How to Listen to God*, puts it this way: "He impresses His will in my spirit or mind, and I hear Him in my inner being."

The more focused time we spend with God, the more we seek him and listen for him, the less we'll have to wonder whether it's him we're hearing. Eventually, there will be no question. We will follow him because we know his voice.

---

*Shepherd of my life, may I be so faithful to spend time
with you that I know your voice.*

To those who use well what they are given,
even more will be given. But from those who do nothing,
even what little they have will be taken away.

LUKE 19:26

Jesus told a parable about being entrusted with something of value, referred to in the New International Version 1984 translation as talents (Matthew 25:14–30; Luke 19:11–26). According to the *NIV Study Bible, talent* originally referred to weight, then to coinage, but its present-day meaning of ability or gift comes from this parable.

God wants us to use the abilities he's given us—no matter how small or insignificant we think they are or how much safer it seems to hide or ignore them. Jesus teaches that if we're faithful to use what we're given, we'll receive even greater abilities and more opportunities to use them.

What abilities has God given you? To what extent are you using each? Are there any you're hiding or ignoring? What could happen if you worked to develop and use them?

I want to give him reason to say to me, too, "Well done, my good and faithful servant" (Matthew 25:21).

Whether my talents be large or small, Lord, grant me
the faithfulness to develop them in the best way I'm able.
May my doing so be to your glory.

I have fought the good fight, I have finished the race,
and I have remained faithful.

2 TIMOTHY 4:7

Sometimes, even when we're faithful, things don't turn out as we'd hoped. We study faithfully but fail the test. We're a faithful friend, but our friend turns on us. We witness faithfully, but our testimony is ignored.

We can learn from Mother Teresa, who said, "I am not called to be successful; I am called to be faithful." Ruth Bell Graham acknowledged, "My job is to take care of the possible and trust God with the impossible." God's definition of success may be different than ours; he may be planning something our limited vision can't see.

The story is told of an elderly preacher who was rebuked because only one person had joined his church in a year, and that person was just a child. Years later, a successful and revered missionary returned to that town. He had been the child saved by that pastor.

Under Moses's leadership, a generation of Israelites turned from God and wandered in the wilderness, yet Moses was lauded for his faithful service (Hebrews 3:2). As a longtime pastor said in *Marks of Maturity* at Bible.org: "Where there is faithfulness to discharge one's duties, regardless of the results, there is success in God's sight. . . . We are to be faithful to the gifts, abilities, and opportunities God gives us and leave the results to Him."

Lord, help me do my part by being faithful,
and leave the rest to you.

A faithful person will be richly blessed.
PROVERBS 28:20 NIV84

I get frustrated that I so often fall short of who I want to be, and that I do and say things I later regret. I'm improving, but I still make plenty of mistakes. I need to remember that living the fruit of God's Spirit takes practice, just like everything else. As philosopher Will Durant said, "We are what we repeatedly do. Excellence, then, is not an act, but a habit."

To achieve excellence in anything, faithful practice is essential. How much practice? According to author Malcolm Gladwell in *Outliers*, researchers have settled on ten thousand hours as the magic number for true expertise, even for "people we think of as prodigies."

Ten thousand hours is a lot of faithfulness. No wonder it's so difficult to perfect a godly character trait! Living the life God wants for us demands faithful practice of following his way.

Faithfulness brings results. It brings blessings. It brings us close to God. The more we practice, the easier it will become.

Whenever I want to quit, Lord, help me keep going.
I never want to give up on anything you want me to do.

I will show you what it's like when someone comes to me,
listens to my teaching, and then follows it.
It is like a person building a house who digs deep and lays
the foundation on solid rock. When the floodwaters rise
and break against that house, it stands firm because it is
well built. But anyone who hears and doesn't obey is like
a person who builds a house without a foundation.
When the floods sweep down against that house,
it will collapse into a heap of ruins.

LUKE 6:47–49

My friend looked at me with bafflement and exasperation. "I just don't see how you've gotten through your tough times without falling apart. Look at me! I'm a mess!"

I knew the answer: I have Jesus as my foundation. She doesn't. It makes a huge difference.

Jesus makes it clear we'll have troubles. He doesn't say *if* the floodwaters rise, but *when*. The only way to stand firm in those times is to build our lives on the foundation of God our Rock. "The Lord is my rock, my fortress, and my savior . . . in whom I find protection. He is my shield, the power that saves me, and my place of safety" (Psalm 18:1–2). I'm praying my friend turns to God soon, for her floodwaters are rising fast.

In this fallen and dizzying world, Lord,
I am glad to have you as my Rock,
the strong foundation for my life.

For everything there is a season,
a time for every activity under heaven.
ECCLESIASTES 3:1

Is there a time to stop? Certainly—when we've fulfilled the commitment we made. But what about when we haven't and want to stop anyway? When that happens, we can ask why we want to stop. Is it because of any of these reasons?

- it's easier
- you don't believe your effort will make a difference
- you have limited time
- it's just not what you want anymore
- you're focusing on short-term impact rather than long-term results
- you're listening to the enemy

All those reasons are red flags. They're self-focused. Any right reason to stop is God-focused—God letting you know it's time to stop, that he has something else planned for you. So talk to him. Be honest about why you want to stop. Ask him to show you reasons to keep going and for help to decide. Having God's blessing when we stop is one thing. Just giving up is another.

Help me, Lord, to know
whether the season is over or ongoing.
May I never stop before it's your time.

You must always act in the fear of the Lord,
with faithfulness and an undivided heart.

2 CHRONICLES 19:9

Almost three thousand years ago, messengers informed Jehoshaphat, king of Judah, that a vast army was approaching (2 Chronicles 20:2). Jehoshaphat was "deeply committed to the ways of the Lord" (2 Chronicles 17:6). Rather than rely on himself, he turned to God for help, recounting God's faithfulness and telling him the details of the impending crisis.

God responded: "Do not be afraid! Don't be discouraged by this mighty army, for the battle is not yours, but God's. . . . You will not even need to fight. Take your positions; then stand still and watch the Lord's victory" (2 Chronicles 20:15, 17). Jehoshaphat and his people obeyed God's instructions and he gave them victory.

God's words to Jehoshaphat are words he still speaks when we faithfully turn to him. We needn't be afraid of nor discouraged by any challenge, for the battle is not ours, but God's.

Lord, when trouble looms or attacks,
may I always turn to you,
to your Word, and to your way.

Believe in the LORD your GOD, and you will be able to stand firm.

2 CHRONICLES 20:20

An internet search of "how to approach problem solving" netted me more than twenty-three million results, but none I reviewed mentioned God. Not one referenced 2 Chronicles 20:1–30, which contains a God-given template for problem-solving through faithfulness:

1. *Turn to God first* instead of relying on our own way.
2. *Thank God for his faithfulness,* honoring him for what he has done and is able to do now.
3. *Pour out our hearts to God,* telling him our thoughts, feelings, and concerns.
4. *Acknowledge our dependence,* admitting we can't handle this situation without him.
5. *Listen for God's response,* hearing God in our heart, being led to a scripture, seeking counsel, seeing circumstances clarify the decision, continuing to pray until we feel peace.
6. *Worship and praise God,* not necessarily *for* the situation, but *in* it.
7. *Obey* what we believe God wants, leaving the rest to him.
8. *Trust God,* knowing he's handling our problem the best way.
9. *Continue to worship and praise God* even after the problem has passed.

Lord, I'm powerless against this mighty army that threatens.
I don't know what to do, but I'm looking to you for help.

[2 CHRONICLES 20:12]

Do not forget this! Keep it in mind!
ISAIAH 46:8

I was concerned about some family issues. I lay awake for hours, mentally playing out scenarios, struggling over what I and others should be doing. Suddenly I remembered 2 Chronicles and solving problems through faithfulness!

I fell asleep, vowing to return to faithfulness, and when I woke up, I grabbed my coffee, curled up under my blankets, and gave my problem to God according to the guidance he offers in 2 Chronicles.

I began by recalling some of the many times God has solved our problems, answered our prayers, and guided us. I told God how I felt, my concerns, uncertainties, frustrations, fears, and need for him. Then I took a deep breath . . . and listened.

I heard God speaking to my heart about a few simple things I should and shouldn't do, saying I should rest in the knowledge that he would deal with the situation in his way and his timing. I thanked him and worshipped him for all he is.

How different I felt from the day before. A huge burden had been lifted from me.

Lord, help me never forget that the first step
in my being faithful is remembering
what it is I'm supposed to do—turn to you.

Never forget the things I have taught you.
Store my commands in your heart. . . .
Tie them around your neck as a reminder.
Write them deep within your heart.

PROVERBS 3:1, 3

Thankfully, God understands we're a people who forget. Several hundred Scripture verses deal with remembering, being reminded, and not forgetting. Moses spoke to the people of Israel: "Commit yourselves wholeheartedly to these commands. . . . Repeat them again and again. . . . Talk about them at home and when you are on the road, when you are going to bed and when you are getting up" (Deuteronomy 6:6–7). Jesus, on the night he was betrayed, used bread and wine to help us remember his sacrifice, saying, "Do this in remembrance of me" (1 Corinthians 11:23–26). He told his disciples he would send someone to help them remember: "the Holy Spirit—he will teach you everything and will remind you of everything I have told you" (John 14:26).

The Bible also tells of people forgetting what God had done for them, "the wonders he had shown them. . . . Their hearts were not loyal to him, they were not faithful to his covenant" (Psalm 78:11, 37 NIV84).

It's one thing to resolve to do something. It's another to remember . . . and do it.

Lord, I want to do what you want me to do.
Too often I forget. Please help me remember.

Make tassels for the hems of your clothing and attach them
with a blue cord. When you see the tassels,
you will remember and obey all the commands of the Lord
instead of following your own desires . . .
as you are prone to do.
NUMBERS 15:38–39

Each morning I ask God to help me to be loving, peaceful, patient, etc. Then daily life steps in and I forget what I've learned. Not eager to wear tassels, I've tried other reminders:

- sticky notes on my bathroom mirror or car dashboard
- a bracelet associated with what I'm trying to remember
- antique button hooks to remind me to button my mouth
- a pacifier on which I wrote "No Regrets Plug"
- framed verses from Scripture on my desk
- a small cross in my pocket or purse

Some of these cues have worked better than others. You know what may best help you. Be creative. Try different ways until you find some that work. (A friend wears a rubber band on his wrist and snaps it hard when he errs.) Try generating computer or cell phone reminders, or leave in plain sight a significant object to help you remember.

The point is not what we do, but that we do something—whatever works—to remind us to faithfully walk with God, turning to him first in everything.

Lord, you know me better than I know myself.
Please give me some good ideas for my reminders—
and help me remember to use them.

Make the chestpiece of a single piece of cloth folded to form
a pouch nine inches square. Mount four rows of gemstones on it.
The first row will contain a red carnelian,
a pale-green peridot, and an emerald.

EXODUS 28:16–17

For me, the highlight of every day is my morning quiet time when I sit with my coffee, my Bible, and God. I worship him, make requests, seek his guidance, study his Word. Then I go about my day, too often overlooking that God wants not just to sit with me in the morning, but to walk with me every minute.

It's in the dailiness that I forget to turn to God. I need him there. We all do. If we'd bring him into not just the big issues, but the small ones, too, not just into the quiet times, but the noisy ones as well, into the dailiness, the details, he'd lead us to live even more beautiful lives.

The Bible is filled with God's interest in detail. Exodus and Leviticus, for instance, contain his comprehensive instructions on building his Tabernacle and its furnishings, on how to worship and how to live. I used to see those passages as culture-specific, antiquated and boring, nothing that applied to me. But I was missing something. Those passages show that God cares about everything, even the minutiae, the dailiness.

As author John Eldredge says in *Walking with God*: "What would it be like to yield to Christ in the details of our lives? . . . to follow his counsel and instruction in all the small decisions that add up to the life we find ourselves living? It would be . . . amazing."

Thank you, Lord, for caring about my days and details.
May I be faithful in sharing them with you.

Take your son, your only son . . .
whom you love so much . . . and sacrifice him.

Genesis 22:2

The story of God asking Abraham to sacrifice his son Isaac is one I can barely stand to read. It's so painful to read, I'd rather it wasn't in the Bible. I don't think I could ever show the faithfulness Abraham did.

I would imagine that as Abraham walked toward the place of sacrifice, he struggled with his faith and faithfulness, greatly tempted to turn around. But God had never failed him, and Abraham had confidence God never would. Abraham remained faithful, trusting that somehow, some way, God would spare his son's life. God did, and blessed Abraham greatly.

I'm humbled by Abraham's faithfulness. His example highlights my limitation and lack. It shows I should never become complacent. My faithfulness can always be stronger.

Abraham's story illustrates the magnitude of God's love, for God did the very thing he asked Abraham to do. God sacrificed his Son for us. This story of Abraham brings home the depth, pain, and intensity of that sacrifice.

The unimaginable may come in some form in our lives. God may ask for our trust in circumstances we cannot imagine. If he does, we can be certain he understands our anguish, for he's been there. We can also know that if we remain faithful, he will provide, and ultimately bless, as he did for Abraham.

Lord, I pray I never have to face the unimaginable,
but if I do, give me strength to trust you.

Let's not get tired of doing what is good.
At just the right time we will reap a harvest
of blessing if we don't give up.

GALATIANS 6:9

I love the Bible's candor. It describes people as they are, including flaws, fears, weaknesses, and failings. Great people of God are imperfect humans struggling to remain faithful to him.

Elijah was a prophet, chosen by God to combat idol worship. He obeyed God's instructions and performed miracles in God's name (1 Kings 17–18). But even Elijah became exhausted and overwhelmed: He "prayed that he might die. 'I have had enough, LORD,' he said" (1 Kings 19:3–4). God didn't berate Elijah for wanting to quit. Instead, he sent an angel who tenderly ministered to Elijah's needs until he regained strength to complete his mission.

Through stories like Elijah's and in various Psalms, God lets us know it's natural and all right to become discouraged and cry out to him. He'll support us and provide what we need.

Because of God's faithfulness, outcries of despair in the Bible are followed by proclamations of trust and praise. God understands life can be difficult. If we remain faithful, we will yet praise him. "Why am I discouraged? Why is my heart so sad? I will put my hope in God! I will praise him again—my Savior and my God" (Psalm 42:11).

Lord, sometimes it's hard not to give up.
Thank you for showing me I'm not alone.
Thank you that with faithfulness, my cries of discouragement
will eventually become songs of praise.

Letting the Spirit control your mind leads to life and peace.

ROMANS 8:6

I identify with the apostle Paul when he says, "I don't really understand myself, for I want to do what is right, but I don't do it" (Romans 7:15).

If Paul, an anti-Christian zealot, a true sinner-turned-saint, could have his life turned around and become a communicator of God's Word, there's hope for us. If Paul, who dedicated his entire later life to serving the Lord, struggled with his weak human nature, we shouldn't feel so badly when we do.

Paul was tenacious. When he believed in something, he fully committed himself to it. He never gave up, no matter what. That may be one reason God chose him. Seeing Paul's misdirected zeal, God knew that once Paul was infused with the Holy Spirit and his wholeheartedness was redirected to Christ, Paul would accomplish great things for God's kingdom. Although Paul struggled with his sinful nature, once Christ entered his life, he was freed from sin's power (Romans 8:2).

Whenever we feel discouraged about our struggle to obey God, we can read Romans 7 and 8. Those verses reassure that with God, we can overcome our sinful natures and produce much fruit.

Thank you, Lord, that there is no condemnation
for those who belong to Jesus.
Help me follow your Spirit and produce your fruit.

Keep on praying.

ROMANS 12:12

When our youngest daughter was eight years old, she asked us for a horse. We said no. For several years she continued to ask. We continued to say no. She added detailed plans for learning how to ride and care for a horse. When she was eleven, we bought her one. Did she wear us down? No. She convinced us this was no idle request, and we decided the time was right.

Jesus told us, "Keep on asking. . . . Keep on seeking. . . . Keep on knocking" (Matthew 7:7). One reason may be to show him that what we're asking truly matters to us and that we'll do our part. We persist in prayer only for our greatest desires. God, our heavenly Parent, may still answer no, or answer differently than we sought. Or, in his perfect timing, God may decide to give us what we've asked for.

Jesus said, "always pray and never give up" (Luke 18:1). Persistent prayer demonstrates our faith. We wait, continue to believe he'll answer, and keep praying. Our perseverance shows we trust him to grant our request if it's in his will and timing. He wants our happiness. He'll decide what's best.

Lord, you've told us to never stop praying.
Thank you for understanding my repeated prayers
are not to wear you down,
but to let you know how much I care and trust.

Remain faithful to one another in marriage.

HEBREWS 13:4

Have you been faithful to your spouse? Before you answer yes because you've never committed adultery, let me suggest that while sexual fidelity is crucial, marital faithfulness encompasses much more.

I said my marriage vows over forty years ago. I made that pledge voluntarily; I eagerly took on that obligation. Yet now I don't even remember specifically what I promised. I presume I said I'd love, honor, and cherish my husband. But have I always done so? Have I always treated him with respect? Have I always treated this man as precious in God's sight? Have my actions and words always been loving and honoring?

Faithfulness in marriage means sticking with our spouse, no matter what. It also means loyalty in what we say to and about them, how we say it, and how we treat them each and every day. We need only open our ears and eyes to know there are plenty of people sexually faithful to their spouses, but unfaithful to them in other ways.

I'm going to dig through my keepsakes and find out exactly what I promised God and my husband all those years ago. And, with God's help, I'm going to grow the fruit of faithfulness to those vows and to my husband in every way, throughout every day, until death do us part.

Lord, may I never forget what I promised
my husband on our wedding day. Help me stay true
to those vows until that time we leave each other
to live with you for eternity.

Direct your children onto the right path,
and when they are older, they will not leave it.

Proverbs 22:6

I vividly remember the first time I held each of our newborn children. I was engulfed in awe, certain I held in my arms the meaning of life. I felt an overwhelming responsibility. God had entrusted this child to me and I committed eagerly and joyfully always to be faithful to them.

As I parented through the years, I learned that faithfulness to my children means more than unrelenting love and devotion, more than teaching and care. It also means living what I teach. Who my children are as adults was influenced more by what I did than by what I said. No matter their age, our children watch us. They become like us in many ways. What an awesome duty to be the followers of Jesus we want them to become.

What better gift than to be a role model of faithfulness, pointing them toward the best life possible on earth and for eternity?

Father, thank you for my children. Help me remember that,
at every age, faithfulness in my own life is the best way
to teach them to be faithful in theirs.

Honor your father and mother.

EXODUS 20:12

On my bookshelf is a box containing some of my most precious possessions: notes from our children. Their words of love and gratitude honor me as a parent—and they make my heart sing.

The fifth of the Ten Commandments is "honor your father and mother" (Deuteronomy 5:16). Notice that God puts no age limits on this commandment, nor does he say to honor our parents only if they do a good job or are perfect people. The command is to be faithful in honoring our parents regardless of our age or their character or behavior.

> Honoring your parents is an attitude accompanied by actions that say, "You are worthy. You have value. You are the person God sovereignly placed in my life. You may have failed me, hurt me . . . disappointed me . . . but I . . . choose to look at you with compassion— as people with needs, concerns, and scars of your own." . . . Many of us do not comprehend the remarkable power we have to bring life and happiness into our parents' lives. (*The Tribute*, Dennis Rainey and David Boehi)

God comprehends this and commands us to be faithful in honoring them.

Lord, help me always focus on what my parents did right and to honor them for that.

*How wonderful and pleasant it is when
brothers live together in harmony!*

PSALM 133:1

Brothers, sisters, aunts, uncles, cousins, nieces, nephews, grand-parents, in-laws—extended families can be large, full of diverse personalities. They can be fun . . . or challenging.

In Old Testament times the extended family was esteemed. People lived, moved, and grew old with their family unit, tribe, or clan. In America today, the extended family is considered less important. Relatives are commonly separated by hundreds or thousands of miles. They may rarely see or speak to each other. What is our faithfulness duty to relatives?

God doesn't require us to like every one of them. We're never to put them before our relationship with God (Luke 9:61–62). We're to care for relatives when they're genuinely in need (Timothy 5:3–8). We're not to stir up conflict: "The LORD hates . . . a person who sows discord in a family" (Proverbs 6:16, 19). As far as possible, we're to live at peace with them (Romans 12:18 NIV84). As Jesus said, "A family splintered by feuding will fall apart" (Mark 3:25).

If Aunt Matilda drives us crazy, we're to keep it to ourselves. If Grandmother Ethel is a widow struggling to pay her bills, we're to help as we can. If the cousins are feuding, we can try to help them reconcile, but not take sides. We're to get along with siblings. We're to love them as ourselves, for they're closer to us than neighbors (see Mark 12:31).

*Lord, help me look on my relatives as the gift they are.
Help me see the good in each, provide for their needs as I'm able,
and be a peacemaker to the extent it depends upon me.*

Two are better than one. . . .
If either of them falls down, one can help the other up.
ECCLESIASTES 4:9–10 NIV84

How do you define a true friend? Someone you enjoy being with? Who has similar interests? Who's fun? Or is it more?

Chances are, you'll include faithfulness: true friends stand by each other through good and bad. The Bible helps us know how to be a friend:

- "A friend is always loyal." (Proverbs 17:17)
- "The heartfelt counsel of a friend is as sweet as perfume and incense." (Proverbs 27:9)
- "Love prospers when a fault is forgiven, but dwelling on it separates close friends." (Proverbs 17:9)
- "Unfriendly people care only about themselves." (Proverbs 18:1)
- "Gossip separates the best of friends." (Proverbs 16:28)
- "Just as damaging as a madman shooting a deadly weapon is someone who lies to a friend and then says, 'I was only joking.'" (Proverbs 26:18–19)

Faithfulness, listening, giving comfort and good advice, accepting them as they are, putting their needs above our own, being trustworthy—being a faithful friend is a tall order. But we have the perfect example in our forever Friend, Jesus (see John 15:12–15).

May I be as true a friend to others, Lord, as you are to me.

Don't let us yield to temptation.

LUKE 11:4

A recent e-mail contained beautiful pictures paired with sayings—but one of those statements was frightening. It said, "There is no bad or good, only choice."

It reminded me of a poem by Alexander Pope that my mother taught me. "Vice is a monster of so frightful mien as, to be hated needs but to be seen; yet seen too oft, familiar with her face, we first endure, then pity, then embrace."

How can we—living when the black and white of right and wrong has faded into gray—avoid being pulled into accepting, then embracing, what goes against our values?

Jesus said, "Keep watch and pray, so that you will not give in to temptation" (Matthew 26:41). Proverbs admonishes, "If sinners entice you, turn your back on them!" (1:10). Peter cautioned, "Stay alert! Watch out for your great enemy, the devil." (1 Peter 5:8–9). Paul asked, "Am I now trying to win the approval of human beings, or of God?" (Galatians 1:10 NIV84). Psalm 1:1 reminds us of "the joys of those who do not follow the advice of the wicked, or stand around with sinners."

When foundations are being destroyed, what can the righteous do? (See Psalm 11:3) Pray. Avoid what and who go against our values. Remember who the real enemy is. Don't give in to him. Care what God thinks, not what people think. And, ask God for strength not to embrace what the world embraces.

Lord, help me stand firm in your truth
in a world of gray, a world bereft of values.

DAY 41

Do not make any vows! . . . Just say a simple,
"Yes, I will," or "No, I won't."
MATTHEW 5:34, 37

Our youngest daughter dated a young man for three years. He said he loved her. He made her ten promises, wrote them out, framed the page—and eventually broke every one of them, along with her heart. Sometime later I asked if she'd ever take him back. "I couldn't," she said. "I'd never trust him." Once broken, trust is difficult, if not impossible, to regain. Forgiveness may occur, but it doesn't reestablish trust.

Remaining faithful to our word means never promising anything, large or small, we're not certain we'll be able to do. Yet people are often cavalier about promises. If every single one had to be kept, no matter what, we'd think harder before making a promise—and fewer promises would be made. It's fine to say we'll try our best to do something or that we'll do it if nothing else comes up, but whatever we promise, faithfulness means we carry it out.

There's rarely a time we're physically incapable of fulfilling a promise. But if that is the case, we aren't breaking trust. If fulfilling a promise is merely inconvenient, or we've changed our mind, or following through is too difficult, we can pray for strength to do it anyway. After all, what's more important to God: our word or our comfort?

Lord, may I follow your example by never promising anything I won't do and always doing what I promise.

DAY 42

Everything comes from him and exists
by his power and is intended for his glory.
All glory to him forever!

Romans 11:36

We're almost at the end of our forty-day focus on faithfulness. We have 323 days left to concentrate on the remaining fruit. It's going to take effort, self-discipline, and faithfulness to remain on this journey. Now is a good time to remind ourselves why we want to do it.

I want to be faithful on this journey because I love God, because he is all things to me, and because I want to be all I can be for him. He has given me an abundant life and the promise of eternal life with him. He has provided for me, delighted me, and stood by me even when my behavior didn't warrant it. His unending patience, lavish love, unimaginable forgiveness, amazing grace, and unrelenting mercy have blessed me. He has given me joy, and I want my faithfulness to bring him joy.

Whatever reasons you have for focusing on the fruit of the Spirit, I invite you to write them down to read every time the going gets tough.

Thank you for what you have taught me
about faithfulness, Lord. Help me keep in the forefront
of my mind why I've chosen this journey.

Our purpose is to please God, not people.

1 THESSALONIANS 2:4

For forty days we've focused on faithfulness—faithfulness in prayer, in marriage, to children, parents, family, friends, values, and promises. We've covered a lot of faithfulness. Your head may be spinning, wondering how you'll ever fulfill all your obligations to all the people and commitments in your life. The answer involves narrowing, not broadening, our focus.

To be faithful to all, we need only be faithful to One: God. If we're faithful to him—to spending time with him, turning to him, talking with him, studying his Word, listening to and following him—he will enable us to be faithful where we need to be faithful. Philip Yancey wrote this in *Rumors of Another World*:

> I ask myself how my life would differ if I truly played to an audience of One, if I continually asked not "What do I want to do?" or "What would bring me approval from others?" but "What would God have me do?"

Many live for the praise and admiration of others. Our best life comes when we choose to please God, not people (1 Thessalonians 2:4).

Thank you, Lord, that I have begun this year focused on faithfulness, which flows from being faithful to you.

SELF-CONTROL

[It is] better to have self-control than to conquer a city.

PROVERBS 16:32

Dear Lord,
Of all the fruit of your Spirit, self-control is the hardest for me to live. I have strong emotions. I feel deeply. I get caught up in the moment. Because of that, I often act based upon my feelings, without thinking or praying first. I do and say things I later regret. Afterward I think; afterward I pray. But words can't be taken back; actions can't be undone.

It's easy to follow what I feel, what I want, and what I think I need immediately. Sometimes those things shout so loudly they drown out all else. It's hard to remember that feelings, wants, and felt needs can be fleeting and deceptive. I need self-control to get over the hump of "right now" and on to the wisdom of consequences, long-term impacts, and true needs.

I need your Spirit guiding me, giving me the strength to listen and follow that guidance before I say and do things I'll later lament. I'm eager to get started, Lord. Please give me self-control.
Amen.

DAY 44

*Those who live only to satisfy their own sinful nature
will harvest decay and death from that sinful nature.*

GALATIANS 6:8

An emotion, an idea, or a desire wells up inside. You want to act on it *now*. But you know that doing so is not best for you or for others, so you ignore the urge. That's self-control.

What is the self we master?

It's our sinful nature, the part that thinks "me" and values immediate gratification—what feels good *now* regardless of long-term impact, right or wrong, or whether it's part of God's plan. Our sinful nature "is always hostile to God. It never did obey God's laws, and it never will. That's why those who are still under the control of their sinful nature can never please God" (Romans 8:7–8).

With self-control, the criterion for action or speech becomes: would God approve? The choice not to act just on feelings takes power that only God's Spirit can provide.

---

*Lord, my sinful nature keeps rearing its ugly head.
I ask for power from you to ignore what my self wants
unless that desire agrees with your will.*

*Anyone who hears and doesn't obey is like a person who
builds a house right on the ground, without a foundation.
When the floods sweep down against that house,
it will collapse into a heap of ruins.*

LUKE 6:49

According to the New Oxford American Dictionary, a foundation is "the lowest load-bearing part of a building." It's necessary if a structure is to withstand the elements. When bad enough weather hits, a house without a foundation will fall apart. Self-control is a foundation for the remaining fruit of God's Spirit. It helps us live them even when times get tough, even when living them is the last thing our emotions want to do. When life is smooth, when nothing is rocking our world, being loving, joyful, peaceful, patient, kind, and good isn't as difficult. But when life's storms hit, it helps to have a solid foundation of self-control in place.

Just as a house's foundation is generally below the ground, our self-control foundation lies deep within us, beneath stress and emotions, enabling us to absorb their blows and still produce God's fruit.

Building a foundation in the midst of a storm, if it can be done at all, is tough. Better to construct it on overcast days, small challenge by small challenge, turning to God for help even with the slightest irritation or most minor temptation. Then, when tempests come, our foundation of self-control will be securely in place: we'll automatically turn to him.

*Lord, help me build my foundation of self-control now,
so when life's bad weather hits, I'll be prepared.*

Let us not be like others, who are asleep,
but let us be alert and self-controlled.

1 Thessalonians 5:6 niv84

The apostle Paul compared lack of self-control to being asleep, a state void of conscious thought. When we're asleep, we're essentially on autopilot. That's a good summary of lack of self-control.

Paul partnered being alert with self-control. Webster's defines *alert* as "watchful and prompt to meet danger or emergency." When we're alert, we're mindful of the potential dangers of what we're contemplating. We're aware that doing what isn't best, isn't best.

Do you operate on autopilot? Or do you stay alert to your actions and their potential consequences? What and who challenges your self-control? When and where? For instance, when it comes to exercising instead of giving in to a preference to take it easy, I do a pretty good job. But when my emotions are running high, I tend to speak and act without thinking first.

It's helpful to know where we're most vulnerable, where we should stay highly alert to our actions and focus our greatest attention, thought, and, most important, prayer.

Lord, sometimes I control my sinful self,
and other times I don't do a good job. Make me aware
of when and where I most need your help.

No discipline is enjoyable while it is happening—it's painful.
But afterward there will be a peaceful harvest
of right living for those who are trained in this way.

HEBREWS 12:11

My phone rang. "I got a package from you, Granmom!" Three-year-old Cayden's sweet voice was a gift to me. "Can I open it?"

Uh-oh. Christmas was still two weeks away. So much for being organized and efficient.

"It would be best to wait until Christmas, sweetheart."

"I don't want to!" Oh, how many times I've said those words. I understood my granddaughter's feelings.

"Think how much fun it'll be to open it on Christmas Day," I tried.

"I don't want to."

"If you open all your presents now, you won't have any to open on Christmas." I could sense her struggle from her silence.

Then . . . "I don't want to."

"It's best to wait, sweetheart. Trust me."

Cayden finally agreed, adding one more time, "But I don't want to."

What a perfect summary of my feelings when faced with doing something I know is right but not wanting to do it. But Cayden and I are in the best of company. Even Jesus, in one of his final days on earth, fell prostrate before the Father, letting him know he didn't want to do what he knew God wanted him to do. But look at the result when Jesus agreed.

Lord, help me remember my actions shouldn't be
determined by what I want, but by what you want
for me—for that's always the best.

DAY 48

*Because my servant Caleb has a different spirit
and follows me wholeheartedly, I will bring him into the land
he went to and his descendants will inherit it.*

NUMBERS 14:24 NIV84

Self-control doesn't mean lack of enthusiasm. God loves enthusiasm. When we are in his will, he wants us to give our all and not hold back. God doesn't want us to mistake our half-heartedness for self-control.

This is how Jesus put it: "I know all things you do, that you are neither hot nor cold. I wish that you were one or the other! But since you are like lukewarm water, neither hot nor cold, I will spit you out of my mouth!" (Revelation 3:15–16).

Moses sent men to explore Canaan. When they returned, most were cautious, warning the Israelites not to go there. But Caleb and Joshua were all in for God. They had wholehearted confidence he'd give them the land. God was so disgusted with the men who urged restraint, he struck them down, declaring only Caleb and Joshua would live to enter Canaan. God doesn't want restraint when it comes to trusting him.

A life of self-control is not subdued. It's all in, lived wholeheartedly for God. It's exuberant gratitude, prolific praise, and overflowing joy because we have our sinfully inclined self under control and are free to live abundantly in God's will, following his Spirit's lead.

---

*Lord, rather than a lukewarm life, may I live
with passion and joy. Help me control only my sinful self
and live with unbridled gusto in the center of your will.*

My heart is confident in you, O God;
no wonder I can sing your praises with all my heart!

PSALM 108:1

Our adult daughter, Rachel, was home for a visit. While I made dinner, I was thinking how wonderful it was to have her here. A waltz was playing on our sound system. When Rachel walked into the kitchen, I turned up the volume, grabbed her, and danced her around the room. As we waltzed, she tried to look at me like I was crazy, but she couldn't curb a grin.

Self-control doesn't mean being stiffly dignified or stifling urges for harmless fun. Self-control is needed only when we want to do something we shouldn't—or not do something we should. Self-control isn't a detached, straight-faced, totally controlled life.

When our heart knows we're in God's will, we can act with abandon. We can praise God with all our heart, dance merrily, laugh till our sides hurt, do something ridiculous, be spontaneous, splurge if we can afford it, plan an adventure, try new things, jump in with both feet, and stop worrying about looking silly.

When we're surrendered to God, losing restraint is the best thing we can do. We make beautiful memories. We make God smile.

Lord, may I not confuse self-control with senseless control.
Let me never become someone who can't have fun
or thoroughly enjoy this beautiful world.

They wouldn't believe his promise to care for them.
Instead they grumbled . . . and refused to obey the Lord.

PSALM 106:24–25

God is completely holy. He has no sinful nature to control. But he does have infinite power. From Genesis through Revelation, God's people disobey, ignore, complain, refuse to believe, worship idols, and forget to trust him. Since creation, God has seen our selfishness, stubbornness, and rebellion. Yet instead of justifiably obliterating a thankless human race, he sent his Son to die in our place, so we could be forgiven and live with him for eternity.

God has never lost self-control. Even when he sent a flood, he was deliberate and controlled (Genesis 6 and 7). After the floodwaters receded, God declared that even though everything we think or imagine is bent toward evil from childhood, he will "never again destroy all living things" (Genesis 8:21). Not that we haven't given him reason. Repeatedly we've "tested God's patience" (Psalm 78:41). Yet he has chosen to control his power.

Whenever we're tempted to lose self-control, we can look to the model of God's self-control—an ability he offers us through his Spirit. "When I think of all this, I fall to my knees and pray to the Father, that from his glorious, unlimited resources he will empower me with inner strength through his Spirit" (Ephesians 3:14–16).

Thank you, God, for giving us your example,
and the ability, through your Spirit, to follow it.
May I always do so.

*When the leading priests and the elders made their accusations
against him, Jesus remained silent.*

MATTHEW 27:12

Jesus had intense emotions and, as the Son of God, unlimited
power, but "he did not think of equality with God as something
to cling to. Instead, he gave up his divine privilege. When he
appeared in human form, he humbled himself in obedience to
God" (Philippians 2:6–8). That is self-control. Jesus had every
reason to use his power to strike down the unrighteous. Many
times he probably felt like doing that. He chose to love instead.

Jesus was flogged, spat upon, humiliated, mocked, and
nailed to a cross. He didn't strike back. He remained calm and
controlled, trusting in his Father's will. Jesus is the epitome
of self-control in the face of understandable reasons *not* to have
self-control.

We may have been terribly wronged and feel retribution is
justified. Jesus offers us the ability to do as he did: to restrain our
negative emotions even when provoked. Jesus was not weak. By
choosing to be controlled, he manifested strength.

When we feel that losing our self-control is defensible, we
can look to Jesus and remember our greatest effectiveness comes
from controlling our self and trusting God. Losing control is
an admission we're too weak to act calmly. Power from God to
exercise self-control is ours for the asking.

---

*Lord, when I know I'm right and others are wrong,
help me remember your example.
Teach me to follow you instead of my emotions.*

> *Love your enemies! Do good to those who hate you.*
> *Bless those who curse you. Pray for those who hurt you.*
> *If someone slaps you on one cheek, offer the other cheek also.*
>
> LUKE 6:27–29

Jesus taught self-control with a capital *S*, instructing us to have not just a little self-control, but a superhuman amount.

- "If you are even angry with someone, you are subject to judgment . . . if you curse someone, you are in danger of the fires of hell." (Matthew 5:22)
- "You have heard the commandment that says, 'You must not commit adultery.' But I say, anyone who even looks at a woman with lust has already committed adultery with her in his heart." (Matthew 5:27–28)

When Jesus's disciples heard the stringent requirements for entry into the kingdom of God, they were astounded and asked, "Then who in the world can be saved?" Jesus answered, "With God everything is possible" (Matthew 19:25–26).

Jesus knew that obedience to his mandate "You are to be perfect" (Matthew 5:48) is humanly impossible, but that nonetheless, God provides a way to enter his kingdom.

Humanness precludes perfection. Christ's redemptive death was needed.

Heavenly Father, you know that my humanness will never
allow the perfection necessary to enter your kingdom.
Thank you, that through Christ, it is mine.

Stay alert! Watch out for your great enemy, the devil.
He prowls around like a roaring lion,
looking for someone to devour.

1 PETER 5:8

Satan knows our weaknesses. And he doesn't hesitate to use them against us. His goal is to steal our joy, kill our love, and destroy our peace (John 10:10). Getting us to act on our emotions is one way he does this. He relishes the damage it causes. Satan knows the power of human emotions. But we know the power of God.

Author Joyce Meyer says in *Managing Your Emotions*, "If I depend upon my flesh through sheer willpower or determination alone, I will fail every time. But if I am determined to resist temptation by calling on the power of the Holy Spirit, I find the strength I need for success."

When we act on our emotions, we play into Satan's hands. His game plan is to get us to act according to our feelings. To defeat Satan, we can take the opposite approach: we can call on the Holy Spirit, listen for his guidance, and follow it instead of our emotions. Then that roaring lion will have to look elsewhere for someone to devour.

Lord, help me remember that Satan wants me
to lose self-control, but I know that when I do, he wins.
Let me never join his team.

SELF-CONTROL

I also pray that you will understand the incredible greatness
of God's power for us who believe him.

EPHESIANS 1:19

Emotions can rapidly become too strong for us to control on our own. But more potent than our emotions is the power God offers us to control them.

To receive God's power, we have to ask. The Bible says the Holy Spirit will teach us, remind us, convict us, and guide us (John 14:26; 16:8, 13). It never says He will force us. We decide whether to ask, listen, and follow. We can either give free rein to our emotions, or we can turn to God. If we elect to go it on our own, God will allow that. A consequence will be lack of self-control.

It's easier to turn to God for help when we discern a trickle of emotion than when we're being swept away by its flood. Asking God for strength before our feelings run amuck requires us to be alert to them. The moment we sense our emotions beginning to build, we can ask God for power—his power—to control them.

Thank you, God, for my freedom of choice.
May I always use it to choose you.

Wisdom is shown to be right by its results.

MATTHEW 11:19

In our many married years, my husband and I have said hurtful things to each other more times than I want to count. We said them because we felt justified at the moment; it felt good, right then, to say them. Letting off steam gave us brief satisfaction. Later, we'd regret our words, but couldn't take them back. We'd acted on our feelings instead of exercising self-control.

Have you ever said, done, bought, or eaten something because it felt *reeaally* good at the time . . . but found it felt *reeaally* bad later? Acting on feelings generally gives us immediate pleasure, but, later, remorse. We give up what we want most for what we want *now.* It's easy to be in the moment and not notice the Holy Spirit's check on our spirit. Or to ignore it. In contrast, exercising self-control sacrifices instant happiness, but generally means long-term gratification.

Self-control is fed by wisdom: "Wisdom that comes from heaven is . . . peace-loving, considerate, submissive, full of mercy and good fruit, impartial and sincere" (James 3:17 NIV84). Joyce Meyer adds this: "Wisdom always waits for the right time to act, while emotion always pushes for action right now! . . . While wisdom calmly looks ahead to determine how a decision will affect the future, emotions are only concerned with what is happening at the moment" (*Managing Your Emotions*).

When you need wisdom, ask God. He promises to give it to us (James 1:5).

Lord, when something feels so right
I know it must be wrong, give me wisdom.

Wise people think before they act; fools don't.

PROVERBS 13:16

Too often, I live the way I play tennis. On the court, instead of planning how to return the ball and where to place it, I just smash it back and hope that, through sheer force and some luck, it will land where it should. But my swift returns often land in the wrong place, and I end up losing. The same thing happens on the court of life: smashing without planning doesn't work out for me.

With every ball and every circumstance that comes my way, there's a time—however brief—when I can think about how I should respond. Using that instant to consider options and likely consequences is critical. Aiming my return rather than just whacking the ball is the only way I'll succeed at tennis. Making considered responses is the only way I'll succeed at life. This is being proactive instead of reactive. Stephen Covey, in *The 7 Habits of Highly Effective People*, says, "Reactive people are driven by feelings, by circumstances, by conditions, by their environment. Proactive people are driven by values—carefully thought about, selected and internalized values."

Lack of self-control and reactive behavior go hand in hand, and reactive behavior can result in regret. If a first impulse will lead to the best result, it will also withstand the test of self-control. A pause allows examination. It enables wise action rather than an emotional reaction. Responding rather than reacting can mean the difference between ultimate success or failure in the game of tennis . . . and in the game of life.

Help me, Lord, to respond, not react,
to be proactive, not reactive.

Trust in the Lord with all your heart;
do not depend on your own understanding.

PROVERBS 3:5

Recently I blurted out the first thing that came to mind. It wasn't the wisest choice of words. I persisted; things got worse. Later, trying to mentally pick up the pieces, I asked God where I went wrong. His answer was immediate: "You tried to deal with the situation without me."

Self-control isn't only a matter of weighing instant gratification against long-term impact (although I'd blown that one too). It's trusting God, acknowledging we need his help. It's restraining our proclivity to jump in without seeking his direction. Sometimes it's just keeping quiet, turning the situation over to him. Failure to do that says, in essence, "I don't trust God to handle this" or "I'll leave God out of this" (always a bad idea). The Bible never says to figure it out on our own. Repeatedly it says to trust God.

Living the fruit of self-control can be a huge relief. We can give all our burdens to God. He'll take care of us (Psalm 55:22). When we're still and we know that he is God (Psalm 46:10), we can be certain the situation will be resolved in the best possible way, at the best possible time.

What a relief, Lord, to know I don't have to deal
with anything on my own. Help me remember
that exercising self-control means I'm trusting in you.

So think clearly and exercise self-control.

1 PETER 1:13

At a restaurant, my husband and I split a salad. I ordered a different dressing for my half. When we got our bill, we'd been charged a dollar for the extra dressing. I complained to my poor husband for nearly an hour not about the dollar, but about the principle of their charging it. Finally, I remembered a story about Benjamin Franklin I'd read in Dale Carnegie's *How to Stop Worrying and Start Living*.

At age seven, Franklin wanted a whistle. He piled his savings onto the store counter and requested the whistle without asking its price. When his siblings discovered he'd paid far more than the whistle was worth, they mocked him. Franklin's happiness turned to tears when he learned he'd paid too much for his whistle. As he grew up, Franklin saw that many people make that same mistake. He observed, "A great part of the miseries of mankind are brought upon them by their giving too much for their whistles."

In the scheme of things, no "whistles" are important enough to warrant losing self-control. The cost of something is the amount of life we exchange for it. We often give more of our lives for our whistles than they're worth. We need to weigh the cost of our actions in terms of what they take out of our very existence.

Having complained to my husband for an hour—no self-control there!—I had definitely overpaid, all over salad dressing.

Lord, help me remember that if I listen to you,
I will never pay too much for a whistle.

*Jesus said, "Come to me, all of you who are weary
and burdened, and I will give you rest."*

MATTHEW 11:28

Marta looked at her friend's pale face, her dark-circled eyes, how she just picked at her lunch.

Marta knew that "You look tired" is never taken as a compliment. So she just said, "Is everything okay?"

A half hour of venting later, Marta's friend smiled. "Don't worry. You can say it. I look frazzled . . . because I am."

"Have you tried sharing all this with God?" Marta said.

"God's got better things to do than deal with my problems," her friend said.

From our human perspective, God does have a lot to do—but the friend's statement wasn't accurate. It implied a limit to God's power, interest in, and love for us. There is no such limit. He cares about and will gladly handle everything we take to him. He promises rest when we're weary and burdened (Psalm 62:5 NIV84).

When we're exhausted, we may not be exercising the kind of self-control that allows the best refreshment possible—controlling our propensity to cope alone. We can restrain our urge to figure it all out and instead lay it at God's feet. We can "Pour out [our] hearts to him" (Psalm 62:8 NIV84). When we're stooped under the weight of problems, we can respond with the self-control of saying "Here I am, Lord. I'm giving this all to you."

*Thank you, Jesus, for inviting me to come to you
and know your rest. Whenever I'm tempted to go it alone,
let me remember your words, "Come to Me."*

DAY 60

Don't use your freedom to satisfy your sinful nature.

GALATIANS 5:13

Everything we do is a choice. "One of the biggest mistakes people make is thinking that life is one big 'have-to.' They have to go to work . . . to school . . . to the store . . . to do a zillion other things. The truth . . . is that we don't *have* to do anything" (Hal Urban's *Life's Greatest Lessons*). Anything but accept the consequences of our choices.

To get an idea of where our choices are taking us, author Stephen Covey suggests imagining our funeral. Ask, "How do I want to be remembered? What legacy will I leave? Are my everyday choices consistent with those outcomes?" Covey calls this "beginning with the end in mind" (Stephen Covey's *The 7 Habits of Highly Effective People)*. Make sure every choice we make supports who we want to have been in our earthly life. Even more important, imagine standing before God. What do you want him to say about your life? Are your daily choices in accord with that?

By choosing to be led by God's Spirit, we'll exercise the self-control needed so that when we leave this earth, who we've been and the life we've chosen will be one that made God smile.

*Lord, help me always to make choices
with my end in mind.*

Test me, O Lord, and try me,
examine my heart and my mind.
PSALM 26:2 NIV84

Our anniversary began well. David, my husband, had made dinner reservations. I'd decided to wear what I'd worn at our daughter's recent wedding rehearsal dinner. I asked David how I looked. "Gorgeous" would've been nice. Instead, he looked hesitant, then said, "Are you sure that's in style?"

I didn't react well. He must have had that same thought the night of the rehearsal dinner! I let David know how upset I was. He didn't react well. He told me I had ruined the night, and he wasn't going. It was not a pleasant time. Then I realized I was being tested. I prayed.

It wasn't easy, but somehow I calmly convinced my husband to get in the car. Not a word was exchanged for the half-hour drive to the restaurant. Every time I wanted to speak, God kept me quiet. For thirty minutes I mentally discussed the situation with him. He pointed out that if I was going to be upset every time David deviated from the mental script I'd written for him, I was going to be upset most of the time. David had arranged this dinner because he loved me, in his own way yes, but he did love me. As we arrived, I reached for David's hand. He didn't pull away.

Instead of a ruined night, we had a wonderful dinner, all because I talked to God and kept my mouth closed.

It felt good to pass that test, Lord. It was close,
but thanks to you, we had a beautiful night.

How can you think of saying "Friend, let me help you get rid of that speck in your eye," when you can't see past the log in your own eye.

LUKE 6:42

My husband doesn't like to be interrupted when he's reading. I feel he shouldn't mind my small intrusions, especially when they're brief. He tries to convince me to stop disturbing him. I try to convince him he shouldn't mind my interruptions. We've argued over this for years. We can't seem to change each other.

This is a small of example of a big reality: we can complain, fuss, fume, and try to convince someone to change, but we can't make them do it. The ability to control others is not listed as a fruit of the Spirit. The only behavior we can control is our own.

Yet how much time do we waste trying to control other people's behavior? How little time do we focus on controlling our own? The human conundrum is that each of us wants to control everything in our lives except ourselves, but we have the power to control nothing in our lives except ourselves. It's ironic that often frustration over our inability to control circumstances or other people leads us to lose self-control.

If I would put my effort into examining and correcting my own behavior instead of my husband's, I'd come closer to becoming who God wants me to be. I should either take what bothers me to God . . . or let it drop.

*Lord, may I focus on my own behavior
rather than the behavior
of others.*

Then the way you live will always honor and praise the Lord,
and your lives will produce every kind of good fruit.

COLOSSIANS 1:10

I was recently convicted by this line from a song by Jaime Jamgochian: "My worship is the life I live."

Too often I've allowed my words and actions to contradict the worshipful attitude I feel in my heart. Too frequently my behavior is not what God would look on with delight or see as an act of praise. I want my life to be a worshipful gift to God by living as he's taught. But in life's daily routine, I forget.

I've pondered how to better thank God for all he is and all he's done. Could this line from a song help me remember how to do it? What better way to thank God than to be able to say with confidence, "My worship is the life I live." Do my actions, choices, and words reflect the worship I feel? Does my daily life consistently honor and glorify God? I need to ask myself this every day. Several times a day.

Living the worship my heart contains takes self-control, for each day has challenges and annoyances along with its beauty and joy. Dealing with those in a way that honors God means not being ruled by emotions. When I choose self-control, my life becomes the worship I feel and the best thanks I can offer God.

Lord, thank you for reminding me that, for better or worse,
"my worship is the life I live." May those words prompt me
to exercise self-control, so I live as you've taught.

People with understanding control their anger;
a hot temper shows great foolishness.

PROVERBS 14:29

Remember old westerns, when the team of horses—rattled by something—wildly took off, dragging the stagecoach behind them? That's a great image of what emotions can do to us when we don't use the reins of self-control. They can take us places we don't want to go, places we shouldn't go.

Imagine a child sitting on that runaway stagecoach, trying to manage the reins and get the horses under control. They're too powerful for him. Just as he needs to turn the reins over to someone strong enough to handle the horses' force, we need to turn our reins over to God when our emotions charge ahead.

When we exercise self-control, we harness the energy of potentially runaway emotions and redirect it to where God wants it to be. It's tough to guide a spooked horse. Emotions, too, are more easily directed when they're calmed first. That requires God's help.

Anger is an emotion to be reined in. "Fools vent their anger, but the wise quietly hold it back" (Proverbs 29:11). Anger is a reaction to expectations not met. We're more concerned about whether others are living up to our expectations than we are about whether we're living up to God's. There's much we can't control, but by giving God the reins, our emotions can be restrained, then repositioned on his path rather than carrying us to where we shouldn't go.

When emotions threaten to pull me headlong
in the wrong direction, take the reins,
Lord, calm and redirect me.

As I stood there in silence—not even speaking of good things—
the turmoil within me grew worse.
The more I thought about it, the hotter I got,
igniting a fire of words.

PSALM 39:2–3

Our dog Montana took a while to housebreak. He would relieve himself in the house whenever he had the urge—and also when his excitement rose above a minimum level. An emotional puppy, he'd get caught up in the moment and lose control. He'd pee on the rug.

Over time Montana learned that the consequences of doing so were not good. Eventually he learned to control himself and not let go where it was unacceptable to do so. What a relief when he was finally housebroken.

After all my years, my tongue still isn't completely housebroken. At times I still verbally pee on the rug, saying whatever I feel like saying, whenever and wherever I have the urge. I need to housebreak my tongue, to hold it when it's not appropriate or best to say what I'm feeling. That takes self-control. When I have the urge to speak what I ought not, perhaps I should go outside, away from others, and verbally relieve myself there.

As Montana learned, lack of control is not an endearing habit. I—and everyone around me—will be happier when I learn never to verbally pee on rugs. Getting word stains out is nearly impossible.

Lord, whenever I see perfectly housebroken Montana,
let him remind me it's high time I housebroke my tongue.

Too much talk leads to sin.
Be sensible and keep your mouth shut.

PROVERBS 10:19

In the heat of the moment, how do we avoid saying things we'll regret? The only sure way is to keep silent and allow God to handle the situation. Of course we can't go through life without talking. But if we truly appreciated the impact our words have, we'd choose silence more often.

The book of Proverbs is blunt about the importance of keeping quiet when we're about to say something we shouldn't: "Opening your mouth can ruin everything" (13:3). "Spouting off before listening to the facts is both shameful and foolish" (18:13). "Watch your tongue and keep your mouth shut, and you will stay out of trouble" (21:23).

When I'm about to lose control, the biblical wisdom I need to obey is, "Keep your mouth shut." I need to focus on keeping my lips together, not on what my emotions tell me would be a zinger of a response.

Knowing when to talk and when not to isn't difficult. God puts a check on my spirit when he wants me to stay silent. It's easy to ignore his guidance, but foolish to do so. We're wise to "open our mouths only if what we're about to say is more beautiful than silence" (anonymous).

Lord, put your arm around my shoulder
and your hand over my mouth.

For the happy heart, life is a continual feast.

PROVERBS 15:15

Anna had everything: good looks, a beautiful home, a loving husband, accomplished children—and a complaining spirit. She claimed to know she was blessed, yet that truth didn't sink in enough to keep her from focusing on the bad, rather than the good. One day Anna's daughter was in a car accident. Doctors gave her child little hope of surviving. After a month in the hospital and weeks of rehabilitation, Anna's daughter not only survived, but healed completely. And Anna changed: she was now keenly aware of the insignificance of all that had formerly ignited her tongue.

Crisis brings perspective; perspective can bring self-control. Maybe crisis brings perspective because it turns us to God and he opens our eyes. Controlling the self becomes easier when we realize that most things that bother us are pretty unimportant.

The lens provided by a crisis helps us recognize our upside-down values and skewed viewpoints. Even looking around at other people's trials can bring the needed perspective. This statement offers a valuable reminder: "I cried because I had no shoes until I met a man who had no feet" (origin uncertain).

Lord, may it never take a crisis to give me self-control

You must all be quick to listen, slow to speak,
and slow to get angry.

JAMES 1:19

King Saul was jealous of David, who seemed to be successful at everything, specially blessed by God, and loved by the Hebrew people. Saul felt threatened, thinking David wanted him off the throne. Obsessed with this erroneous belief, Saul hurled his spear at his imagined rival (1 Samuel 19:10). Ruled by emotions and blind to David's loyalty, Saul sought to kill David.

Saul's action was prompted by his emotional reaction to his perceived reality. What we think may or may not be true. It may only be our best guess. Like a first draft, it may need to be revised or even discarded. If, however, we use self-control to put our feelings on hold and then investigate the facts, we can determine whether our assessment is accurate.

Self-control uses emotions as starting points for exploring, not commands to obey. Our emotions should be a cue to seek to know more. Too often I act on them without determining if they're appropriate for reality. We rarely need to respond with fight or flight, or to act instantaneously based on emotions. Instead, they can protect us by making us cautious instead of precipitous, by guiding, not propelling us.

Lord, give me the self-control to not act
until I've examined my emotions in your light of truth.

You are controlled by the Spirit if you have
the Spirit of God living in you. . . .
You have no obligation to do
what your sinful nature urges you to do.
ROMANS 8:9, 12

I had a small victory today: I chose self-control when I felt slighted and hurt. I wanted to let the person involved know my feelings, but the way I was about to do that would have ruined their day—and mine. Instead, I was calm and polite. I briefly said my feathers had been ruffled and why. Then I dropped the matter. We ate lunch together. I said nothing further about the incident. Nor did I let my hurt feelings impact our conversation.

I was surprised to find my tension dissipating. As our conversation became more and more a normal exchange, my hurt feelings began to disappear. By meal's end I was in a good mood, not even thinking about the hurt that had threatened to disrupt the day.

Self-control works. I need to remember that when I'm tempted not to exercise it. Self-control takes the wind out of our ship's sails when we're approaching stormy seas. It redirects us back to calm waters. The effort may be great; the rewards are greater. God will give us the power we need.

My mother used to say, "A journey of a thousand miles begins with a single step." Today I took a step.

Lord, thank you for walking with me,
one small step at a time.

Be my rock of protection, a fortress where I will be safe. . . .
For the honor of your name, lead me out of this danger.

PSALM 31:2–3

"Time out!" We use this with our children. We see it in sports. We can also use it with ourselves when we're in danger of doing something we may regret. A time-out removes us from the heat of the moment. It allows us to calm down and reassess. It can save us from unwise behavior.

Elijah was a prophet used by God to turn Israel away from its idol worship. Israel was ignoring Elijah's message. When he became discouraged and afraid, God led him to take a time-out. "Go out and stand before me on the mountain," God said (1 Kings 19:11). There, in a gentle whisper, God told Elijah what his next steps should be.

Psalm 57:1 says, "I will hide beneath the shadow of your wings until the danger passes by." That is what we can do when we're overwhelmed or risk making a wrong choice. We can take a time-out in the shadow of God's wings and listen for his whisper of guidance, for he will surely lead us. That's a promise: "I will guide you along the best pathway for your life. I will advise you and watch over you" (Psalm 32:8–9).

Lord, when I'm about to lose self-control,
help me call "Time out!" and spend the time with you.

*I pondered the direction of my life,
and I turned to follow your laws.*

PSALM 119:59

I couldn't decide between the tiger and the giraffe.

I was buying puppets for two of my grandchildren, brother and sister. I knew I wanted the lion with the adorable shaggy mane for one, but I liked both the tiger and the giraffe for the other. Then the salesperson said something that made my decision easy.

"What story do you want to tell? The lion and the tiger will have conflict. The lion and the giraffe can be friends and make a happy story." I bought the lion and the giraffe.

I'd been looking only at which puppet I thought was cuter. I hadn't thought about the impact each one could have. "What story do you want to tell?" What great advice, not only for my purchase, but for our lives. How often do we make decisions based only on surface appeal? What if, before every choice, we were to exercise the self-control to ask, "What story do I want my life to tell?" and "Will this choice help tell that story?"

My life story can be one of conflict or one of joy, of complaining or contentment, self-indulgence or self-discipline. Asking, "What story do I want to tell?" will help avoid choices that look appealing but would make my life a story neither I nor God want it to be.

*Lord, when my life is done, it will tell a story.
Give me the self-control to ensure my every choice contributes
to the story you want my life to have told.*

DAY 72

SELF-CONTROL

These people are grumblers and complainers.

JUDE 1:16

The Israelites Moses led through the desert were complainers. They bemoaned their thirst, their hunger, and that Moses took too long in his Mount Sinai meeting with God. They protested that they never should have left Egypt. Despite their bad attitude, disrespect, and lack of trust, God met their needs. But they went too far: fed up with their complaining, he refused to let that generation enter the Promised Land.

A complaint is an expression of dissatisfaction without any attempt to solve the problem. Complaining distances us from others. No one wants to be around a complainer.

So why do we complain? Perhaps to release stress. If so, there are more effective ways to do that (like exercise!). Whiners zero in on the negative. The Bible says to fix our thoughts on the positive (Philippians 4:8). If something is bothersome, we can take it to God not as a complaint, but as a prayer: "Pray about everything. Tell God what you need, and thank him for all he has done. Then you will experience God's peace" (vv. 6–7).

Complaints surface when we focus on self, perhaps offering a running commentary on our emotions: "I'm upset. . . . He irritates me. . . . That is so annoying. . . . I'm so angry, concerned, afraid, outraged, hurt."

Like a kaleidoscope, feelings continually change. It's normal to experience them, but we don't need to express them all.

Lord, I find it too easy to complain. Forgive me.

Those who are dominated by the sinful nature think
about sinful things, but those who are controlled
by the Holy Spirit think about things that please the Spirit.

ROMANS 8:5

Be careful of your thoughts, for your thoughts become your words. Be careful of your words, for your words become your actions. Be careful of your actions, for your actions become your habits. Be careful of your habits, for your habits become your character. Be careful of your character, for your character becomes your destiny. (origin unknown)

It all begins with thoughts. They have enormous impact. Our words, actions, habits, and character are all rooted in them. We can let them run anywhere, or we can control them. Controlling our thoughts is the best way to gain mastery over our words and actions.

The Bible says, "Take captive every thought to make it obedient to Christ" (2 Corinthians 10:5 NIV84). We're promised peace when we fix our thoughts on God (Isaiah 26:3). Yet John Ortberg says that "our thought patterns become as habitual as brushing our teeth. We get so used to bitter . . . or selfish thoughts that we don't even notice" them (*The Me I Want to Be*).

When Peter lasered his thoughts on Jesus, he walked on water. When he lost that focus, he sank (Matthew 14:2–31). Our thoughts affect us physically, emotionally, and spiritually. They can even change our world.

Lord, keep me aware of my thoughts and their potential impact.
Guide them first and foremost to you.

The man replied, "It was the woman you gave me
who gave me the fruit, and I ate it."...
"The serpent deceived me," she replied. "That's why I ate it."
GENESIS 3:12–13

Humans blame. What began with Adam and Eve continues in today's litigious society. People act without prayer or thought. Then, when bad consequences result, they look for a scapegoat.

Today's society is reluctant to label sin for what it is and places little importance on accountability, for that would require drawing a distinct line between right and wrong. People rationalize sin by renaming it "choice," and replace black and white with gray.

When we can blame, rationalize, and make excuses, who needs self-control? As Philip Yancey said in *Rumors of Another World,* self-control isn't following rules set by "God as a frowning Enforcer." It's living according to the plan of our "loving Creator who desires the best for us in life, with sin as the main obstacle preventing it."

God can give us the ability to replace blame with accountability. When we make that choice, we're more likely to exercise self-control.

Lord, help me take full responsibility for my actions.

Better to hear the quiet words of a wise person
than the shouts of a foolish king.

ECCLESIASTES 9:17

When I'm angry or upset, the volume of my voice automatically increases (a kind way of admitting I lose self-control). When it does, my effectiveness decreases.

I've heard that to get a child's attention, whisper. That works with adults too. People tend to tune out yelling or become too defensive to listen. The best way to convince is to lower, not raise, your voice. That takes self-control.

Though yelling may appear to work for parents, over time it not only teaches children this bad habit, its result is that we lose their attention and eventually their respect. "Talking with quiet confidence will always beat screaming with obvious insecurity" (origin unknown).

In *When You Feel Like Screaming*, authors Pat Holt and Grace Ketterman say this about screaming: "The lasting effect of screaming is that psychological calluses form on the eardrums. . . . True strength is expressed only through gentleness and self-control." This principle applies to every relationship. Legitimate, important messages can be lost through angry delivery.

Lord, when I feel my volume rising,
help me speak with quiet confidence instead.

Don't you realize that your body is the temple of the Holy Spirit,
who lives in you and was given to you by God?

1 CORINTHIANS 6:19

Everyone wants to be attractive, healthy, energetic, and in great shape. And people know God doesn't want us involved in sexual sin. Nevertheless, we human beings overeat, overimbibe, choose unhealthy food, smoke, take illegal drugs, let ourselves get out of shape, and/or are sexually immoral. When it comes to bodies, lack of self-control is rampant.

Perhaps we would take better care of our bodies if we lived according to what the Bible says about them: the Spirit of God lives in the believer (Romans 8:10–11; John 14:20). Our "bodies are actually parts of Christ" (1 Corinthians 6:15). We're to honor God by taking good care of our bodies and avoiding sexual sin (1 Corinthians 6:18, 20). Letting our bodies "be a living and holy sacrifice" is a way of worshipping God (Romans 12:1). Each of us is to "control his own body in a way that is holy and honorable" (1 Thessalonians 4:4).

This is a lot to think about when we reach for that extra piece of cake or watch TV instead of exercising or are tempted by a physical desire we know is wrong. As with all aspects of self-control, when we're tempted, God will show us a way out (1 Corinthians 10:13).

Help me remember my body is your earthly temple, Lord,
and to care for it accordingly.

Honor the LORD with your wealth.

PROVERBS 3:9

A young man said, "Dad, you told me to put my money in that big bank, and now that bank is in trouble."

"But that's one of the most solid banks in the state."

"I don't think so," the son replied. "They just returned my checks with a note that said, 'insufficient funds.'"

Many people spend more than they can afford. It's not surprising. "Advertising is the art of convincing people to spend money they don't have for something they don't need" (Will Rogers). Credit cards make it easy.

God has nothing against money. He asked Israel's King Solomon, "What do you want? Ask, and I will give it to you!" (2 Chronicles 1:7). When Solomon requested wisdom to lead, God was pleased: "Because your greatest desire is to help your people, and you did not ask for wealth, riches . . . but for wisdom and knowledge . . . I will also give you wealth, riches . . . such as no other king has had before, or will ever have!" (vv. 11–12).

Because Solomon had his priorities right, God had no problem with Solomon having wealth. What angers God is not money but a focus on money, on stuff. If we value money and possessions more than we value him, he objects (Matthew 6:24). Jesus said, "A person is a fool to store up earthly wealth but not have a rich relationship with God" (Luke 12:21).

*Lord, may I never let money or things
become more important to me than you are.*

Give honor to marriage.

HEBREWS 13:4

If something is in the Bible, we can be certain it's important to God. If he wanted something in the Bible four times, we'd better pay attention. A "quarrelsome wife," one who doesn't control her tongue or her behavior, who lacks self-control, makes the mark four times in Proverbs:

- "It's better to live alone in the corner of an attic than with a quarrelsome wife in a lovely home." (21:9; 25:24)
- "It's better to live alone in the desert than with a quarrelsome, complaining wife." (21:19)
- "A quarrelsome wife is as annoying as constant dripping on a rainy day. Stopping her complaints is like trying to stop the wind or trying to hold something with greased hands." (27:15–16)

These scriptures are just as applicable to husbands. No one likes to be around—certainly not married to—a person who lacks self-control. We can't control our spouse's words or actions, but we can control ours. Our marriage is impacted by how well we exercise self-control.

The woman whose husband praises her is one "clothed with strength and dignity" (Proverbs 31:25), a perfect description of someone who exercises self-control.

Lord, my marriage is an easy place for me to lose self-control,
yet a most important place to maintain it.
Please help me do so.

Lead them by your own good example.

1 PETER 5:3

Our children watch us, no matter their age. They can pick up our habits, good and bad. Regardless of what we say, they're most impacted by what we do. If we lose our temper, overeat, are financially undisciplined, complain, or react rather than respond, they'll likely do the same. Conversely, even if we don't talk about self-control, they will probably live in a self-controlled manner if that's what they see in us. What they learn in childhood will influence who they become as adults. The good news is, if we direct our "children onto the right path, when they are older they will not leave it" (Proverbs 22:6).

Amaziah, a king of Judah, "did what was pleasing in the LORD's sight. . . . He followed the example of his father, Joash" (2 Kings 14:3). The most important thing we can do for our children is—like Joash—be a good example of a person who honors God with their life.

The actions of Jesus were always in line with his teachings and commands. "I have given you an example to follow," he said. "Do as I have done" (John 13:15).

Lord, help me lead my children
by living the fruit of self-control.

A cheerful heart is good medicine,
but a broken spirit saps a person's strength.

PROVERBS 17:22

Emotions are contagious. That's great when they're positive. But when they're negative, is it fair to subject others to them?

Self-control means keeping our destructive emotions from spreading. If we lay low, stay away from others, take good care of ourselves, and seek God's guidance, negative emotions will likely go away more quickly than a cold. This four-pronged approach beats infecting others with our negativity.

Negative emotions are not only contagious, they can also harm our bodies. Emotions are symptoms of a root cause. They alert us to an underlying issue we can deal with rationally, a better option than shedding them onto others.

Self-control involves subjecting our emotions to the test of time. We can take control and tell the emotion to sit in a waiting room until we've examined it to determine if it's fleeting or needs attention. Then, an expert, the Holy Spirit, can help us diagnose the origin of our emotion, deal with it to bring healing, and keep others from catching it.

Lord, when I feel a negative emotion coming on,
remind me to take it to you and keep it from others.

SELF-CONTROL

People who accept discipline are on the pathway to life.

PROVERBS 10:17

I'm good at making mountains out of molehills. Many of my upsets haven't been worth the time or energy I spent on them. Here are two ideas to help prevent unnecessary emotional expenditure:

1. *Keep an Upset Journal.* Choose one day each week to write in it. When something irritates or upsets you, use self-control and don't let anyone other than God know. When you feel annoyed, remind yourself you can write about it later. Then, on your chosen day, write in the journal all you want, about everything that bothered you the past week. Monthly, review what you've written. Cross out what no longer bothers you. I find that even though those situations seemed important in the moment, I'm thankful I kept quiet. Pray about anything that's still on the list.

2. *If you didn't keep quiet, rate the level of your upset/reaction.* Using a scale of 1 to 10, rate the seriousness of what upset you— how important it will be a year from now—and the intensity of your reaction. Anything with a seriousness rating of less than 5 and a reaction rating greater than 1 means you're making a mountain out of a molehill. In most cases, a reaction rating of more than 5 is wasting energy that could have been invested in prayer. Even though your reaction has already occurred, this exercise increases awareness. Eventually we can learn to apply the upset/reaction exercise before we let our response get out of control.

Lord, help me stop making mountains out of molehills.

Jesus said, "Now you are my friends."

JOHN 15:14

It's wonderful to have friends to turn to, complain to, vent to, share with, and ask for advice. But many people don't know how to handle another person's emotions. They may listen, but not know how to help, no matter how much they want to. They may think they're giving good advice, but it may be worldly or unwise. It's best to control our urge to let it all out.

The only friend to whom we can always confidently and safely express our emotions is God. He understands every emotion, for he created them. He never tires of hearing us, and he's never too busy to listen. He can help us sort the important from the unimportant, the fleeting from the more enduring, the better from the good. He will calm and guide us. God knows our heart, and past, present, and future—as well as that of everyone involved. No one else has that perspective.

God will let us know whether the issue or feeling should be shared with others. Going to him first can save us headache, hassle, and heartache. It can preserve friendships that might be harmed by sharing emotions and problems that should have remained private.

When troubles strike, turn to a friend first—as long as that friend is your *best* Friend. We'll never regret exercising the self-control to do that.

Thank you, Jesus, for being the best Friend I could ever have.

Don't copy the behavior and customs of this world.

ROMANS 12:2

From oversized restaurant servings to enticements to buy the latest in everything, from the sexual revolution to encouragement to do whatever feels good, the world shouts invitations to indulge. Peer pressure and constant exposure inure us to self-focused living. The Bible warns about the time when "people will love only themselves and their money. They will be boastful and proud, scoffing at God . . . and ungrateful. They will consider nothing sacred. They will be unloving and unforgiving; they will slander others and have no self-control . . . love pleasure rather than God . . . [and] reject the power that could make them godly" (2 Timothy 3:2–5). God also says, "Do not love this world nor the things it offers you" (1 John 2:15).

At first, I had difficulty accepting the admonition not to love this world. After all, it's amazing and beautiful, and Jesus came to give us "a rich and satisfying life" (John 10:10). But now I believe the world Scripture refers to here is not God's natural world, but cultures, politics, philosophies, social systems, and values man has fashioned within it. We're to enjoy what God created, but not love the self-indulgent, man-produced world.

As Christians, we're to be the light of the world (Matthew 5:14). But, without self-control we're like a city with broken-down walls, exposed to the enemy's attacks (Proverbs 25:28).

---

*Lord, when I'm tempted to idolize the world's self-gratifying ways,
remind me it's the fruit of self-control that will help me
know the rich and satisfying life you came to give.*

PATIENCE

Patient endurance is what you need now,
so that you will continue to do God's will.
Then you will receive all that he has promised.

<small>HEBREWS 10:35–36</small>

Dear Lord,
Life is filled with challenges and difficulties. When things get tough, it's tempting to get angry or give up. Please fill me with patient endurance instead.

So many things require waiting. Waiting is hard. When I want something, I want it right away. When someone or something isn't to my liking, I want change immediately.

Rather than responding with impatience, may I always seek you before I act and speak, for you have perspective that I do not. You know all things, see all things, and understand all things. I tend to see what I want to see, know so little, and understand even less. When I become impatient, remind me that impatience will not get me what I truly want or need.

I am grateful, Lord, that you have perfect patience—with me, and with mankind. May this fruit blossom in me, no matter what urge I feel. Help me to always pray with trust, knowing that your answer, whatever it is and whenever it may come, will be the right answer at the right time, even if the wait seems long to me.

Amen.

*If we look forward to something we don't yet have,
we must wait patiently and confidently.*

ROMANS 8:25

Daniel Webster, in his 1848 dictionary (which he wrote with a strong Christian faith), defined patience as "a calm temper which bears evils without murmuring or discontent . . . endurance without . . . fretfulness." Endurance is essential because, as Jesus said, "Here on earth you will have many trials and sorrows" (John 16:33). The Holy Spirit gives us the patience to keep on keeping on no matter what we face.

This ability to endure applies to every aspect of life, from things as insignificant as a slow grocery checkout line to as critical as keeping our faith in God through crisis and tragedy. Patience is a combination of acceptance and trust—acceptance that people and circumstances won't always be as we want, trust that no matter what, God is in control. We need patience when we look forward to something that can't come quickly enough as well as when we face something that can't end soon enough. When, with calm acceptance, we do what's in our ability and God's will for us to do, then wait, trusting God for the rest, we're living this fruit.

*Thank you, God, for the strength to continue no matter what.
May I always have the faith to accept and trust,
knowing you're in control.*

*We also pray that you will be strengthened
with all his glorious power, so you will have
all the endurance and patience you need.*

COLOSSIANS 1:11

Life includes waiting. Often, it's the only option we have. We face trials and challenges. There may be no choice but to somehow survive. We deal with trying situations and complicated people. Sometimes we're unable to get away from them. Does this mean we're patient?

Getting through doesn't equal patience. Patience is attitude as well as behavior. It's tolerance for what is, while doing our part, according to God's will. If we continue on, but complain, whine, or let our temper flare, we're not being patient. If we survive, but haven't done what we should, we've not been patient. Patience is "reaching up as far as we can and letting God reach down all the rest of the way" (origin unknown).

When situations or people aren't to our liking, how do we respond? When life gets tough, do we opt out or persevere? When we wait, do we wail as well?

Some of us are calm in crisis and fall apart over little things. Some can handle small things well but are defeated by major trials. Others face both with composure. Some can deal with neither and are always flaring up or caving in.

In what areas of your life do you most need to cultivate patience?

*Lord, help me be patient at all times
and in all things, most especially when . . .*

Create in me a pure heart, O God,
and renew a steadfast spirit within me.

PSALM 51:10 NIV84

"Nobody likes a quitter." How many times did we hear that growing up? And it was true. No one respected or wanted to be friends with someone who couldn't hack it, who said, "I quit" when frustrated or disappointed. Yet, as we became adults, quitting somehow became more acceptable, often painted over with excuses, costumed with blame, or labeled with euphemisms.

Hoping for something better, people drop one pursuit and pick up another. Like someone with a remote control constantly switching channels, never giving any show a chance, those people switch relationships, jobs, friendships, homes, and even marriages they find boring, uncomfortable, or challenging. Or they tap their fingers and wait, calling attention to their frustration and impatience. What's happened to determination, to persistence, to Churchill's "Never, never give up"? While alive and well in many, they've disappeared in others.

"If something isn't fun anymore, it's not for me" is a sad, and shallow, mentality. Too often the downs in the normal ups and downs of life are seen as a sign to move on. God included patience as a fruit of his Spirit so we won't give up. For no one, including God, likes a quitter.

Lord, I'm your child. I refuse to be a quitter.
Give me strength to keep my resolve.

Since God chose you to be the holy people he loves,
you must clothe yourselves with . . . patience.

COLOSSIANS 3:12

Picture someone who is impatient. How do they look? How do you feel about them?

Impatience is unattractive at best, quite ugly at worst. It can bring frowns, glares, and general unpleasantness, things I don't want to be around. My opinion of an impatient person spirals down. Could it be that when I'm impatient I look that way, too, that people want to get away from me, and their opinion of me plummets?

When I think of impatience, words that come to mind are *angry, reactive, irritated, intolerant, hasty, rash, hotheaded.* And how does an impatient person cause us to feel? Tense, on edge, stressed, defensive, upset, resentful, bothered?

What words describe patience? I think of *calm, peaceful, kind, understanding, pleasant, controlled,* and *accepting.* Those words make me think of Stephen, "a man full of God's grace and power," who patiently endured false accusations of the Sanhedrin, yet "his face was like the face of an angel" (Acts 6:8, 15 NIV84).

God offers us the ability to clothe ourselves in the beauty called patience. Why would we want to wear anything else?

Help me remember, Lord, that being dressed
in impatience is never attractive.

Do not fret—it leads only to evil.

PSALM 37:8 NIV84

Isabel glared at her children who were laughing as they ate breakfast. "Hurry up, I haven't got all day!"

Her stomach churned, but she wasn't hungry. Today she might hear about the promotion for which she'd waited so long. She hustled her kids to the car and fumed as she pulled into a long line of vehicles. Her children sang as she drove, but she didn't listen. She was too busy grumbling about the traffic.

"You're taking forever!" she said as her kids gathered their backpacks and exited the car at school.

At work Isabel stared at her watch. *Why haven't I heard anything?* Her head pounded. She slammed her mouse down as her computer locked up yet again. *I've prayed and prayed for this promotion, God. Why haven't you done something?*

Driving to the grocery store, Isabel leaned on her horn and passed a car. In the store's express line, her chest tightened. Both shoppers ahead of her violated the posted item limit. Isabel called her husband. "Did you pick up the kids?" He'd been delayed. Her blood pressure rose along with her voice.

After dinner Isabel, exhausted, went to bed. Her husband read to the kids, tucked them in, then joined her. He noticed the deep furrow between her brows even as she slept.

Impatience closes our eyes to our blessings, stresses our body, damages our relationships, mars our character, and wears us out. It does no good, no good at all.

Help me choose patience, Lord.

Better to be patient than powerful.
PROVERBS 16:32

When I was a practicing litigation attorney I attended a hearing before a judge known for his careful reasoning as well as his volatility. The opposing attorney told the judge he'd been waiting for a ruling on a Motion and asked when he'd get a decision. The judge replied, "You want a decision? Okay. I'll give you one." He banged his gavel. "Your Motion's denied."

My daughter and I were on a road trip. We got behind a car barely going the speed limit on a seemingly deserted highway. I encouraged her to pass. She did, exceeding the speed limit, and was immediately pulled over by a state patrolman who wrote her a ticket.

I wanted an avocado for lunch. All the ones I had were hard, but I cut one open anyway. It was tasteless and inedible. I threw it away.

Those are just a few examples of a larger truth: impatience gets results, but not the ones we want. Most things take time for a reason. The judge may have had other pressing priorities or planned to write a well-reasoned opinion. The other car may have seen the cop or known of some road danger we didn't see. And that avocado? Well, ripening just takes time, pure and simple.

Lord, help me remember that if I force things,
I'll generally regret it.

It is to our glory to overlook an offense.

PROVERBS 19:11

When we don't get what we desire or expect, we may feel anger. Anger is a form of impatience. It says, "I don't like this. I want it to change right now." God has given us anger as a cue that something may need to change. But uncontrolled, anger can be a slippery and treacherous slope. That's why the Bible says, "Don't sin by letting anger control you" (Ephesians 4:26).

Patience can stop anger. Proverbs reminds that "A patient man calms a quarrel" (15:18) and "Don't say 'I will get even for this wrong.' Wait for the Lord to handle the matter" (20:22).

At least nine times the Old Testament says the Lord is "slow to anger" (Exodus 34:6; Numbers 14:18; Nehemiah 9:17; Psalm 86:15; 103:8; 145:8; Joel 2:13; Jonah 4:2; Nahum 1:3). God gets angry, but he tempers his anger with patience. Scripture says we're to do the same: "You must all be quick to listen, slow to speak, and slow to get angry" (James 1:19).

When we feel an inner explosion of anger, we can curb its outward impact by choosing patience. We can pray for wisdom: "Don't let me do something stupid, Lord." "Wisdom gives us patience" (Proverbs 15:18). Why? Because it opens our eyes to the truth that uncontrolled anger gets us nowhere good.

Lord, may I never try to solve anything when I'm angry.

This a trustworthy saying . . .
1 TIMOTHY 3:1

The apostle Paul was fond of passing along "trustworthy sayings" (1 Timothy 1:15; 3:1; 4:9; 2 Timothy 2:11; Titus 3:8). I've collected some of my own sayings about patience, to use as reminders when I'm in danger of losing it.

- "Faith in God means faith in his timing." (Neal Maxwell)
- "The moment you're ready to quit is usually the moment right before the miracle happens. Don't give up." (anonymous)
- "You are going to want to give up. Don't." (anonymous)
- "A diamond is a piece of charcoal that handled stress exceptionally well." (anonymous)
- "I'm not telling you it's going to be easy. But it's going to be worth it." (anonymous)
- "Patience is the ability to idle your motor when you feel like stripping your gears." (Barbara Johnson)
- "The key to everything is patience. You get the chicken by hatching the egg, not by smashing it." (Arnold Glasgow)

Thank you for trustworthy sayings, Lord.
Help me remember that turning to trustworthy you
is the best thing I can do.

The LORD is my shepherd; I have all that I need.

PSALM 23:1

The words of Psalm 23 exemplify the attributes of patience. Patience means faith the Lord is leading and caring for us. If we never get more than we have, we know we have enough. We have peace and strength to endure, no matter what. We don't charge ahead on our own but look to God for guidance. We don't fear, but trust, knowing God is working all things for good (Romans 8:28).

What else does patience do? It's a witness of our trust in God; it injects calm, provides opportunity for change for the better, reduces stress, prevents quarrels, respects others, builds character, acknowledges the sovereignty of God, encourages enjoying what we do have, brings perspective and clarity, allows response rather than reaction, lets life unfold according to God's plan, frees us to use our energy productively, sets a good example, and avoids regret.

There's a lot of good in patience.

Lord, please help me choose patience more often.

I was pouring out my heart to the Lord.

1 SAMUEL 1:15

My sister, a Christian counselor, introduced me to the concept of stress buckets. Everyone carries one. Small daily stresses drip into it, merging with the stream of more significant ones. The total amount of stress in our bucket determines how well we'll handle additional stressors.

Have you ever become impatient when you normally wouldn't have? Have you felt you were handling a challenge well, but suddenly couldn't deal with it? What happened? Your stress bucket overflowed.

We all have different size stress buckets. Some are huge, others tiny, yet all can fill up and overflow as impatience. Even a small stress will cause an almost-full bucket to spill over. Add a big enough stressor, and it will flood over.

At some point, our stress bucket will reach its limit and not be able to hold any more. But if we continually give our stresses to God, the contents in our bucket will remain manageable. Whether it's a few drops or a brimming bucket, God welcomes us pouring it at his feet. We need never hesitate to give all our worries and cares to God, for he cares about us (1 Peter 5:7).

Lord, remind me when my stress bucket needs emptying,
and to empty it only before you.

Surely I spoke of things I did not understand.
JOB 42:3 NIV84

I e-mailed a couple we'd met on a cruise vacation. I didn't hear back and mentally wrote them off. Three months later I received a long e-mail from them, apologizing for not writing sooner. Just after my e-mail had arrived, the wife's father had become ill. He had died two weeks later.

How often a lack of patience is due to a lack of understanding. How much more patient we are when we know the reasons for things we're bothered by. Evaluating a situation only from our own limited perspective fails to consider other possible explanations. "People with understanding control their anger" (Proverbs 14:29).

The biblical definition of *understand* is "to perceive with the mind, as distinct from perception by feeling . . . to know, to come to know . . . to inquire." We often become impatient based on "perception by feeling," not facts. Understanding sees from another's viewpoint; facts can align our thinking with reality. Sometimes, to understand, we need to ask.

Lack of understanding has been defined as "to be ignorant." When we're ignorant of the facts, we're more likely to become impatient. Understanding something doesn't mean we agree, but it increases the likelihood we'll be patient.

Lord, help me seek to understand.

What is impossible for people is possible with God.
LUKE 18:27

When I was young, I enjoyed singing "High Hopes," a song made popular by Frank Sinatra. It was about an ant that was determined to move a rubber tree plant, a seemingly impossible feat. But that ant had "high hopes," and the song ended with "Oops, there goes another rubber tree plant."

That simple song holds an important truth. It's hope that keeps us going. It's hope that fuels endurance. When we have hope, we acknowledge the possibility that what we want will happen, so we don't give up.

The good news for Christians is that, no matter what occurs, we always have hope, because "nothing is impossible with God" (Luke 1:37). We're to "rejoice in our confident hope . . . as we wait patiently for God's promises to be fulfilled" (Romans 12:12; 15:4).

When discouraged, we can have hopes far higher and more real than that ant's. As Jesus said, "Anything is possible if a person believes" in him (Mark 9:23). With Christ as our hope, those rubber tree plants don't have a chance.

Next time I'm found—like the ant—with my "chin on the ground," may I look to you, Lord, and find hope to endure.

You will keep in perfect peace, all who trust in you,
all whose thoughts are fixed on you!

Isaiah 26:3

Life requires patience. Whether we're waiting for the arrival of happy events like weddings, childbirth, and vacations, or nervous about job offers, test results, or selling homes, or waiting for a friend to show up for lunch, patience is called for.

Assuming our stress bucket level is comfortably low, we can be patient in lots of daily things, like waiting for coffee to brew, tedious meal preparation, or our turn at the gas pump. We don't think twice about being patient with babies, airport security, the disabled, or the elderly. Every day we're patient in certain situations and may not give it a thought.

Today, make a mental note of every person and situation that requires your patience. Pay attention to how you respond. You may notice you're patient when you focus on the other person(s) needs and situation, and impatient when you focus on your own needs or desires.

Key is where our focus is, where we fix our thoughts. When we elevate ourselves to primary position, we're likely to lose patience.

Help me put you first Lord, others second, me last.

The Lord said, "My power works best in weakness."

2 CORINTHIANS 12:9

I was leaving work for a long-awaited family vacation to England and Scotland when a colleague stopped me. "I know you're excited about your trip," he said. "Just don't expect it to be perfect."

During our vacation, his advice echoed. I remembered it when our children fell asleep in the car, oblivious to my ongoing exclamations of "Ooh, look! Another castle!" I recalled it when we got rain-soaked walking to a castle . . . only to learn upon arrival that it was closing time. I thought of it when we got lost, as we navigated roundabouts, and when we ate potato chips for dinner because by the time we found a hotel, the restaurants had closed. "Don't expect it to be perfect" turned frustrations into adventures we still laugh about.

How much aggravation do I subject myself and others to because—even subconsciously—I expect perfection? Patience comes more readily when our expectations are closer to reality. Not much in life goes without a hitch.

———————————

Lord, when I start expecting perfection, remind me that nothing and no one is perfect except you.

A cheerful heart is good medicine.

PROVERBS 17:22

Something to think about: heartfelt laughter and impatience can't occur together.

It can be difficult to let ourselves laugh, especially when it means laughing at ourselves. There have been times I've stifled a smile or held back laughter because I didn't want to admit my situation really was laughable. How ridiculous! To avoid looking foolish I've chosen to be impatient instead of letting myself laugh. But how much more foolish I look when I'm impatient. I'm sure anyone would appreciate me more if I laughed at myself rather than lose my cool.

Sometimes Winston Churchill could be talking about me: "Madam, you are like the woman who keeps chickens in her yard and goes around picking up the chicken droppings instead of the eggs." How much better to find the eggs of humor in a situation rather than the droppings of irritation.

Learning to look for and find what's funny, and not taking ourselves, others, and situations more seriously than they deserve, can be excellent patience creators. Like the proverbial duck, we can let things roll off our backs and laugh them off if they don't roll off by themselves. As a man named Michael Pritchard observed, "Laughter is like changing a baby's diaper. It doesn't change things permanently, but it makes everything okay for a while." This "while" allows us to garner patience. It can even be a game: when tension wells up, see how quickly we can find humor in the situation. There almost always is some.

*Lord, help me never be afraid to laugh . . .
especially at myself.*

For the happy heart, life is a continual feast.
PROVERBS 31:25

I'd ordered birthday flowers to be delivered to our daughter Rachel's workplace. When I hadn't heard from her by midday, I called the florist and was put on hold for twenty-five minutes. They finally assured me the flowers had been delivered.

"Are you positive? I know my daughter. She'd have thanked me by now."

Silence. "No, they weren't delivered—but they will be right away."

I decided to try patience, so I thanked them and left to go for a bike ride. Putting my bike in the car, I realized my bike tires needed inflating, extracted my bike, and hooked up the electric pump. Nothing. I called my husband for tips—and saw he'd left his phone at home. I chuckled.

I finally figured out the problem with the pump and drove to the bike path. When I put in my earphones, I discovered my iPod battery was dead. I shrugged. My odometer had stopped working. *Oh, well.* My phone rang. It was Rachel's ring . . . *probably calling to thank me.* She whispered she was in a meeting and had pocket-dialed me. I laughed. Riding again, I was about to pass a jogger. I said hello but forgot to say, "On your left." She jumped and gave me a dirty look. I apologized.

Eventually the flowers were delivered, but the arrangement wasn't what I'd ordered. I called the florist and waited thirty-eight minutes on hold, chuckling frequently.

It beat losing my patience.

Lord, help me see the humor in everyday frustrations.

A day is like a thousand years to the Lord,
and a thousand years is like a day.

2 PETER 3:8

God's concept of time differs from ours. He's not time-bound or time-focused. He's results-focused. God isn't looking at how long something takes, but at whether it occurs. And he's willing to wait: "He is being patient for your sake. He does not want anyone to be destroyed, but wants everyone to repent. . . . The Lord's patience gives people time to be saved" (2 Peter 3:9, 15).

Further, God wants those who are saved to become more like Christ: "God knew his people in advance, and he chose them to become like his Son" (Romans 8:29). He patiently waits for each of us to become more like Jesus, guiding us in our struggle. As the psalmist said, "The Lord directs the steps of the godly. . . . Though they stumble, they will never fall, for the Lord holds them by the hand" (Psalm 37:23–24).

Like the parent of a toddler learning to walk, God is exceedingly patient with our bumbling attempts to live a godly life. He understands our humanness. He forgives our repeated mistakes. But one day, "we will all stand before the judgment seat of God. Yes, each of us will give a personal account to God" (Romans 14:10, 12). Let's pray it includes patience.

Thank you for your patience, God, and for not giving up
on your efforts to make me more like Jesus.

When troubles come your way, consider it an opportunity
for great joy. For you know that when your faith is tested,
your endurance has a chance to grow.

JAMES 1:3

I've tried to grow tomatoes. If I'm lucky, I might get a few, each about golf ball size. Recently a friend showed me her tomato plants. In each of her twelve large pots was a jungle of vines laden with tomatoes the size of grapefruits.

"What's your secret?" I said.

She held up a bag: "Fertilizer."

My tomatoes had been bathed in sunshine and water, but I'd forgotten fertilizer.

Trials and challenges are God's fertilizer for growing our endurance. The apostle Paul put it this way: "We can rejoice, too, when we run into problems and trials, for we know that they help us develop endurance" (Romans 5:3).

Are we to rejoice over pain? No, but we can rejoice because of the results pain can bring: robust patience, hardy endurance, strength of character. God focuses on what grows within us because of trials. We can focus on that as well, pressing on "to possess that perfection for which Christ Jesus first possessed [us]" (Philippians 3:12).

It's tempting to ask God for only sunshine and showers of blessings. But without the fertilizer of trials, our patience and endurance will remain puny and weak.

Lord, may I rejoice in the fact that you use the hardships
I face to help me become more like Jesus.

Think of all the hostility he endured from sinful people;
then you won't become weary and give up.

HEBREWS 12:3

Jesus had to deal with human selfishness, blindness to truth, lack of understanding, forgetfulness, pride, doubt, and fragile faith. Many were oblivious to his identity and ungrateful for his healing and wisdom. Some people rejected him outright.

Jesus had much to teach in a short time. People were slow to grasp truth. No wonder there were times Jesus, who was both human and divine, displayed irritation.

- "Unbelieving and perverse generation . . . how long shall I stay with you? How long shall I put up with you?" (Matthew 17:17 NIV84)
- "Are you still so dull?" (15:16 NIV84)
- "Do you still not understand? Don't you remember?" (16:9 NIV84)
- "Woe to you . . . hypocrites! You blind fools!" (23:13, 17 NIV84)
- "You snakes! You brood of vipers! How long will you escape being condemned to hell?" (23:33 NIV84)

But, reflecting his divinity, Jesus patiently suffered our shortcomings for the greater good. Patience brings results that would not occur if we quit. We have a Lord who can empathize with our feelings of impatience, yet who demonstrated the rewards of endurance.

Lord, I'm glad you understand my impatience.
Help me learn to endure for a greater good.

*Put on every piece of God's armor so you will be able
to resist the enemy in the time of evil.*

EPHESIANS 6:13

It's easy to become exasperated and angry at individuals and circumstances. But they are not where our true battles lie. Satan uses them to get to us. As the apostle Paul says, "We are not fighting against flesh and blood enemies, but against evil rulers and authorities of the unseen world, against mighty powers in this dark world, and against evil spirits in the heavenly places" (Ephesians 6:11–12).

Satan is glad when we don't recognize he's behind our frustration and pain. He wants us to blame anyone and anything but him. When we do, relationships are damaged. That's what he's seeking. Satan doesn't want us to achieve a greater good. He doesn't want us to have any good. His goal is for us to quit and never obtain what we would have if we'd endured.

God supplies everything needed to defeat Satan. We're to put on God's armor of truth and righteousness, peace from the gospel, faith in God, knowledge of our salvation, and the Word of God. We're to pray in the Spirit "at all times and on every occasion, stay alert, and be persistent" (Ephesians 6:13–18).

Patient endurance means standing firm, not in our own strength, but in God's. He'll handle the rest.

---

*Help me keep your armor on, Lord, and to pray unceasingly.
If I do these things, Satan has no chance.*

Don't you see how wonderfully kind, tolerant,
and patient God is with you?
Does this mean nothing to you?

ROMANS 2:4

God knows we're not perfect and, on this side of heaven, never will be. Yet, "while we were still sinners, Christ died for us" (Romans 5:8). Through his death, our sins are forgiven, giving us access to our Holy God. "Well, then, should we keep on sinning so that God can show us more and more of his wonderful grace? Of course not!" (Romans 6:1). Yet we do.

When it comes to living a sinless life, we're slow learners. Thankfully, God accepts us as we are. He waits patiently for us to repent of our sins, turn away from them, and turn to him for forgiveness. When we seek him, we will find him (Jeremiah 29:13).

The apostle Paul, who once persecuted Christians, told his story: "God had mercy on me so that Christ Jesus could use me as a prime example of his great patience with even the worst sinners. Then others will realize that they, too, can believe in him and receive eternal life" (1 Timothy 1:16).

Patience is an aspect of God's character available to us as a fruit of his Spirit. When we need endurance, we can draw from his immense reservoir. When others sin against us, we can be patient with them. Seeing that, they may want what we have and turn to Jesus. What greater gift can we give someone? What greater gift can we give God?

Patient Father, may I not only turn from my sin,
but be patient with others.
Use me—use my patience—to draw them to you.

Why are you downcast, O my soul?
Why so disturbed within me? Put your hope in God,
for I will yet praise him, my Savior and my God.

PSALM 42:11 NIV84

The Bible is silent about the interval between Christ's crucifixion and resurrection. I imagine that for those who followed Jesus, it was a hushed time of trying to assimilate what had happened. Or maybe they were just numb. Their Messiah had suffered the horrific execution of a common criminal. He was dead.

It wasn't what they'd expected. They'd seen his miracles, watched him walk on water, witnessed crowds gather to hear him teach. Now he was gone, and so was their hope. Or so they thought. Jesus had told them he would die and rise again, words not understood and now likely forgotten.

Christ could have avoided the cross. He chose not to, for the cross was part of God's plan. God's plan also included a time of waiting before the resurrection.

When an unexpected and unwanted event occurs, we may forget God's promises and feel despair. Let's instead remember Easter waiting. We don't need to understand; just patiently trust. Be it soon or in eternity, resurrection from our time of distress will come. As sunshine follows rain, "weeping may last through the night, but joy comes with the morning" (Psalm 30:5). That is the message of Easter waiting. At the proper time, God "will turn the desert into pools of water, and the parched ground into springs" (Isaiah 41:18).

Lord, when something terrible happens,
give me strength to patiently wait for you to use it for good.

I am waiting for you, O Lord.

PSALM 38:15

God has plans to prosper and not harm us, to give us hope and a future (Jeremiah 29:11). Timing is up to him, and not for us to know (Acts 1:7). Our role is to patiently wait for God's appointed time in all things. "For everything there is a season, a time for every activity under heaven" (Ecclesiastes 3:1). God has given us his Holy Spirit so we'll have patience to wait for his perfect timing. His Word says:

- "Be still in the presence of the LORD, and wait patiently for him to act." (Psalm 37:7)
- "The LORD is a faithful God. Blessed are those who wait for his help." (Isaiah 30:18)
- "As for me, I look to the LORD for help. I wait confidently for God to save me, and my God will certainly hear me." (Micah 7:7)
- "I wait for the LORD, my soul waits, and in his word I put my hope." (Psalm 130:5–6 NIV84)
- "I waited patiently for the LORD to help me, and he turned to me and heard my cry. He lifted me out of the pit of despair." (Psalm 40:1)

Lord, help me remember that when I choose to wait for you,
I will never be disappointed.

Rejoice in our confident hope.
Be patient in trouble, and keep on praying.
ROMANS 12:12

My father was a good, but stubborn man. He struggled with his Christian faith, wanting more scientific proof, more hard evidence. For years I prayed for him, but Daddy remained resolute.

When he reached his eighties, however, his questions about faith became more persistent. I sensed God working. When, at age eighty-five, Daddy told me, "Jesus Christ is my Savior," I experienced the joy of patient prayer answered.

The psalmist said, "Each morning I bring my requests to you and wait expectantly" (Psalm 5:3). Our wait may last seconds, years, even decades. God's answer may be exactly what we asked for, it may be different, or it may be "no." If we cease praying when we don't feel God is responding quickly enough, we may never receive an answer. But if we're patient, as patient as God requires, God will answer—in his perfect way, timing, and will.

Jesus told his disciples a parable "to show that they should always pray and never give up" (Luke 18:1). A widow was relentless in her petition to an unjust judge. After much time, the judge said yes. If an unjust judge will answer a persistent request, "don't you think God will surely give justice to his chosen people who cry out to him day and night?" (Luke 18:7).

Lord, give me the patience to never stop praying
about whatever you put on my heart.

*We do not want you to become lazy,
but to imitate those who through faith and patience,
inherit what has been promised.*

HEBREWS 6:12 NIV84

Patient endurance is exemplified throughout the Bible. Noah displayed it when he followed God's instructions and built the ark and, after the rains, when he waited for the waters to recede. Moses illustrated it in the wilderness for forty years. Abraham eventually showed it as he waited for God's promise of an heir. Jacob demonstrated it as he labored fourteen years to receive Rachel as his wife. Joseph lived it as he languished in prison and, later, served Egypt's Pharaoh. And those examples are only from the book of Genesis! Throughout both Testaments, patient endurance is taught by example. The apostle Paul said, "In everything we do, we show that we are true ministers of God. We patiently endure troubles and hardships and calamities of every kind" (2 Corinthians 6:4).

In the end times, our patience will be noted. Jesus commended the church in Ephesus: "I know your deeds, your hard work and your perseverance. . . . You have persevered and have endured hardships in my name" (Revelation 2:2–3 NIV84). In his words to the church in Philadelphia, we see that patience may save us from ultimate trial: "Since you have kept my command to endure patiently I will also keep you from the hour of trial that is going to come upon the whole world to test those who live on the earth" (Revelation 3:10 NIV84).

*Lord, you know what's important for me
now and in the future. Thank you for equipping me
through your Word and your Spirit.*

Though he slay me, yet will I hope in him.

JOB 13:15 NIV84

Job had a large family and immense wealth. He was "blameless, had complete integrity, feared God, and stayed away from evil" (Job 1:1). Then Satan struck. Job lost his family, his home, his wealth, his health.

In my Bible, the book of Job is forty-five pages long. Over half are Job's laments and vehement complaints about unfairness: "I will not keep silent; I will speak out in the anguish of my spirit, I will complain in the bitterness of my soul" (Job 7:11 NIV84). And he does, page after page.

We've heard of "the patience of Job." But doesn't patience mean silent endurance, no complaints, sucking it up? If it does, Job was hardly patient. He bemoaned that God had "shattered" him (Job 16:12). But look again. Peppered amongst Job's wailings are words of heartfelt praise: "The Lord gave me what I had, and the Lord has taken it away. Praise the name of the Lord!" (Job 1:21); "God is so wise and so mighty" (Job 9:4) and "True wisdom and power are found in God; counsel and understanding are his" (Job 12:13).

Our pain—emotional, and/or physical—may be so great we're unable to stay silent. Job teaches us that this is all right. We can cry out to God and even at him. Job's patience was that, despite everything, he retained his reverence for God.

Job became a symbol of patience, defined not as silent acceptance, but as enduring faith.

Lord, thank you for understanding my need to vent.
Even if I vent loudly and long,
may I also display the patience of enduring faith.

*Consider the farmers who patiently wait
for the rains in the fall and in the spring.
They eagerly look for the valuable harvest to ripen.
You too, must be patient.*

JAMES 5:7–8

When my granddaughter Cayden was four, we were playing with a phone app: we put our photos on top of dancing bodies and watched ourselves perform some pretty impressive moves. We'd inserted our faces and were watching the phone's revolving circle which said "Video loading. Be patient." I read it to Cayden. She replied, "I don't like to be patient. Do you?"

At age four Cayden touched on a universal truth: no one likes to be patient. But her matter-of-factness told me she'd already learned that often we must do things we don't like. Not everything is fun. Most things take time. Cayden knows and loves God. He's teaching her wisdom. "The Lord gives wisdom, and from his mouth come knowledge and understanding" (Proverbs 2:6 NIV84). As she grows older, she'll no doubt learn other lessons in patience—people disappoint; plans change; the unexpected happens; progress is a process.

We have opportunities to learn patience early because, in countless forms, waiting is always necessary. We learn that impatience rarely gets us what we want in the short term and, in the long term, never does. Learning patience is learning wisdom.

By the way, the dancing video was worth waiting for!

Thank you for the wisdom of patience Lord.

The trouble is with me, for I am all too human.

ROMANS 7:14

I'd been feeling good about how I was doing. I was thinking before speaking, turning first to God for guidance, and letting things go. I thought I might finally have it all figured out. Then I blew it. I felt devalued by someone and struck back verbally. I apologized, but my peace had vanished.

I admitted my failure to God. He assured me that I am forgiven, but also that I'll blow it again. I was taken aback. I want to be perfect with no weeds in my fruit orchard. But God is telling me that's not going to happen, that I need to be patient with myself.

Lysa TerKeurst's words in *Unglued* encourage me:

> Progress. Just make progress. It's okay to have setbacks. . . . Just make sure you're moving the line forward. . . . Take baby steps, but at least take steps that keep you from being stuck. Then change will come. And it will be good.

God isn't expecting perfection. He's looking for a right heart and progress. Jesus says in Revelation: "I have seen your love, your faith, your service, and your patient endurance. And I can see your constant improvement in all these things" (2:19).

Pastor Chuck Swindoll wrote a book titled *Three Steps Forward, Two Steps Back*. I can identify with that pace. At least I'm headed in the right direction.

Lord, as long as I'm making progress, help me be patient with myself.

DAY 112

PATIENCE

A servant of the Lord must . . . be patient with difficult people.

2 TIMOTHY 2:24

People can be annoying and upsetting. (Not us, of course. Just others.) When they're thoughtless, hurtful, or even cruel, it's okay for us to be impatient with them. We have the right to tell them off!

Unfortunately, not.

God doesn't discriminate when it comes to patience. He says, "Be patient with everyone" (1 Thessalonians 5:14). That includes people who are acting like jerks. "God is pleased with you when you . . . patiently endure unfair treatment" (1 Peter 2:19).

When we're impatient with a difficult person, we are, in effect, saying, "Your behavior is improper. I'm going to punish you by not being nice to you." We're judging, and we're not to judge (Matthew 7:1). Judgment is different from "speaking the truth in love" (Ephesians 4:15), those times we patiently and lovingly point out the problem and leave the results to God.

Often we let other people's impatience beget ours. We allow ourselves to be sucked into their poor behavior. When we respond to a challenging person with patience, we can turn down the heat of their impatience. "A hot-tempered man stirs up dissension, but a patient man calms a quarrel" (Proverbs 15:18).

People can be jerks. God realizes that, but says, "Be patient with each other, making allowance for each other's faults because of your love" (Ephesians 4:2).

Lord, help me be patient with everyone,
even and especially those I feel don't deserve it.

Don't store up treasures here on earth. . . .
Store your treasures in heaven.
MATTHEW 6:19–20

Less than a year ago, we replaced a glass door at our house. It cost seven hundred dollars. Today my husband was weed-wacking. A stone flew up and shattered the door. Another seven hundred dollars down the drain. Thankfully, I'm in the midst of writing about patience.

I wanted to blame. I felt like yelling. Instead, I prayed for patience—and God gave it to me. He also reminded me that everyone encounters unexpected occurrences—the washing machine breaking, needing a new roof, car repairs—that cost money but are basically hidden and just not fun. You know, the "think of all the things I've wanted to buy but didn't, and now I have to spend more than those things would have cost just to get things back to the way they were" times.

Today, as I prayed, God spoke to my heart: he told me to keep my mouth closed. He reminded me I have everything that matters, most importantly, our family, our health, and our safety. The glass door wasn't critical. It was only money.

Unanticipated and unproductive expenses happen. They're a fact of life. We should probably budget for them. Losing patience over them won't change anything but our stress level. When unexpected expenses threaten to make me lose my cool, I'm learning to take a deep breath, pray for patience, thank God for my blessings, keep my mouth closed . . . and move on.

Thank you, Lord, for another lesson in patience.

Now please listen to me patiently!

ACTS 26:3

Listening—*really* listening—takes patience.

Often, instead of truly listening, I'm looking for an opening to talk. But "answering before listening is both stupid and rude" (Proverbs 18:13 MSG). Patient listening waits until the other person is finished. It not only hears words, it notices tone, inflection, emotion, and body language. It seeks to understand. Its result is the acquisition of additional and more accurate information, allowing a more appropriate response. Patient listening shows respect for others and strengthens relationships.

Listening to God also requires patience. We may not recognize his voice at first, or we may not really be listening. As the psalmist said, "Let all that I am wait quietly before God, for my hope is in him" (Psalm 62:5). Listen too for his voice in nature. How much beauty we can hear from birdsong to breeze, thunderclap to rustling leaves, rushing water to cricket melody, and even the sound of silence.

We can discover new worlds with people, with nature, and with God. We need only be patient . . . and listen.

Lord God, whether I'm listening for you, to others,
or to your creation, give me the patience
and ability to truly hear.

Love is patient . . . and endures through every circumstance.

1 CORINTHIANS 13:4, 7

IACETEPN. That was an easy one.

The object of the bridal shower game was to see who, in five minutes, could unscramble the most words associated with marriage. While I didn't get them all, I certainly recognized *IACETEPN. Patience.* Every marriage requires it. Lots and lots of it. The thrill of new unity may blind newlyweds to this reality.

When two lives are joined as one, differences in habits, personalities, interests, needs, desires, preferences, methods, opinions, beliefs, and more become apparent. Some differences are more significant than others; some are easier to live with than others. Still, husbands and wives need patience to accept, understand, compromise, overlook, tolerate, endure, and trust each other and God.

Patience includes accepting each other and not giving up when rough roads appear and life is, frankly, difficult. Many disagreements will extinguish themselves if the fuel of impatience isn't poured on them. "Sensible people control their temper; they earn respect by overlooking wrongs" (Proverbs 19:11). Impatience can end a marriage. At the least, it can change a good marriage day into a bad marriage day, week, month, or longer . . . much longer.

——————————

Lord, help both my spouse and me accept our differences
and give each other the gift of patient love.

Be patient, bearing with one another.
EPHESIANS 42 NIV84

Some people rub me the wrong way. We just don't click.

Actually, everyone annoys me sometimes. I'm certain I affect them the same way. "We all stumble in many ways. If anyone is never at fault in what he says, he is a perfect man" (James 3:2 NIV84). Everyone provokes and is provoked by some people all the time, and by all people, some of the time. God calls us to bear with it: "Be patient with each other, making allowance for each other's faults because of your love" (Ephesians 4:2). While we're thinking, *Please accept me for who I am*, the other person is probably thinking the same thing. Overlooking faults and forgiving (Colossians 3:13) aren't easy, but God can give us the patience to do it.

Just a reminder. No one's perfect. Shortcomings are part of being human and patience is critical, for "if you keep on biting and devouring each other, watch out or you will be destroyed by each other" (Galatians 5:15 NIV84). As the apostle Paul prayed,

> May God, who gives this patience and encouragement, help you live in complete harmony with each other, as is fitting for followers of Christ Jesus. Then all of you can join together with one voice, giving praise and glory to God, the Father of our Lord Jesus Christ. (Romans 15:5)

After all, that's what it's all about.

Lord, give me the patience to accept the weaknesses of others—
and please instill in others the patience to accept mine.

Be imitators of God, therefore, as dearly loved children.
EPHESIANS 5:1 NIV84

When I think how long it's taken me to learn much of what I routinely expect from my kids, it's humbling. I'd like to wrap up all my hard lessons in a big box with a beautiful bow and present them to my children to painlessly apply to their lives.

It doesn't work that way. Our sons and daughters must learn the toughest lessons the hard way, for they absorb lessons best by making the same mistakes we did. Though we want them to learn from our experience and be spared the ache of their own, that's not realistic. How much did we heed our parents' warnings or learn from their experiences? Probably about the same amount our children have benefited from ours.

I'm not saying we shouldn't teach our children. We should, by our words and our example. But we also need to patiently allow them to forge their own paths, overcome their own obstacles, and find their own way. Once we've helped them build the right foundation, including a close relationship with God, we often need to hold back, bite our tongue, and let them discover and learn . . . sometimes the hard way.

---

*Lord, give me patience to realize when it's best
to let my children figure something out.*

Do not exasperate your children.

EPHESIANS 6:2, 4 NIV84

Our parents need us to be patient with them. We need our children to be patient with us. For parents don't always say or do what's best. It's not for lack of love or effort. It's because parents are just grown kids struggling to be good adults, and children don't come with an instruction book. But life does. It's called the Bible, and it tells children to honor their parents (Exodus 20:12; Ephesians 6:2). One way we honor people is by being patient with them.

Children—of all ages—may be impatient because they think their parents don't understand what they're dealing with. Oh, but our parents do understand, and we parents do too. That's often the problem. Parents have been there.

Children can also be impatient when their parents don't give them what they want when they want it. (Any similarity to us with our heavenly Father?) Or they may have forgotten that parents are human, with all the flaws, faults, and struggles that entails. Parenthood doesn't equal sainthood. We march directly into parenthood with our weaknesses and idiosyncrasies. No wonder God told parents not to exasperate their children, and children to honor their parents. And he gave us the fruit of patience, knowing we'll need it.

Lord, help me be patient with my parents—
and forgive me for those times I haven't been.

Greedy people try to get rich quick. . . .
A person who wants quick riches will get into trouble.

Proverbs 28:22, 20

Get-rich-quick schemes abound. So do stories of those who fell for them and lost everything. A few people win big in the lottery. Most don't. Some get temporary wealth by gambling or lucky investments. Most don't. Furthermore, every so-called big win can be followed by great loss—of the riches gained or, more tragically, the winner's values.

Even traditional investments like land, personal property, homes, and stocks are subject to ups, downs, gains, and loss. During the down times, patience may prevent loss by enabling us to hold on until values go up again.

One of the best paths to financial success remains hard work over time: "Hard work brings rewards" (Proverbs 12:14). Those rewards are not only financial. They also include character building as lessons in perseverance, determination, accountability, responsibility . . . and patience. The possibility of missing these critical lessons may be why the Bible warns, "An inheritance obtained too early in life is not a blessing in the end" (Proverbs 20:21).

It's fine to strive for more, as long as we don't give material wealth undue priority, and we remember that "true godliness with contentment is itself great wealth" (1 Timothy 6:6). What a blessing to be able to say, "I have learned to be content whatever the circumstances" (Philippians 4:11 niv84).

Lord, teach me that if it sounds too good to be true,
it probably is. Help me invest wisely, wait patiently,
and to be content with what I have.

We too, wait with eager hope for the day
when God will give us . . .
the new bodies he has promised us.

ROMANS 8:18, 23

God has indeed promised us new bodies—in heaven. Yet many of us hope for new bodies here on earth, asking, "How long must I wait?" (Psalm 119:84).

The world looks for ways to rapidly reverse the effects of years of poor eating habits and lack of exercise. People don't want to "eat the bitter fruit of living their own way" (Proverbs 1:31). No wonder "weight loss is a $55 billion-a-year industry globally. . . . Americans alone . . . spend $40 million of the total" (Livestrong.com). According to "The Shape of the Nation" at Diet.com, "the majority of American adults (54.1%) do not engage in the recommended minimum amount of physical activity."

We want the results, but not the hard work or waiting it takes to get them. Rather than look for quick, effortless fixes, we can accept that our bodies take time to change. Forgoing temporary pleasures, undergoing the discipline of healthy eating, and regular working out require perseverance and endurance. As the Bible says, "If we look forward to something we don't yet have, we must wait patiently and confidently" (Romans 8:25).

Lord, give me the patience I need to put in the time
and effort it takes to achieve the healthy body
we both want me to have.

We do not know what to do, but our eyes are upon you.

2 CHRONICLES 20:12 NIV84

Dogs in general, and my Australian shepherds, Sage and Montana, in particular, amaze me with their patience. . . .

Sage and Montana are eager to go out each morning, yet they patiently let me sleep. They're lucky to get fifteen minutes a day of my undivided attention, yet, hoping for extra petting, follow me from room to room. When I do pet them, they wag happily and then lounge by me, content. Other than chew toys, they don't have much to occupy their time. When I return after being out, Sage and Montana wiggle with delight. They lie at our feet during meals. When we're done, they gobble any tidbits we offer. If I forget to fill their food bowls, they merely eat the food gratefully when I remember. They anticipate the magic word *walk* and leap with joy when they hear it. No matter how long I'm occupied, no matter how protracted their vigil, their enthusiasm for me remains.

How can they be so patient? I think one reason is because they don't watch the clock. They focus not on time, but on me, their master. They love me and depend on me. I care for and provide for them. Their eyes are ever on me, patiently waiting and simply wanting to be near me. They concentrate not on their needs, but on the desires and actions of the one who cares for them. A perfect prescription for patience.

Lord, help me learn patience—and gratitude
and joy in simple pleasures—from my dogs.

Where can I go from your Spirit?
Where can I flee from your presence?
PSALM 119:7–8 NIV84

We all know people who aren't believers. We worry about and pray for them. We witness to them, but our words seem to fall on deaf ears. What else can we do? We can be patient. We can remember that Jesus said, "No one can come to me unless the Father . . . draws him" (John 6:44). God pursues us with unimaginable love and patience. Many people refuse for years to accept Christ as their Savior. Then God reaches down and takes hold of them (Psalm 18:16 NIV84). Some do ignore him forever. Most resist only for a time.

> I fled Him, down the nights and down the days;
> I fled Him, down the arches of the years. . . .
> "Whom wilt thou find to love ignoble thee
>   Save Me, save only Me?
> All which I took from thee I did but take,
>   Not for thy harms.
> But just that thou might'st seek it in My arms.
>   All which thy child's mistake
> Fancies as lost, I have stored for thee at home;
>   Rise, clasp My hand, and come!"
>   (Francis Thompson, "The Hound of Heaven")

Lord, when I've done all I can to lead someone to you,
please give me patient trust in your pursuit.

May the Lord lead your hearts into a full understanding
and expression of the love of God
and the patient endurance that comes from Christ.

2 THESSALONIANS 3:5

Our world calls for us to have oodles of patience every single day. Yet, many people don't have much patience at all. We see evidence of this—in the ubiquity of anger, dropping out, giving up, violence, crime, and the insatiable desire for instant results.

Though we're surrounded by impatience, we don't have to succumb to it. Having the fruit of patience enables us to shine "like bright lights in a world full of . . . perverse people" (Philippians 2:15). Producing this fruit requires seeking God. Having created a world that requires patience for success—and the inability for us to have patience without him—God motivates us to depend upon and draw our strength from him.

> By his divine power, God has given us everything we
> need for living a godly life. We have received all of this
> by coming to know him. . . . [He] has given us great
> and precious promises . . . that enable you to share his
> divine nature and escape the world's corruption caused
> by human desires. (2 Peter 1:3–4)

In Christ, God provides the example. Through his Spirit, he provides the power. Our responsibility is to ask for the power and follow the example.

Thank you, Lord, that in a world crying,
"Give it to me now!" I can—by your grace
and in your power—have the patience to wait.

GENTLENESS

Let your gentleness be evident to all.

PHILIPPIANS 4:5

Dear Lord,
Please help me with this fruit of gentleness. May I see it, not as a weakness, but as the strength it is.

Often I've taken the easy way and been harsh in my thoughts, words, and actions. I've experienced the damage this can cause. It builds walls where they shouldn't be.

Even though I don't always act with gentleness, I respond positively to it in others. It makes me feel loved, valued, cared for, understood, and grateful. Please remind me of this when I'm tempted to be less than gentle. Help me treat others the way I want them to treat me. You've put the need for gentleness inside all of us and, through your Spirit, given us the ability to fulfill that need for each other.

Help me remember the truth that when I choose gentleness, I'm choosing your way, and your way is always best. Grant me the strength to be gentle.

Amen.

Caress me with your gentle ways.

PSALM 18:35 MSG

Interestingly, the Greek word "*epieikés*, translated as *gentleness* in the New Testament, is considered one of the most untranslatable words in the New Testament" (Bible.com). Yet we do try: *gentleness*, per *Vine's Expository Dictionary*, "denotes [something] . . . 'equitable, fair, moderate, forbearing,' . . . It expresses that considerateness that looks 'humanely and reasonably at the facts of a case.'"

I had always thought of gentleness as tenderness, but I've learned it's also a balance between alternatives. "People who display true *epieikés* live with a Christ-like virtue of being able to precisely balance justice and mercy. . . . *Epieikés* describes the ability to extend the kind of consideration that we wish to receive ourselves" (Bible.com). Jesus demonstrated *epieikés* when he refused to condemn a woman who had committed adultery (John 8:1–11).

Gentleness is complex, a combination of self-control, patience, peace, love, and kindness topped with compassion, grace, mercy, understanding, acceptance, forbearance, and wisdom.

Gentleness also deals with both the content and the manner of delivery. It means using less force than we could use. It's the outward expression of empathy and compassion. It's tenderness. But it's also much more.

Lord, gentleness sounded so simple, but it's complex and truly beautiful. Teach me more.

*Remind the believers . . . they should be gentle
and show true humility to everyone.*

TITUS 3:1–2

Does gentleness come easily for you? When, where, and with whom are you most gentle? What about least gentle? Would others describe you as gentle?

I believe I have a gentle heart, but I don't always have gentle ways. Perhaps my less-than-gentle ways are my attempt to protect my gentle heart. I often act gently but *react* less than gently. I'm most gentle when the people I'm around are gentle, vulnerable, and compassionate. Like elicits like.

When I'm with people who are abrasive, I find it difficult to react gently. Yet that can be when gentleness is most important. It's easy to be gentle when others are. But throw in some harshness, and defenses go up. Defenses usually aren't gentle.

Gentleness isn't weakness. It takes strength not to react in kind to what's coming at us. It takes strength to put ourselves in another's position, to see and speak in a way that brings justice yet extends grace.

Gentleness calms and quiets. It elicits the best in people. But when faced with its opposite, gentleness may go into hiding. That's when we most need God's help to nurture this important fruit.

───────────────

*Lord, I want to be a gentle person—not only when
others are being gentle, but most especially when they're not.
I ask for your help.*

Correct me, Lord, but please be gentle.

JEREMIAH 10:24

God has formidable power and is free to use it as he will. . . .

Nadab and Abihu, sons of the Israelite priest Aaron, flagrantly disobeyed God and got a lesson in his power: "fire blazed forth from the Lord's presence and burned them up" (Leviticus 10:2). The psalmist acknowledged, "In anger [God] rebukes [nations that plot against him], terrifying them with his fierce fury" (Psalm 2:5). Mankind has rebelled against God, disobeyed him, turned their backs on him, and been faithless (Psalm 78:56–57). God could have and can respond in fearsome ways. More often than not, he chooses to be gentle: "He does not punish us for all our sins; he does not deal harshly with us as we deserve" (Psalm 103:10).

The Bible is replete with examples of God's gentleness. In fact, God was so gentle with the sinful city of Nineveh that Jonah was angry at him and decided to run in the opposite direction . . . and ended in the mouth of that great fish. Paul warned Jesus's followers to "make sure you stay alert to these qualities of gentle kindness and ruthless severity that exist side by side in God—ruthless with the deadwood, gentle with the grafted shoot" (Romans 11:22 MSG).

Perhaps God's gentlest act of all was Jesus coming to earth to bear our sins instead of requiring us to suffer the penalty ourselves. How gentle to forgive our sins and ask in return only that we believe in him and follow him.

Holy God, I'm eternally grateful for your great gentleness toward your people, including me.

I hear this most gentle whisper from
One I never guessed would speak to me.

PSALM 81:5 MSG

Isn't it amazing that the God of the universe speaks to us individually? If I didn't know God, I'd be like the ancient Israelites; "Do not have God speak to us or we will die" (Exodus 20:19). Indeed, in the Old Testament, God's voice was sometimes overwhelming:

> There was thunder and lightning, with a thick cloud over the mountain and a very loud trumpet blast. . . . Then Moses led the people out of the camp to meet with God. . . . The smoke billowed up . . . the whole mountain trembled violently, and the sound of the trumpet grew louder and louder. (Exodus 19:16–19 NIV84)

I'd expect God's voice to be booming and thunderous. God can speak that way (Psalm 18:7–15). Yet—as the prophet Elijah experienced—God usually chooses to speak gently.

Elijah had worked to turn Israel from idol worship back to God, but he became discouraged and afraid. "I have had enough, Lord," he said (1 Kings 19:4). In response, God sent an angel to gently minister to Elijah until he regained strength. Then God, in a gentle whisper, mercifully instructed Elijah on the anointing of the prophet's replacement (1 Kings 19:11–18).

Like the psalmist, we can say, "Let your gentle Spirit lead me in the right path" (Psalm 143:10 CEV).

Thank you, God, that your gentleness
is as awesome as your power.

Come to me . . . for I am gentle and humble in heart.
MATTHEW 11:28–29 NIV84

The almighty God with the thunderous voice chose to send . . . a gentle Savior.

The prophet Zechariah foretold the Messiah's coming: "See, your king comes to you . . . gentle and riding on a donkey" (Zechariah 9:9 NIV84). Jesus entered this world as a helpless baby, requiring gentle care. And because "anyone who has seen me has seen the Father!" (John 14:9), God demonstrated his gentleness through the gentleness of Jesus.

I can hear the gentleness in Jesus's heartbroken words: "Oh Jerusalem, Jerusalem, the city that kills the prophets and stones God's messengers! How often I have wanted to gather your children together as a hen protects her chicks beneath her wings, but you wouldn't let me." (Matthew 23:37)

The apostle Paul also spoke of Christ's gentleness, writing to the church at Corinth "with the gentleness and kindness of Christ" (2 Corinthians 10:1–3). Jesus didn't wage war as humans do, or as kings do, or as he could have done since he is God. Jesus chose gentleness: he balanced justice and mercy.

Jesus also treated his disciple Peter gently. After he denied knowing Jesus not once but three times, "the Lord turned and looked straight at Peter" (Luke 22:61). I picture Jesus's look as one of understanding, love, and gentleness. That gentleness, like all gentleness, was powerful, for "Peter left the courtyard, weeping bitterly" (Luke 22:62).

Through you, Lord, I understand the power of gentleness.

*What do you prefer? Shall I come to you with a whip,
or in love and with a gentle spirit?*

1 CORINTHIANS 4:21 NIV84

At some point, we're going to irritate (intentionally or unintentionally), every single person in our lives. We're going to do or say something they don't like. How do we want them to respond? Figuratively speaking, with a whip, or with love and a gentle spirit?

Likewise, every person in our lives is going to irritate us at some point. They'll all do or say something we don't like. How will we respond? How does God want us to respond?

Jesus has a straightforward answer to that question: "Do to others whatever you would like them to do to you" (Matthew 7:12). We want others to be gentle with us. If they come at us with a whip, we won't respond well. Neither will they if that's how we approach them. When we don't like someone's behavior and are tempted to give them a piece of our mind, we can instead choose to live by the Golden Rule and—with God's help—respond with the gentleness we want to be treated with.

---

*I'd prefer gentleness every time, Lord.
In light of that truth, help me be gentle with others.*

A gentle answer deflects anger,
but harsh words make tempers flare.

PROVERBS 15:1

Nineteenth-century American settlers tried to keep prairie fires from getting out of control by starting their own small fires. Their goal was to remove flammable material in the path of a larger fire, thereby depriving it of fuel. "This literal 'fighting fire with fire' was often successful, although the settlers' lack of effective fire control equipment meant that their own fires occasionally got out of control and made matters worse rather than better" (Phrases.org.uk).

Since then, *fighting fire with fire* has come to mean responding to an attack in the same or similar way. While fighting fire with fire sometimes worked well for the settlers, the Bible tells us it *never* works with our speech. If we try to fight fire with fiery words, we'll be like those fires that made prairie fires worse.

When someone speaks to me in anger, my first reaction is to fight fire with fire. Like the settlers, I try to stop fire coming at me with flames of my own. But all that does is add fuel. Fiery words plus fiery words equal an often-uncontrollable inferno that burns, deeply hurts, even scars.

It's gentleness that quenches anger's fire (Proverbs 15:1). A gentle answer calms; it deprives a word-fire of fuel. If we continue in gentleness, the fire directed at us will eventually go out.

Lord, when the fires of anger threaten me,
help me reach for quenching buckets of gentleness
instead of grabbing flamethrowers.

DAY 131

GENTLENESS

*Reckless words pierce like a sword,
but the tongue of the wise brings healing.*

PROVERBS 12:18 NIV84

When our son was in elementary school, he had a crush on a classmate. He decided to phone her, but before he did, he thought about what he'd say. He even wrote down his ideas and practiced them out loud. When he finally made the call, it went well. (He wasn't the only one relieved!)

Life's pace doesn't always allow us to think through our words ahead of time. But have we gone too far in the other direction? Today's social media encourages us to speak without thinking. Yet "wise people think before they act; fools don't" (Proverbs 13:16).

Do we choose our words carefully? Do we consider our listener's sensitivities? Do we build barriers or bridges? Are our words harsh or gentle? Harsh words can be interpreted as an attack and cause others to get defensive, but "gentle speech breaks down rigid defenses" (Proverbs 25:15 MSG). Gentle words open ears; harsh words close them.

As the Bible and life experiences teach, it's wise to consider the effect our words may have *before* we speak them: "the wisdom of the prudent is to give thought to their ways" (Proverbs 14:8 NIV84). Wisdom "gives gentleness to words" (Ecclesiastes 8:1 MSG).

Lord, prompt me to act wisely and to think before I speak.

Gentle words are a tree of life.

PROVERBS 15:4

I cook. My husband does the dishes. The problem is, he doesn't like to wash pans. Recently I used a large cast-iron pot. He didn't want to clean it. He communicated that fact with words and a delivery that were less than gentle. I was not happy. But paying attention to my response, I used some self-control in my choice of words. But when I spoke them, I sounded and looked harsh. Because we both failed to speak gently, a little thing became big.

Maybe you've heard the adage "It's not what you say, but how you say it." I'd change that to "It's not *only* what you say, but also how you say it." We may not realize it, but we're influenced not only by words, but also by how they're spoken, by the speaker's tone, volume, pitch, emphasis, timing, body language, and facial expression. I've often wished people could see their expressions or hear their own voice. Less often do I pay attention to, and more often I should realize, how my expressions look and how my voice sounds. Those visuals might help me choose gentleness more readily!

The Bible says, "A gentle tongue can break a bone" (Proverbs 25:15 NIV84). Gentleness, in both word choice and delivery, has strength. It can persuade where harshness would trigger defiance.

Job knew the power of gentleness: "My words fell gently on their ears. They waited for me as for showers and drank in my words as the spring rain" (Job 29:22 NIV84). That is the impact of words gently spoken.

When I speak, Lord, help me pay attention not only to what I say, but also to how I say it.

Turn my eyes away from worthless things.

PSALM 119:37 NIV84

I own a lighted magnifying mirror. When I look into its harsh light, I see every wrinkle, spot, and imperfection my face holds. The older I get, the more of these I see. I don't like that mirror: it doesn't give me gentle eyes.

While the magnifying mirror discourages and deflates me, when I catch a fleeting glimpse of myself in a mirror that's farther away, I feel I'm not doing too badly for my age. That's because I'm not studying myself. I'm seeing the overall picture, not the less attractive details. I'm looking at myself with gentle eyes.

When others see me, I pray they look with gentle eyes. I have a lot of—shall I gently say—imperfections, not only in my appearance, but also in my actions and words. If others look too closely, they'll see me in my worst light. But if they look at me with gentle eyes, they will, I hope, see some good.

I also need to have gentle eyes when I look at others. We are all a mixture of good and not-so-good. When we look at others closely, harshly, we focus on the not-so-good. But when we look with gentle eyes, we see the good. In photography that's called airbrushing: we remove imperfections so the beautiful is seen. We can do that with each other: use gentle eyes, give the benefit of the doubt, see only the good. If something is unpleasant, let it blur and fade next to the overall good. Airbrush it away. Let the best be all we see (Philippians 4:8).

Lord, help me always look with gentle eyes.

Your beauty should not come from outward adornment. . . .
Instead it should be that of your inner self,
the unfading beauty of a gentle and quiet spirit,
which is of great worth in God's sight.

1 PETER 3:3–4 NIV84

This scripture reminds me of my daughter-in-law Courtney. She has great outward beauty, but she also has "the unfading beauty of a gentle and quiet spirit." That quality is what I've appreciated most about her since the day we met. I'd guess it's what first attracted our son to her.

That kind of spirit isn't necessarily appreciated by the world, interested as it is in the external. Recently, after looking in the mirror too closely, and influenced by the world, I considered a face-lift. I decided against it because there's a better way to achieve beauty, whatever our age. (Besides, it was too expensive.) That way is to cultivate a gentle and quiet spirit. My spirit has often been more like a raging sea than a flowing river. But the stronger my relationship with Jesus grows, the more my spirit will become gentle and quiet. That's the beauty I want to have. It will never grow old and never need a face-lift.

I believe that regardless of age, a woman with a gentle and quiet spirit will always be more beautiful and respected than the loveliest of younger women who have a mean, harsh spirit. "A woman of gentle grace gets respect" (Proverbs 11:16 MSG), but most important, her gentleness is of great worth in God's sight (1 Peter 3:4).

Holy Spirit, may I remember that lasting beauty
comes from a gentle spirit. Please help me to have one.

You, man of God . . . pursue . . . gentleness.
1 TIMOTHY 6:11 NIV84

Ladies love gentlemen. Though originally *gentleman* involved rank and social status, it came to be associated with respectful behavior and good manners. Yes, ladies love gentlemen.

Ladies also love gentle men. Not weak men, but gentle men—for it takes a strong man to be gentle. Women know this; not enough men do. Men who are gentle are confident enough in their masculinity to reveal their tender core. A strong man has no need to flaunt his power.

I think most women, if asked to rank the importance and attractiveness of gentleness in a man, would put that quality near the top. God placed in us a need for our men to be gentle with us. After lauding the virtues of a woman with a gentle spirit, the apostle Peter wrote, "In the same way, you husbands must give honor to your wives. Treat your wife with understanding" (1 Peter 3:7).

The apostle Paul looked into the future: "People will be boastful, proud . . . without self-control, brutal . . . treacherous, rash . . . lovers of pleasure rather than lovers of God" (2 Timothy 3:2–4 NIV84). Frighteningly, that indeed describes some common notions of masculinity today—and not at all what a woman wants in a man. The Bible says, "Stay away from people like that!" (2 Timothy 3:5). Women agree.

Ladies do love gentle men.

Lord, open the eyes of this world to see that a gentle man is a strong man.

Be merciful, just as your Father is merciful.

LUKE 6:36 NIV84

I act most poorly when I'm misunderstood, hurt, or treated like I don't have value. I justify my behavior by thinking that those who mistreated me deserve my response. Yet God wants us to be merciful (Hosea 6:6; Matthew; Zechariah 7:9). And having mercy means *not* giving someone the negative we think they deserve.

"God is a merciful God" so "rich in mercy" that often we take his mercy for granted, forgetting what a gift it is (Deuteronomy 4:31; Ephesians 2:4). What if God treated us as our sins deserve? What if, when we acted wrongly, he would "cast us from his presence or take his Holy Spirit from us" (Psalm 51–1 NIV84)? He won't, and he wants us to extend to others the mercy he gives us.

The Holy Spirit enables us to do exactly that, for mercy is an aspect of gentleness. It "forgives when justice gives the right to condemn" (*Vine's Expository Dictionary*). As C. S. Lewis observed in *The Weight of Glory*, "To be a Christian means to forgive the inexcusable, because God has forgiven the inexcusable in you." We who don't hesitate to accept God's gift of mercy are to offer mercy to others. The bonus is that mercy "is twice blest: It blesseth him that gives and him that takes" (William Shakespeare).

Lord, when I'm tempted to retaliate, help me instead
to give the gift of gentle mercy I receive so freely from you.

*In him we have redemption through his blood, the forgiveness
of sins, in accordance with the riches of God's grace
that he lavished on us with all wisdom and understanding.*

EPHESIANS 1:7–8 NIV84

God calls us to go even further than giving mercy. He wants us
to add grace. Mercy is *not giving* someone the negative they *do*
deserve; grace *is giving* someone the positive they *don't* deserve.
Grace is not just holding back retribution. It's treating someone
well when you think they deserve to be treated poorly.

Philip Yancey notes in *What's So Amazing About Grace?* that
although the world preaches giving people what they deserve,
Jesus disagrees:

> Jesus gave us . . . stories about grace . . . to call us to
> step completely outside our tit-for-tat world of ungrace
> and enter into God's realm of infinite grace. . . . Grace
> demands of me that I step over that wounded part of
> my heart that feels hurt and wronged.

Giving grace does not come naturally. When we hurt, it's
normal to want to hurt back. Yancey adds, "Only by living in
the stream of God's grace will I find the strength to respond
with grace toward others."

When tempted to act on the thought that people don't
deserve our gentleness, God gives us the grace to give it anyway.

---

*Lord, thank you for the gentleness of your grace to me.
Enable me, I pray, to generously give to others
the kind of grace you give me.*

If you are always biting and devouring one another, watch out!
Beware of destroying one another.

GALATIANS 5:15

Why do we handle an antique vase gently? Because if we don't, it could break. Why do we hold an infant gently? Because if we don't, they could be injured. Why do we hug elderly people gently? Because they can be fragile.

But why aren't we gentle with everyone all the time? Why aren't we unfailingly gentle, especially toward the people closest to us? Is it because we feel irritated, upset, or angry? If so, is that a good reason to withhold gentleness?

Next time you react less than gently to someone, look into their eyes. Eyes give insight into hearts and souls. Could they be breaking within, trying to hide it?

Everyone is breakable; all of us can be hurt by harshness. Some of us are more delicate than others, at least on the outside. But we all have an inner self that can chip, crack, or shatter when treated badly. We may not admit it, but we feel the pain in those moments.

No matter who we are with, we can envision "Fragile: Handle with Gentleness" written across their foreheads. It's not visible, but it's there.

Lord, help me deal with others gently,
so I never damage their inner selves.

I have stilled and quieted my soul, like a weaned child
with its mother, like a weaned child is my soul within me.

PSALM 131:2 NIV84

My almost one-year-old son was not yet fully weaned, so we both eagerly awaited my return from work each day. He'd nurse; I'd savor cuddling and nourishing him.

One time I'd just gotten home when our minister paid a surprise visit, which postponed nursing time. I held my squirming child and tried to make polite conversation. Finally, my son could stand it no longer. With both hands he pulled my blouse open. I don't know who was more embarrassed, the minister or me.

Once my son was weaned, he was often content just to be held. That is the picture of the gentle worship I see in Psalm 131.

We can worship God in many ways. We can "shout with joy to the Lord" (Psalm 100). We can "pour out our hearts to him" (Psalm 62:8). We can cry out to him (Psalm 57:2). We can honor him with music and dance (Psalm 150:3–5 NIV84). Yet sometimes our worship is most wonderful when we are like a weaned child, not clamoring for anything, just satisfied to simply rest in our Father's arms.

As I worship you, Lord, you still and quiet my soul.
Thank you.

Help me abandon my shameful ways.

PSALM 119:39

Brain science is a fascinating study. For example:

> Special neurons in the brainstem of rats focus exclusively on new, novel sounds and help them ignore predictable and ongoing noises. . . . Similar neurons . . . almost certainly exist in the human brain. . . . The "novelty detector neurons," as researchers call them, quickly stop firing if a sound or sound pattern is repeated. . . . This allows people to ignore sounds that don't require attention. ("How the Brain Tunes Out Background Noise," LiveScience.com)

Perhaps this is how our brains deal with people who are habitually harsh. We eventually ignore them because we get used to their harshness.

We know the story of the boy who cried, "Wolf!" This bored shepherd would, for some excitement, yell, "Wolf! Wolf!" To the boy's delight, the villagers would come running . . . only to find there was no wolf. One day there really was a wolf, but when the boy cried, "Wolf! Wolf!" the villagers ignored him, assuming he was fooling again. The wolf destroyed the flock.

A habit of harshness can do the same thing: people will stop listening. Harshness on a regular basis loses all possibility of effectiveness. But if we're normally gentle, when the time to be forceful comes, people pay attention.

Lord, help me save forcefulness for when it's truly needed.

Fix your thoughts on Jesus.
HEBREWS 3:1 NIV84

Gentleness is magnetic. I believe humans' need for gentleness extends to our surroundings. There, as with people, lack of gentleness brings stress.

How much environmental gentleness we experience depends upon where we live and what we do. My home in Colorado is encircled by rolling hills, trees, and cows, but you may live in a less-than-gentle city. The corporate world was not gentle when I worked there. Others may have a more easy-going occupation. Regardless, if our external world isn't gentle, we can make sure our internal world is.

What does the word *gentle* bring to mind? I think of a breeze, the rain, a baby sleeping, a whisper, a lush blanket, steaming coffee, soft music, quiet time, dim lights, a knowing look from one I love. For me, gentle words include *mild, calm, hushed, peaceful, soft-spoken, light, airy, gradual, soothing, mellow,* and *restful.* Just thinking about gentleness is relaxing, whatever is going on around us.

Close your eyes and think "gentle." Picture gentle people you know, envision gentle things, repeat gentle words. In the midst of a not-so-gentle day, we can create our own mental oasis of gentleness. Better yet, when we're surrounded by clamor and craziness, we can fix our thoughts on Jesus. "He leads me beside quiet waters. He restores my soul" (Psalm 23:2–3 NIV84). It doesn't get much better than that!

Lord, I can't always control my environment,
but I can control my mind. Lead me beside still waters.
Restore my soul.

This is what he requires of you:
to do what is right, to love mercy,
and to walk humbly with your God.

MICAH 6:8

Think about yesterday. How much gentleness did you experience? Who was or wasn't gentle? What difference could more gentleness have made? As you go through today, ask yourself similar questions: Am I being as gentle as I should? Do they need gentleness right now?

We all appreciate gentleness, respond well to it, and feel stress when it's absent. As always, it's a matter of becoming more aware and recognizing that a lot of little not-so-gentle things can have the cumulative impact.

We can make an effort to incorporate more gentleness into every day. Get up earlier, have a quiet time, watch the sunrise, speak softly, take a walk, notice trees, enjoy the breeze, smile, buy flowers, watch the sunset, stay rested, hold someone's hand, give the benefit of the doubt, control our tongues, and seek to understand. "When you encounter difficulties and contradictions, do not try to break them, but bend them with gentleness and time" (Saint Francis de Sales). Do whatever feels gentle, say a prayer of thanks, and wrap ourselves and others in God's love.

Lord, open my eyes to the possibilities
for gentleness in every day.

Consider how the lilies grow. They do not labor or spin.
Yet I tell you, not even Solomon in all his splendor
was dressed like one of these.

LUKE 12:27 NIV84

When you're feeling stressed, would you choose to walk on a forest path or the sidewalk of a bustling city? What's more relaxing for you: being at a mall or strolling through a garden? Which activity brings peace to your inmost being: gazing at a mountain range or a row of skyscrapers? I'll take nature every time, God-made over man-made, hands down.

Picture in your mind—and hear the sounds, of people, places, creatures, and things God has made. Now do the same with things created by man. God's creations contain an innate gentleness missing from man-made creations. Perhaps that's why God's handiwork decreases our stress and fills a void that man-made things cannot.

Yet the ultimate wonder of God's creation is this: his creation is a reflection of God himself, the perfect blend of awesome power and breathtaking gentleness.

Thank you, God, for surrounding me with evidence
of your flawless blend of gentleness and might.

God's servant must not be argumentative, but a gentle listener.

2 TIMOTHY 2:24 MSG

An elderly couple was sitting on their porch, relaxing in their rocking chairs. One spouse said to the other, "I love you."

The other said, "What? Can't hear you!"

"I love you," the first repeated.

"Huh? What'd you say?"

"I love you."

"Still can't hear you!"

"I LOVE YOU!"

"Oh. I'm tired of you too!"

Let's not wait until we can't hear to start listening! Focused listening respects and values the speaker. Listening with genuine interest and caring, without interjecting our thoughts, is a gift everyone craves. Stifling our rebuttals says, "I care enough to want to know your feelings, opinion, and perspective." That's gentleness.

God also wants us to listen to him. My *NIV Exhaustive Concordance* contains about 450 references to listening. Many are requests or commands to listen to God. Yet we may be so busy making requests of God that we don't listen for what he has to say to us.

The fruit of gentleness can help us listen, for true listening requires gentleness. It compels us to calm down and abandon self-centeredness. As Proverbs 1:5 says, "Let the wise listen and add to their learning" (NIV84). Let the wise be gentle, for there's a lot to learn.

Lord, give me the gentleness I need to truly listen,
not only to others but, most important, to you.

Show a gentle attitude toward everyone.

PHILIPPIANS 4:5 GNT

I don't know if you're a Pinterest person, but it offers lots of great sayings about gentleness. Some of my favorites are:

- "Nothing is so strong as gentleness and nothing is so gentle as real strength." (R. Sockman)
- "10 percent of conflict is due to difference of opinion and 90 percent is due to wrong tone of voice." (anonymous)
- "People will forget what you said, but people will never forget how you made them feel." (Maya Angelou)

Had Pinterest existed in biblical times, it might have contained repinned verses such as these:

- "Be completely humble and gentle, be patient, bearing with one another in love." (Ephesians 4:2 NIV84)
- "As GOD's chosen people . . . clothe yourselves with compassion, kindness, humility, gentleness, and patience." (Colossians 3:12)
- "Make a clean break with all cutting, backbiting, profane talk. Be gentle with one another, sensitive." (Ephesians 4:31–32 MSG)

Gentleness acknowledges that everyone has inner and outer battles. It's "we're in this together" instead of "every man for himself." Pinterest is new. The message is not.

Lord, may I repin onto my mind and heart your reminders to live with gentleness—and then do so.

We have all had human fathers who disciplined us,
and we respected them for it.
HEBREWS 12:9 NIV84

Children see parents as, well, *parents.* They may not give any thought to what worries, frustrates, hurts, or concerns their parents as individuals. A child's world is "me"-focused: what *I* want, can, can't, should, and shouldn't do; what's expected of *me*; what everyone thinks of *me*.

Having been a parent for many years, I realize big-time that parents are just people, people with feelings—that can be hurt, stepped on, trampled, or ignored. Not only do we have our own feelings, but many parents—I'm one of them—live out our children's feelings vicariously as well. That's a lot of feelings to deal with!

For these reasons and others, all parents need their children to be gentle with them and to try to understand them as individuals. Children need to realize parents are imperfect human beings who, like everyone else, are vulnerable, breakable, and in need of acceptance, appreciation, and love.

Children of all ages can give their parents the gift of gentleness by recognizing that moms and dads do their best and by not judging them when their best doesn't seem good enough.

Everyone is someone's child, Lord, and many of us
are parents as well. Help my children and help me
remember that parents need gentleness too.

Always be prepared to give an answer to everyone
who asks you to give the reason for the hope that you have,
but do this with gentleness and respect.

1 PETER 3:15–16 NIV84

On a visit to Lima, Peru, I watched a woman standing in a city square, Bible in hand, shouting a message to passersby. I don't speak her language, but I'm certain she was trying to spread the gospel. The problem was, no one was listening.

I struggle with how I'm to be an effective witness for Christ. Loud, argumentative, in-your-face witnessing doesn't work for me, and it's not what God recommends: "Remind the believers . . . they should be gentle and show true humility to everyone" (Titus 3:1–2). We can't force people to change their beliefs, and an aggressive approach only puts them on the defensive. For some reason "religious" issues are sensitive topics. People become offended, withdrawn, critical, and worse—all in defense of their beliefs.

Christ wants us to witness (Matthew 28:18–20), but we're to "be courteous. . . . If they welcome you, be gentle in your conversation. If they don't welcome you, quietly withdraw. Don't make a scene" (Matthew 10:12–15 MSG). The apostle Paul recognized the importance of gentle witnessing: "as apostles of Christ, we could have been a burden to you, but we were gentle among you" (1 Thessalonians 2:5 NIV84).

Words are important. But living our beliefs may be the gentlest and most effective way to help nonbelievers come to see the truth of Christ.

Jesus, help me to gently share the gospel with my words, yes,
but, more important, with my life.

A leader must be well-thought-of . . .
cool and collected . . . not pushy but gentle.

1 TIMOTHY 3:3–7 MSG

I once had a boss who wasn't happy with something I'd done. He came into my office and yelled at me. He didn't just raise his voice; he shouted. I kept my composure, but after he left, I went to my car and cried. I didn't tell anyone, but apparently coworkers heard him and reported him. Within days he was fired.

I have no recollection of what he was upset about, but I do know he was a poor leader. This man had been the company's second-in-command, yet because his manner was offensive, it wasn't tolerated.

It's a shame potential talent is lost because of inability to lead gently. Not lead weakly, but gently. Huge difference. Gentle leadership is firm but calm. It's strong, with the wisdom and self-control to use only the degree of forcefulness necessary.

My husband and I once had the excitement of operating a tank simulator under our officer son Kirk's leadership. The simulation felt real. What a composed and capable leader Kirk was. When we made mistakes, he didn't get riled. He repeated concise instructions with unruffled clarity. The strength of Kirk's gentle leadership kept me from being rattled. His calmness made us calm. We learned and, eventually, performed well because of that.

Two kinds of leadership . . . at opposite ends of the spectrum. Gentle leadership wins every time.

Lord, I pray for leaders everywhere.
Give them the strength to lead gently.

I think of you through the watches of the night.
Because you are my help.

PSALM 63 NIV84

One Mother's Day our adult son sent me an e-mail listing some of his childhood memories. One was my gently placing my hand on his forehead as he was going to sleep and softly reciting the poem "Sleep Sweetly" by Victor Hugo, which my mother had said to me:

Sleep sweetly in this quiet room
Oh thou who'er thou art;
And let no mournful yesterdays disturb thy peaceful heart.
Nor let tomorrow scare thy rest with thoughts of coming ill,
Thy maker is thy changeless friend,
His love surrounds thee still.
Forget thyself and all the world
Put out each feverish light.
The stars are watching overhead;
Sleep sweetly then . . . goodnight.

Our son says the poem to his children. One of them told him, "Daddy, I'm going to say that poem to my children, and they're going to say it to their children." I think that will happen. I still say the poem to myself when I have trouble sleeping. As I do, I remember my mother's gentle voice and touch as well as the peace and love I experienced when I said it over my children. The gentleness of its words calms spirits and speaks to souls. That's what gentleness does.

Thank you, Jesus, for the gift of sweet sleep and gentle memories.

Gentle thoughts bring happiness.
PROVERBS 12:20 CEV

It was usually our mother's job, and as gentle as her personality was, she approached hair brushing like a woman on a mission. But when our father brushed her hair, as my sister Judy remembers, "No one had ever been so gentle with my hair. He didn't pull at it. He brushed slowly, like he feared I'd break if he brushed faster. It felt easy, relaxing. He didn't talk, but I felt cared about, special." His gentleness so impacted Judy that she remembers it more than sixty years later.

Other people have their own memories of gentleness. My friend Susan recalls, "Grandma used to get up early to read her Bible. I'd sit on her lap while she told me what she'd learned that morning. I carry that gentle memory with me to this day." My friend Linda says, "When I was little, my grandfather was quite elderly. A man of few words, his gentle actions spoke volumes. He knew exactly what to do to make me feel better, be it sitting on a park bench, sharing a bag of licorice while he listened, nodded, and made me laugh, or walking hand in hand in silence, appreciating God's creation." That gentleness took place over fifty years ago.

Gentleness positively impacts us. Memories of gentleness stick with us. Whether those gentle moments occurred years or minutes ago, remembering them brings back what we felt as they happened.

Gentleness has a long life. What we give today may be happily recalled years from now.

Lord, thank you for memories of gentle words and actions.
Please use me to create such memories for others.

Do not merely listen to the word,
and so deceive yourselves.
Do what it says.
JAMES 1:22 NIV84

We can use our newly recharged faithfulness, self-control, and patience to bolster our ability to be gentle. Gentleness requires all these fruits. They build upon each other.

Faced with daily distractions, I can slip into autopilot, let my sinful nature take over, and end up being not so gentle. Faithfully listening to God's Spirit, receiving his power to be self-controlled and patient, enables us to be gentle as well. When we "let the Holy Spirit guide [our] lives . . . [we] won't be doing what [our] sinful nature craves" (Galatians 5:16).

It's simple to learn about the fruit of the Spirit. It takes effort to live them. Since I began this journey, the Holy Spirit has been tapping me on my shoulder—and working overtime. He says things like "Are you being faithful? Are you letting your emotions lead you? Is this being patient? Were you gentle just then?" Sometimes I ignore him. When I do, the result isn't good. But I'm learning to listen to him more often.

I'm making progress, Lord.
Keep the fruit of your Spirit in the forefront of my mind.
I want to follow you, not my sinful nature.

We all stumble in many ways.

JAMES 3:2 NIV84

In my humanness, I'm far from perfect. I never will be perfect. But I'll never stop trying. I agree with the apostle Paul: "Not that I have already obtained all this, or have already been made perfect, but I press on to take hold of that for which Christ Jesus took hold of me" (Philippians 3:12 NIV84).

"While we were still sinners, Christ died for us" (Romans 5:8 NIV84). God has "rescued [you] because he delighted in [you]" (Psalm 18:16 NIV84). What awesome truths. God knows us and chooses us anyway.

When we choose Jesus, God gives us his Spirit, who makes us holy (1 Peter 1:2). Holy, not perfect. *Perfect* means never sinning. *Holy* means set apart for God in order to have a relationship with him. Christ's death erased our sins so we can have that relationship, but all of us will sin again.

God knows we won't achieve perfection on our earthly journey, but step by step, we'll get closer to being the person God wants us to be. God understands we're not going to get it right every time. Thankfully, he "looks at the heart" (1 Samuel 16:7). When he sees its with him, he's gentle with us in our journey. We should be gentle with ourselves as well.

Lord, you forgive my sins, and I am beyond grateful.
Please help me forgive myself.

I will discipline you, but with justice.

JEREMIAH 30:11

We've all felt uncomfortable watching parents being harsh with their misbehaving children. In stores we've seen them pull their screaming child by the arm, yelling, "Be quiet!" My guess is those children will continue to misbehave, will lose respect for their parents, and grow up to be harsh adults who yell at and shame their children. This may be why we're told, "Do not irritate and provoke your children to anger, do not exasperate them to resentment, but rear them tenderly in the training and discipline and the counsel and admonition of the Lord" (Ephesians 6:4 AMP).

I'm happy to say that our son and daughter-in-law parent gently. Kirk and Courtney don't raise their voices. When their kids misbehave, they calmly lead the offending child to a private area and point out their improper behavior and its consequences. An apology is required; sometimes there's a time-out. They may firmly but gently insist their child look the in the eyes and listen. Yelling is not part of the equation.

Gentle discipline exhibits and instills respect. It corrects behavior without stomping on spirits. It also raises up adults who understand boundaries, responsibility, and accountability—and who will parent their own children the same way. The Bible assures, "Train a child in the way he should go, and when he is old he will not turn from it" (Proverbs 22:6 NIV84).

Lord, help me train my children gently
so when they grow up, they will be gentle as well.

A wise woman builds her home,
but a foolish woman tears it down with her own hands.

PROVERBS 14:1

When we live with someone a long time, we can easily take that person for granted. It may also become easier to notice what's wrong with them instead of what's right. A negative focus is harmful. So we're to think about *anything* that is excellent or praiseworthy, not the flaws or annoyances (see Philippians 4:5, 8).

Focusing on what we don't like about our spouse can ruin a marriage. It injects a destructive harshness into the relationship. It's impossible to have a happy marriage when one or both partners are spewing negativity.

Continual nagging or complaining isn't gentle or constructive. Gentleness holds back. It doesn't judge or criticize or use the forcefulness that could be used. Gentleness recognizes our spouse isn't perfect *and* that we aren't either. Appreciating that we're all flawed people doing the best we know how, gentleness is grateful for what we do have. Gentleness in marriage is a choice, a wise choice that can make the difference between happiness and misery.

The Bible gives this recipe for a successful marriage: Wives, "clothe yourselves . . . with the unfading beauty of a gentle and quiet spirit" (1 Peter 3:4). Husbands, "give honor to your wives. Treat your wife with understanding" (1 Peter 3:7). God knows gentleness is best.

Dear God, when I'm inclined to see, think of,
and speak of my spouse harshly, please let me see,
think, and speak gently instead.

*Morning by morning he wakens me
and opens my understanding to his will.*

ISAIAH 50:4

When I had a career and was raising three children, every weekday morning was a whirlwind. Each began with a blaring alarm clock, assembling food for five, prodding and supervising the kids' preparations, and still getting myself ready and everyone out the door. Those years were precious, but I often felt stressed and harried.

Now my career is behind me. Our children are grown. Mornings are gentle. My internal clock wakes me before dawn. The house is hushed, dark. The stillness soothes. I feel peace, knowing that "because of God's tender mercy, the morning light from heaven is about to break" (Luke 1:78). A sliver of brilliance eases above the horizon and grows into a dazzling ball surrounded by luminous orange, red, pink, and magenta clouds. Truly, "the heavens proclaim the glory of God; the skies declare the work of his hands" (Psalm 19:1 NIV84). With praise overflowing my heart, I retreat for my quiet time with God, a time I know will be tranquil and refreshing.

What a difference a gentle start to the day makes. I realize it's not an option for everyone, but each of us can do what we're able. Maybe get up earlier. Use a dimmer on lights. Step outside and drink in the fresh air. Take time to thank God and ask his will for this day.

---

*Bathed in morning light, I pray that the lantern
of my life will move gently this day
into all those places where light is needed.*

[ADAPTED FROM "RISE EARLY" BY MACRINA WIEDERKEHR]

*Be at rest once more, O my soul,
for the Lord has been good to you.*
PSALM 116:7

Reading the poem "Let Evening Come Upon Us" by Judith Brower, I'm reminded that just as gentle mornings set a solid foundation for the flurry of every day, a dusk that gently descends lays groundwork for a restorative night's sleep:

Let day sink into nighttime and darkness close around.
We lift our hearts to praise you, to seek and to be found.

The activities of our evenings depend upon our stage in life. Whatever stage we're at, all of us can focus on gentleness as day fades into night. Dusk can include a time of reflection. We can deliberately slow down, embrace the day-to-night transition, and review our day with God, letting go of any worries and thanking him for the blessings. We can calm our souls and prepare to enter a nighttime of rest in his embrace.

I like to watch sunset's glow fade into evening's gray and the birds that swoop and soar in a pewter sky. From the vantage point of dusk, the eyes of my heart see God's goodness, and I praise him for it. No matter how crammed-full our days, let's try to take even a few minutes to pause and be grateful for the gift of gentle dusk.

*At day's end, Lord, may I decelerate long enough
to breathe deeply of your gentle love.*

Like a lily among thistles is my darling among young women.
Like the finest apple tree in the orchard
is my lover among other young men.

SONG OF SONGS 2:2–3

Our son and daughter-in-law were taking a walk with their children. Cayden, age four, spotted an injured butterfly on the sidewalk, struggling to fly. She knelt. "Poor little butterfly," she said, "I'm sorry you're having trouble. I wish I could help you." Wyatt, age two, stomped the butterfly with his foot.

Girls tend to be gentler than boys. That's the way God made us. Yet, while the proportions may be different, God gave both sexes the capacity to be both gentle and strong. It's this combination that's appealing.

Have you noticed that men seem most attracted to externally gentle and internally strong women, and that women seem most attracted to externally strong and internally gentle men? We complement each other with our blends of gentleness and strength: strong but gentle, gentle but strong. When one of these two qualities is missing, attractiveness wanes: Men don't generally seek women who have no inner strength. Women aren't usually looking for men who have no inner gentleness.

In 1956, through preorders, Elvis Presley's "Love Me Tender" became a gold record before it was even released. I believe its popularity, then and now, is due, in part, to the lyrics: "Love Me Tender" sums up that both sexes want to be loved with the strength of gentleness.

Lord, make us strong but gentle . . . gentle but strong.

He leads me beside quiet waters, he restores my soul.

PSALM 23:2–3 NIV84

My adult daughters tease me about my cure-all. When they're facing anything from a stressful workday to the beginnings of a head cold, they finish my sentence for me. "I know, I know," they say. "Put a warm washcloth over your eyes and take a hot bath."

It works for me. The soothing gentleness of this double remedy helps restore my soul. That's just one of the infinite benefits God gave us when he created water. Its gentleness is soothing, restorative, powerful. Fountains, streams, rivers, gentle rain—there's something about the sound and sight of water flowing that calms our spirit, renews our strength.

Moses said to the Israelites, "Let my teaching fall on you like rain; let my speech settle like dew. Let my words fall like rain on tender grass, like gentle showers on young plants. I will proclaim the name of the Lord; how glorious is our God!" (Deuteronomy 32:2–3). God's glory expressed in gentle waters. How like him to instill the gentle with strength and the strong with gentleness.

It was with gentle water that John baptized Jesus. "After his baptism, as Jesus came up out of the water, the heavens were opened and he saw the Spirit of God descending like a dove and settling on him" (Matthew 3:16–17). Infinite power emerging from gentle water.

May I be like a tree Lord, planted by streams of water, which yields its fruit in season.

[PSALM 1:3 NIV84]

I will take away their stony, stubborn heart
and give them a tender, responsive heart.

EZEKIEL 11:19

Images from a church play I saw years ago have stayed with me. A woman clutched to her chest various implements, like a thorn bush, she had accepted from Satan to protect her heart from being hurt by others. Throughout the play, Jesus stood silently behind her, but she had no interaction with him. As others spoke to her of Jesus, item by item she became convinced to drop Satan's tools. When she was finally free of them all, Jesus spoke and asked her to hand him her heart. She did. It was a large rock. He took it and handed back to her a soft heart made of cloth.

Stubborn, hardened hearts may form to protect their owners from pain. But, as even the late actress Celeste Holme observed, "The trouble with putting armor on is that, while it protects you from pain, it also protects you from pleasure." The trouble with hardening our hearts is that while it may protect us from some short-term pain, it keeps us from allowing Jesus to enter and give us a life, while not pain-free, so much more exquisite than we could ever have without him.

Lord, I give you my stony, stubborn heart.
Please give me a gentle, compassionate heart
that welcomes you and reaches out to others.

You place your hand of blessing on my head.
Such knowledge is too wonderful for me,
too great for me to understand!

PSALM 139:5–6

In 1915, Dr. Henry Chapin reported that in U.S. orphanages with a "no coddling" policy, nearly every infant under age two died, despite clean facilities and adequate nourishment. After further study, psychologist Harry Harlow determined that the babies had died from lack of touch.

An infant has over five million skin sensory cells and thrives on sensation. Touch enhances bonding as well as trust between parent and child. Touch not only helps calm babies, it boosts their development. With gentle touch, infants cry less and sleep better. Their brain's maturation may be facilitated, and their parents' stress levels reduced. This need for touch continues throughout adulthood. Touch alleviates depression, reduces pain, decreases stress, and improves immune function.

Even more impactful is God's gentle touch. His hand "laid the foundation of the earth, and [his] right hand spread out the heavens" (Isaiah 48:13). The touch of Jesus healed (Matthew 8:3) and even brought the dead to life (Luke 7:12–15).

Lord, help me notice when someone needs my gentle touch.
May they know its power comes from you.

*Agrippa interrupted [Paul], "Do you think you can
persuade me to become a Christian so quickly?"*

ACTS 26:28

In his fascinating book *The Tipping Point*, author Malcolm
Gladwell discusses the art of subtle persuasion. He maintains
that slight physical movements in face and body can have significant persuasive impact:

> Non-verbal cues are as or more important than verbal
> cues. . . . How we say things may matter more than
> what we say. . . . Simple physical movements and
> observations can have a profound effect on how we feel
> and think.

Our effectiveness as a communicator is related to how we
speak, not just to what we say. Facial expressions, body language, pitch, volume, pace, and mannerisms are consciously or
subconsciously noticed and responded to. A bulldozer approach
often elicits a bulldozer response. A gentle approach eliminates
the need for defensiveness and paves the way for less-guarded
listening and more open-minded reception.

Jesus didn't yell his message in hell, fire, and brimstone
tones. He didn't speak with blaring messages of superiority. He
didn't intimidate. He spoke thoughtfully and, I would imagine,
almost always quietly, calmly, gently.

Lord, when I want to persuade, help me be gentle.

Blessed are the meek, for they will inherit the earth.
MATTHEW 5:5 NIV84

The word *meek* has long been maligned. It brings to mind images of a milquetoast mousy person. Dictionary.com defines *meek* as "docile . . . overly submissive . . . spiritless; tame." That is not the biblical definition. *Vine's Expository Dictionary* defines biblical *meek* as "gentle" but offers much more:

> In its use in Scripture . . . [meekness] is an inwrought grace of the soul. . . . It is that temper of spirit in which we accept His dealings with us as good, and therefore without disputing or resisting; it is closely linked with the word *humility.* . . . Meekness . . . commonly used, suggests weakness . . . whereas [scriptural meekness] does nothing of the kind. . . . The meekness manifested by the Lord and commended to the believer is the fruit of power. . . . The Lord was "meek" because he had the infinite resources of God at his command.

Biblical meekness flows from strength. It is strength under control.

No wonder the apostle Paul sought "the meekness and gentleness of Christ" (2 Corinthians 10:1–4). According to Scripture, "The meek will inherit the land and enjoy great peace" (Psalm 37:11 NIV84), and when God judges the nations, he'll "remove from this city those who rejoice in their pride. . . . But I will leave within you the meek and the humble who trust in the name of the Lord" (Zephaniah 3:11–12 NIV84).

God, grant me the "grace of the soul" that is true meekness.

DAY 163

The trouble is with me, for I am all too human.

ROMANS 7:14

Too frequently I forget to be gentle. I forge ahead without asking God for help with this fruit. I end up thinking—like the apostle Paul—"Oh, what a miserable person I am!" (Romans 7:24). I came up with this analogy to help me remember to be gentle:

I'm driving a car (I'm the car) toward my desired destination (gentleness). To get there, my car must be in good condition (healthy and not overly stressed). Reading the car's instruction manual (the Bible) helps me navigate safely. My GPS (prayer) is essential. A clear windshield (an alert mind) will allow me to watch for obstacles (Satan and his schemes). I need to remember my car can hurt others (my words). Rather than charge through intersections (those times when I need to make a choice), I must stop, look, and listen before proceeding. A manual transmission (which requires I pay attention!) will help me be aware of how I'm driving. Revving my engine (becoming angry and harsh) accomplishes nothing. Speeding (my tongue moving faster than my thinking) may cause an accident. Driving gently, with less force than I'm capable of and no more than necessary, I'll arrive at gentleness without crashes along the way.

Corny analogy, I know—but fun. Just remember, there are many other cars (people like us) on the road. Drive gently with God. He'll get us there every time.

Lord, we've spent the past forty days thinking about gentleness.
May this fruit bring me closer to my ultimate destination
of being more like you in all ways.

KINDNESS

We beg you not to accept this marvelous gift
of God's kindness and then ignore it.

2 CORINTHIANS 6:1

Dear Lord,
Often I struggle to be kind. I wish that weren't the case. Kindness
makes helping others and meeting their needs more important
than meeting my own needs, and that's not something I always
feel like doing.

Please help me set aside my self-centeredness. I want to be
a kind person, putting you first; others, second; and myself, last.
Too frequently I reverse that order. May I remember that it's in
giving I'll receive what truly matters; it's in dying to myself that
I will fully live.

Your Spirit can help me share the kindness that points
people to you. Help me live with kindness, serving others and
glorifying you.

Amen.

Please be kind to me.
GENESIS 34:11

When I looked up the definition of *kindness* in the dictionary, I found it comes from the New Testament Greek *chrestos*, meaning "serviceable, good, pleasant." I then looked up *serviceable*. It means "helpful, useful" (*Merriam-Webster*). Neither of those definitions was very helpful or useful. Even a can opener is serviceable! So I dug deeper, but not in dictionaries. I opened the Bible to learn more about the kindness God wants us to live.

Scripture says, "Serve one another in love" (Galatians 5:13): biblical kindness involves actions and words that help someone, make them feel better physically or emotionally, are offered without being asked, and done without any expectation of receiving something in return. "If you do good only to those who do good to you why should you get credit? Even sinners do that much!" (Luke 6:33).

Kindness comes as we obey the Golden Rule: "Do to others as you would like them to do to you" (Luke 6:31). Kindness puts others first regardless of the impact doing so will have on us. It's doing something not required, going the extra mile, lightening another's burden, or brightening their day.

The Bible says, "Show mercy and kindness to one another" (Zechariah 7:9). The good news is, that's gratifying and fun. That's not why we're to be kind, but it's generally the result. Other fruits aren't necessarily pleasant at the time. Kindness almost always feels wonderful both short and long term.

*Lord, help me take every opportunity to be kind—
and thank you that you often bless me when I am.*

If you have a gift for showing kindness to others, do it gladly.
ROMANS 12:8

When I was thinking about kindness, I realized I'm not as proactive as I'd like to be. I'm kind when the opportunity presents itself—I'll let someone go ahead of me in the checkout line—but I don't regularly think of other people's needs first.

I also realized that kindness exists in varying degrees. My grocery cart kindness is at the "tiny" end of the spectrum; donating a kidney to someone is at the "big" end.

Being consistently kind is another consideration. What keeps me from being consistent? Am I too involved with my own activities? Is it just easier to turn a blind eye? And how important is convenience to me?

Malcolm Gladwell tells of some seminary students who were to give a talk across campus. Some were told to hurry because they were late; others were informed they had plenty of time; all of them would walk past a man clearly in distress, planted there by the researchers. Of the group told to hurry, "10 percent stopped to help. Of the group who knew they had a few minutes to spare, 63 percent stopped" (*The Tipping Point*).

To assess how we're doing on the fruit of kindness, we can consider to what degree we are kind (small to large kindnesses), how consistent we are, and how big a factor convenience is. Do we seek out opportunities to be kind, or just respond to those that present themselves? These are important questions, for God wants us to be "examples of the incredible wealth of his grace and kindness toward us" (Ephesians 2:7).

Lord, help me to be kind not only when it's easy and convenient.
May my kindness be proactive and generous.

*Though the mountains should depart and the hills be shaken
or removed, yet My love and kindness shall not depart from you.*

ISAIAH 54:10 AMP

God is kind in all ways, from small to huge, from his daily mercies to his ultimate gift of Jesus. The Bible contains abundant recognition of his extravagant kindness:

- "You are a gracious God and merciful, slow to anger and of great kindness." (Jonah 4:2 AMP)
- "He is so rich in kindness and grace that he purchased our freedom with the blood of his Son and forgave our sins." (Ephesians 1:7)
- "Don't you see how wonderfully kind, tolerant, and patient God is with you?" (Romans 2:4)
- "Show me unfailing kindness like that of the Lord as long as I live." (1 Samuel 20:14–15 NIV84)
- "He has showered his kindness on us, along with all wisdom and understanding." (Ephesians 1:8)
- "The Lord is righteous in everything he does; he is filled with kindness." (Psalm 145:17)
- "'With everlasting kindness I will have compassion on you,' says the Lord your Redeemer." (Isaiah 54:8 NIV84)

Today, let's think of how kind God has been in our own lives. We can even make these verses personal to us: "He purchased my freedom. . . . How patient God is with me. . . . He has showered his kindness on me. . . ."

*Thank you, Lord, for being so kind. I will tell of your kindness,
the deeds for which you are to be praised.*

Neither . . . could repay him,
so he kindly forgave them . . . canceling their debts.

LUKE 7:42

God filled his Word with illustrations of kindness to inspire us to be kind as well. Kindness has many faces. We can make some of them our own.

- Before Jonathan died, he asked his best friend, King David, to make a promise: "Do not ever cut off your kindness from my family" (1 Samuel 20:15 NIV84). Although David had a cultural prerogative to kill Jonathan's son, Mephibosheth, as a potential threat to the throne (he was King Saul's grandson), he restored his land, and gave him a permanent seat at the king's table.
- A kind woman built a room for the prophet Elisha to stay in when in town. Elisha wanted to repay her with a kindness of his own. Learning she had no son and an old husband, Elisha prophesied she would have a son within a year. His prophecy was fulfilled (2 Kings 4:8–36).
- When Joseph learned Mary was pregnant, even before discovering she'd conceived by the Holy Spirit, he had planned to break their engagement privately rather than disgrace her publicly (Matthew 1:18–25).
- The apostle Paul wrote to Philemon asking him to act with kindness and grace by welcoming back his runaway slave Onesimus, not as a slave, but as a new brother in the Lord.

Thank you, God, that through your Word you inspire me
to be kind; and through your Spirit you enable me.

*You are becoming progressively acquainted with
and recognizing more strongly and clearly the grace of
our LORD JESUS CHRIST (His kindness, His gracious generosity,
His undeserved favor and spiritual blessings).*

2 CORINTHIANS 8:9 AMP

Jesus consistently lived the kindness he taught. Ever compassionate, he healed the blind, the lame, and lepers (Matthew 8:1–4). He welcomed children after his disciples had shooed them away (Matthew 19:13–15). When a woman washed his feet with precious perfume, Jesus recognized her heart of gratitude for the forgiveness she had received, and defended her (Luke 7:36–50). He spoke kindly to Mary sitting at his feet and to her sister, Martha, who was busy preparing the meal (Luke 10:38–41). Jesus invited the Samaritan woman at the well to accept him as the Messiah (John 4:4–26), and he refused to condemn the adulteress who had been framed (John 8:3–11). These are just a few examples of Jesus's boundless kindness.

Jesus's life was not only a lesson in daily kindness, but a gift of supreme kindness: he died so we could live forgiven and for eternity with him. Jesus knew the cost, yet he put us first. As Paul said, "When the kindness and love of God our Savior appeared, he saved us, not because of righteous things we had done, but because of his mercy" (Titus 3:4 NIV84).

---

*Lord Jesus, thank you for teaching me kindness
and for giving me the gift of ultimate kindness—
your life for mine.*

*Do not grieve the Holy Spirit of God,
with whom you were sealed for the day of redemption.*
EPHESIANS 4:30 NIV84

Surprise, surprise! Over the years there have been times of normal sibling conflict among the Henry children. But they have also shown kindness to each other and experienced special closeness. When they're kind and close, I'm joyful. When unkindness and discord occur, I'm grieved.

We are made in God's image, so it's no surprise that the Holy Spirit is grieved when we act with "bitterness, rage and anger, brawling and slander, along with every form of malice" instead of choosing to "be kind and compassionate to one another, forgiving each other, just as in Christ God forgave you" (Ephesians 4:31–32 NIV84).

I'm certain God feels joy when we, his children, treat each other with kindness. I never want to grieve my heavenly Father; I want to give him joy by making sure kindness reigns in my life.

As Jesus's disciple Peter said, we're to "sympathize with each other. Love each other as brothers and sisters. Be tenderhearted, and keep a humble attitude" (1 Peter 3:8). God will bless us for it (v. 9).

---

*Holy Spirit, may I never grieve you, but bring you joy
as you enable me to extend kindness to others.*

O Lord, please hear my prayer! . . .
Put it into his heart to be kind to me.
NEHEMIAH 1:11

Chances are, every person we encounter on any given day is dealing with some kind of problem, challenge, or heartache we know nothing about. Even if we ask how they're doing, we'll hear, "Fine." I'm guilty of that too. During a family crisis I responded "Good" to every checkout clerk who asked, "How are you?" Only God and close friends knew my pain. I'm not alone in this. "Be kinder than necessary for everyone is fighting some kind of battle" (anonymous). Often the best we can offer are gestures of kindness and faithful prayer.

At the conclusion of a Bible study I taught, I'd ask for prayer requests. My heart has been overwhelmed by the needs those women shared as well as by the multitude and magnitude of prayer requests in e-mail forwards and church group gatherings. It seems everyone is undergoing a trial of some kind or knows someone who is.

Recently, a friend expressed surprise that a woman at Bible study had remained silent during prayer requests. "She has two children in college, her husband lost his job, and she has major surgery next week," this friend told me. Yet she'd said nothing.

It's true that "the strongest people are . . . those who win battles we know nothing about" (origin unknown). We don't know what people are carrying, but chances are good everyone we have contact with is carrying something difficult. We can help . . . with kindness.

Lord, help me to freely share the healing water of kindness,
for everyone is thirsty.

The Lord bless you for showing this kindness.

2 SAMUEL 2:5 NIV84

A nurse led the soldier to the old man's bedside. "Your son is here," she said.

The patient's eyes never opened, but his hand inched toward the edge of the bed in the darkened room. The soldier wrapped his hand over the old man's limp fingers and squeezed them gently. "I'm here," he said.

Through the night the soldier sat by the man's bed and held his hand. Near dawn the old man died. The soldier went to get the nurse.

"I'm sorry," she said.

"Tell me about that man," the soldier said.

"He's not your father?"

"No. I never saw him before last night."

"But when you asked to see Mr. Smith I assumed . . ."

"When you took me in to him, I realized he needed his son. I knew his son couldn't be there. I chose to stay with him. You see, I was assigned to tell him his son was killed in action yesterday. I decided he didn't need to know."

I don't know who first relayed that story, but its lesson is timeless. As first-century Roman philosopher Seneca put it so many years ago, "Wherever there is a human being, there's an opportunity for kindness."

---

*Lord, open my eyes to every opportunity for kindness
that comes my way and help me act on it with generosity,
compassion, and love.*

What have I done to deserve such kindness?
RUTH 2:10

Probably most of us have found ourselves, at one time or another, trying to figure out what to give someone who has everything—or even someone who doesn't. My suggestion? Forget material things. Instead, give a gift of kindness. Even when kindness includes a financial aspect, the kindness part is appreciated most.

I read this story from the website kindnessusa.org: Zeb, a twenty-two-year-old Marine, had returned to the States and was going to college. Needing a washer and dryer, he found a front-loading set on eBay. Shortly after it arrived, he received an e-mail from the seller: "Your PayPal has been refunded. Thank you for serving our country."

Selling Lemonade for Free by Chuck Wall is a book filled with stories of kindness ranging from the life-giving donation of a human heart, to tying notes and birthday balloons to the doors of elderly apartment residents, to even simply saying "thank you." Wall relates, "I was sitting next to some parents during a graduation ceremony. . . . One of the parents . . . turned to me and said, 'Thank you for being a teacher!' I was thrilled!"

We can show kindness anytime and in many ways. Send a heartfelt e-mail of appreciation, bake someone's favorite cookies, pay someone a sincere compliment, babysit for free, rake a neighbor's leaves, learn what a young couple on a budget loves to do and make it happen. Think of ways to warm people's hearts, make them smile, or show them they matter. Kindness is the best gift you can give.

Lord, grant me the insight and creativity to give gifts of kindness.

I want to show God's kindness to them.

2 SAMUEL 9:3

Dairy Queen employee Joey Prusak of Hopkins, Minnesota, saw unkindness and responded with kindness. Prusak was waiting on a visually-impaired customer. When the man pulled out a credit card to pay, a twenty-dollar bill fell on the floor. Prusak saw the woman next in line snatch the bill and stash it in her purse.

"Take no part in the worthless deeds of evil and darkness; instead, expose them" (Ephesians 5:11). Prusak said, "Ma'am, please return the gentleman's money." The woman denied taking it. "There was kind of a scene," Prusak said. "I told her that what she had done was extremely disrespectful, and she had to leave." She did, but she kept the money. So Prusak reached into his own pocket and handed the customer twenty dollars.

"May the LORD reward you well for the kindness you have shown me today" (1 Samuel 24:18–19). A few days later Prusak's manager received an e-mail from a customer who'd witnessed the exchange, praising Prusak for his kindness. The manager asked Prusak why he hadn't mentioned the incident. Prusak said he hadn't thought to. It had just "felt like the right thing to do."

"Whenever we have the opportunity, we should do good to everyone" (Galatians 6:10). Prusak's story, posted online, generated over ten thousand comments cheering his kindness and booing the unkindness of the woman who had gained twenty dollars but lost the respect of many.

Lord, thank you for people like Joey Prusak,
people who are willing to be kind
even at some cost to themselves.

As God's chosen people, holy and dearly loved,
clothe yourselves with compassion [and] kindness.

COLOSSIANS 3:12

You've undoubtedly heard the phrase random acts of kindness, but you may not know about its humble beginnings.

In 1982 Anne Herbert wrote on a placemat at a Sausalito, California, restaurant: "Practice random acts of kindness and senseless acts of beauty." Somehow, these words spread. So did the kind deeds. In 1993 *Random Acts of Kindness,* a collection of true stories about kindness, was published. Academia got involved when a California professor gave his students a class assignment to do a random act of kindness. That unleashed another flood of stories, and the concept spread even more.

Years later, these kindnesses still abound. I googled "random acts of kindness" and netted 32.1 million sites. I even discovered a Random Acts of Kindness Day and a Random Acts of Kindness Foundation.

Why is random kindness so popular? I think because kindness feels good, not only to receive, but also to give. Try it and see. At the beginning of each week for a month, make a list of seven small kindnesses you could do for family, friends, neighbors, coworkers, and/or strangers. Then do one each day. At the end of that month, note how you feel.

God says, "Always try to be kind to each other" (1 Thessalonians 5:15), and he makes doing those acts fun.

Lord, thank you for the pleasure I receive when I'm kind.
May random acts of kindness continue!

*Here is another bit of wisdom that has impressed me
as I have watched the way our world works.*

The word *wisdom* comes from the New Testament Greek *sophia,* meaning "insight into the true nature of things." Here's some kindness wisdom I've come across:

- "Today will never come again. Be a blessing. Be a friend. Encourage someone. Take time to care. Let your words heal and not wound." (anonymous)
- "Always be kinder than you feel." (anonymous)
- "Never miss an opportunity to make others happy, even if you have to leave them alone to do it." (anonymous)
- "Kindness: It's not doing something for someone else because they can't, but because you can." (Andrew Iskander)
- "You can't live a perfect day without doing something for someone who will never be able to repay you." (John Wooden)
- "The true meaning of life is to plant trees under whose shade you do not expect to sit." (Nelson Henderson)

Lord, give me the wisdom to be kind.

What a relief to see your friendly smile.
It is like seeing the face of God!
GENESIS 33:10

When I was in corporate management, I often visited the company's manufacturing plant. One day a union officer told me that some plant employees thought I looked mean. I was floored. Mean is not how I'd ever acted, nor how I thought I looked. But after that I made it a point to smile when I visited. This experience was an embarrassing reminder that facial expressions matter and that not paying attention to them can communicate the wrong message. I hadn't realized that my look of concentration could be misinterpreted as unkindness.

Have you ever passed a stranger and smiled only to receive a blank expression in return? That response bothers me. We can smile anyway. As H. Jackson Brown, Jr. said, "Give a stranger one of your smiles. It might be the only sunshine he sees all day." When a stranger smiles at me, it feels nice. My impression of that person becomes more positive. How much more meaningful a smile to or from someone we know.

As Mother Teresa said, "Be the living expression of God's kindness: kindness in your face, kindness in your eyes, kindness in your smile." Recently I met a woman I liked immediately. Whenever I saw her, I felt good. Then I realized why. She was always smiling, and her smile was contagious. I found myself not only smiling back, but smiling after we parted. A smile is an easy gesture, a kindness that can make a difference.

Lord, may my smiles make others smile.

Do not repay evil with evil or insult with insult,
but with blessing.
1 PETER 3:9 NIV84

"If your enemy is hungry, feed him; if he's thirsty, give him something to drink. In doing this, you will heap burning coals on his head" (Proverbs 25:22). I love that scripture. To me, it reflects God's sense of humor. He understands it's hard to be kind to someone who's not kind. But he makes an excellent point. The godly way to inflict pain on an "enemy" is through kindness. It will contrast with their actions, and, hopefully, cause them to realize the error of their ways. They may expect reciprocally poor treatment and feel remorse when treated kindly instead. Put more graphically, "Never wrestle with a pig. You'll both get dirty and the pig loves it" (George Bernard Shaw), and "One man cannot hold another man down in the ditch without remaining down in the ditch with him" (Booker T. Washington).

If you want to get back at someone you dislike, be kind to them. Whether or not they reciprocate, you'll have nothing to regret. "Treat everyone with politeness, even those who are rude to you—not because they are nice, but because you are" (origin unknown).

God says, "Do not be overcome by evil but overcome evil with good" (Romans 12:21).

We often don't know why people act as they do. Maybe those who repel us have their own private burdens. Perhaps they're hungry for kindness. We can "be kind to unkind people—they need it the most" (A. Brilliant).

Lord, give me strength to be kind to those who are unkind.

He never thought of doing a kindness.

PSALM 109:16 NIV84

She was only twelve years old when she hanged herself. She left a suicide note, and police reported that she mentioned being a target of online bullying. Tragically, events like that one—reported by CNN a while ago—happen all too often. Unkindness can have horrific consequences. If, instead of being bullied, those children had been befriended and encouraged, they'd probably still be alive.

Adults can be bullies too. We've all seen individuals who snap at people, wear a permanent scowl, put others down, and look at the world through vacant, cold eyes. When we see such people, we know right away they're unhappy. In fact, I'd bet there's no such thing as a happy bully. J. M. Barrie, the creator of *Peter Pan*, noted that "Those who bring sunshine to the lives of others cannot keep it from themselves." No doubt those who bring the darkness of unkindness to others cannot keep that gloom from themselves.

A friend's niece was dealing with depression. My friend gave her a Bible. Her niece didn't read it. One night, the girl decided to take her life. But then she saw the Bible, began to read, and invited Christ into her life. Thoughts of suicide disappeared.

Kindness can make the difference between life and death— figuratively and literally.

Lord, make me an instrument of your peace:
where there is hatred, let me sow love; . . .
where there is despair, hope; where there is darkness, light.
[FROM PEACE PRAYER OF ST. FRANCIS OF ASSISI]

You gave me life and showed me kindness.

JOB 10:12 NIV84

One Christmas, our son, Kirk, and daughter-in-law, Courtney, asked my husband, David, me, our daughters Rachel and Lauren, and Lauren's then-fiancé Chris to meet them and their children at a store. They wouldn't tell us why.

After we arrived, Kirk said, "We're blessed. There's nothing any of us needs. So instead of buying you something, our children are handing each of you forty dollars. You have thirty minutes to buy gifts for kids at Children's Hospital. Then we'll meet, each of us will explain why we chose what we did, and we'll vote on whose we like best. The winner gets fifty dollars."

We were off and running, literally, throughout the store. When our thirty minutes were up, we raced to the meeting place and shared our choices. Chris had bought a tricycle, remembering his delight when he'd received one as a child. David bought a basketball hoop and other games. Lauren, too, focused on sports, complete with team-logo slippers. Rachel showed off a ride-on car. My theme was creativity with blocks and craft supplies. Chris and Rachel tied for the prize. They dashed off and purchased a trainer bike with their winnings.

Our Christmas gift culminated with a trip to Children's Hospital to drop off the toys and bike and tour the facility. None of us will forget the joy this gift of kindness brought us. Our grandchildren were more excited about delivering the gifts than they would have been to receive them.

Lord, thank you for the joy of realizing
it truly is more blessed to give than to receive.

KINDNESS

Love is kind.

1 CORINTHIANS 13:4 NIV84

Husbands and wives can be kinder to strangers than to each other. "We flatter those we scarcely know; we please the fleeting guest, and deal full many a thoughtless blow, to those who love us best" (Ella Wheeler Wilcox). I'd bet the divorce rate would plummet if all married couples consistently loved each other with the love described in 1 Corinthians 13:4–7. Too often "for better or worse" turns into "for bitter and worse."

In *The Proper Care & Feeding of Marriage*, relationship expert Dr. Laura Schlessinger talks about "the incredible power of making the other feel cared about and appreciated." In *Woman Power*, Dr. Laura told of one woman who decided to try that "incredible power":

> I realized what I had been doing. I wasn't being nice to my husband. I started to be more loving and kinder. And it's true—my husband wants to please me because I'm making him happy too. This is incredible— all we're doing is being nice and kind to another!

Kindness in a marriage makes a difference. We read in Proverbs 19:22, "That which is desired in a man is loyalty and kindness" (AMP). A man wants the same in a woman. As William Shakespeare noted, "A woman would run through fire and water for such a kind heart." So would a man.

Lord, help me remember that marriage thrives on kindness.

We appreciate the kind concern you have shown us.

2 KINGS 4:13

- A pharmacist tells a customer, "To buy arsenic you need a legal prescription. A picture of your mother-in-law just isn't enough."
- The doorbell rang this morning. When I opened the door, there was my mother-in-law on the front step. She said, "Can I stay here for a few days?" I said, "Sure you can." And I shut the door.

Are these jokes funny? Yes. Kind? No. Why are mother-in-law jokes so popular? What happened to the respect and loyalty Ruth showed her mother-in-law? (Ruth 1:16). Yet that may not have been the norm. We see that 2,700 years ago the prophet Micah said, "The daughter-in-law defies her mother-in-law" (Micah 7:6).

Vanessa had arranged a family photo shoot in an autumn setting for a portrait to hang in her home. She even sent her daughter-in-law a check to buy clothes for her grandchildren for the picture, but the young mom spent the money on frilly outfits in spring colors, completely at odds with the autumn theme, and refused to let her children wear anything else. Despite her hurt feelings, Vanessa decided her ideal photograph wasn't worth damaging her relationship with her daughter-in-law. But she wished she'd been shown more kindness.

Lord, may everyone remember that in-laws
need kindness too.

*He who withholds kindness from
a friend forsakes the fear of the Almighty.*

JOB 6:14 ESV

Job's three friends, at first, just sat with him and said nothing. Words weren't needed or wanted. Unfortunately, each later broke their silence and offered less-than-helpful perspectives and overwhelming ideas. Silent listening is often kinder.

> Oh, the comfort—the inexpressible comfort of feeling
>   safe with a person,
> Having neither to weigh thoughts,
> Nor measure words—but pouring them
> All right out—just as they are—
> Chaff and grain together—
> Certain that a faithful hand will
> Take them and sift them—
> Keeping what is worth keeping—
> And then with the breath of kindness
> Blow the rest away. (Dinah Maria Craik)

The kindest thing a friend can do is be there, in the good times and the bad. Does a friend have a dream, a victory, exciting news? Are they discouraged, down? Either way, encourage them (1 Thessalonians 5:11). "The greatest good you can do for another is not just to share your riches but to reveal to him his own" (Benjamin Disraeli).

---

*Lord, thank you for friends. May I remember
that kindness is the soil in which friendship blossoms.*

Has she been kind to strangers? . . .
Has she always been ready to do good?
1 TIMOTHY 5:10

Our professor gave us a quiz. I breezed through the questions until the last one. "What's the first name of the woman who cleans the school?" Surely this was a joke. I'd seen her, but how would I know her name? I asked if the question would count toward our grade. "Absolutely," the professor said. "In your careers you'll meet many people. All are significant. They deserve your attention and care, even if all you do is smile and say hello." I've never forgotten that lesson. I also learned her name was Dorothy. (Adapted from InspirationPeak.com)

Kindness matters. Jesus says refusal to be kind to strangers brings "eternal punishment;" kindness brings inheritance of the kingdom (Matthew 25:31–46). God considers our treatment of each other to be our treatment of him (Matthew 25:35, 40, 45).

God may let people cross our path for a reason. He may even send them (Genesis 18; Judges 6; 13). Unbeknownst to us, they may even be angels (Hebrews 13:2 NIV84). Even if not angels, "everyone is afraid of something, loves something, and has lost something" (H. Jackson Brown, Jr.). And, like us, they'd love a kindness.

Lord, help me remember how important kindness
to strangers is—to them, to me, and to you.

Is it against the law for me to do what I want with my money?
Should you be jealous because I am kind to others?

MATTHEW 20:15

My then-four-year-old granddaughter Cayden was on the floor surrounded by coins, intently shaking her upside-down polka dot piggy bank.

"What're you doing?" I said.

She didn't look up. "Counting my money so I can buy Wyatt a birthday present." Her brother, Wyatt, was turning three.

I sat down and helped her sort the coins into piles. Then we counted her treasure: a grand total of over fifteen dollars.

Cayden scooped the money into her purse. Later we went shopping. After carefully considering her options, she chose a toy shaving kit for Wyatt. She knew he likes to imitate his dad.

As Cayden emptied her purse to pay, I thought of how financial giving is a form of kindness, of putting others first without heed to its impact on us. Cayden gave no thought to what she could have bought for herself with her long-collected wealth (well, she did hesitate at some animal-shaped backpacks), but all she really wanted was to buy Wyatt something that would make him happy.

Jesus noticed a widow drop two small coins into the temple's collection box: "I tell you the truth, [she] has given more than all the others. . . . For they gave a tiny part of their surplus, but she . . . has given everything she had" (Mark 12:43–44).

Lord, may I be generous with the money
you have entrusted to me.

Honor one another above yourselves.

ROMANS 12:10 NIV84

"The fruit of the Spirit is financial gain, a rewarding career, a great social life, instant gratification of all your wants, and unlimited material things." Of course, that is *not* Galatians 5:22–23!

The fruit of God's Spirit is not self-oriented. It's other-directed. The fruit of a tree nourishes and gives pleasure, not to the tree, but to those who experience its fruit. Similarly, we're to produce the fruit of God's Spirit to share with others. How we treat them reflects who we are as well as whose we are (Matthew 7:20 NIV84). Through God's power, we can become more like Jesus who "made himself nothing, taking the very nature of a servant" (Philippians 2:7 NIV84). That kind of humility enables us to put the needs of others before our own desires.

Kindness moves self to last place. St. Francis of Assisi said: "Above all the grace and the gifts that Christ gives to his beloved is that of overcoming self." God first. Others second. Self last. That's the key to kindness. That's the key to living every fruit of God's Spirit.

Lord, remind me that kindness comes more easily
when I have my priorities in the right order—
you, others, then me.

I am unworthy of all the kindness and faithfulness
you have shown your servant.

GENESIS 32:9–10

We want to please God. He wants us to be kind to others. He cares about and is kind to us. It makes sense he wants us to be kind to ourselves.

We mess up. We're not perfect. We have a long way to go. But we're making progress. So when we stumble, let's not beat ourselves up. Let's give ourselves the kindness of grace and mercy by acknowledging our humanness, our need for God, then moving on.

Being kind to ourselves also includes getting enough sleep, exercise, and healthy food. Our bodies "were made for the LORD, and the LORD cares about" them (1 Corinthians 6:13). We should too. If we neglect ourselves, at some point we won't be as effective for others or for God.

Focus on our accomplishments instead of our mistakes, enjoy a nap or a workout, savor a bowl of fresh strawberries, read a book, pursue that hobby, indulge in some little luxury, have coffee or take a walk with a friend, soak in a sunrise, linger with a sunset. We can give ourselves the kindness of doing something that brightens our day. With our renewed energy, we can brighten someone else's.

Lord, in living a life of kindness,
remind me to be kind to myself.

Show to me . . . the same kindness I have shown to you.

GENESIS 21:23 NIV84

What's your first impulse when someone is kind to you? Chances are, you want to be kind in return. Chances also are that remembering that kindness gives you a desire to be kind to someone else. When you are, that person may not only want to return your kindness but pass it on to others as well. "Remember, there's no such thing as a small act of kindness. Every act creates a ripple with no logical end" (Scott Adams).

The kindness of the Philippians to Paul was no small act. We can hear his gratitude in his words: "How I praise the LORD that you are concerned about me again. . . . I want you to receive a reward for your kindness" (Philippians 4:10, 17). Paul also expressed his gratitude for kindness in 2 Timothy 1:16—17.

Kindness is contagious. It's a great thing to spread. It's wonderful to catch.

Have you had a kindness shown? Pass it on.
'Twas not given for thee alone,
Pass it on;
Let it travel down the years,
Let it wipe another's tears,
'Til in Heaven the deed appears—
Pass it on. (Henry Burton)

Lord, thank you for making kindness infectious.
May I catch it and pass it on!

If you are kind only to your friends,
how are you different from anyone else?
Even pagans do that.
MATTHEW 5:47

The small town where I grew up had a small l café. Stella Ellis was its waitress. She was tight-lipped and had a stern, wrinkled face. I thought she was mean, though my mother suggested Stella Ellis probably just didn't know how to be nice. Typical of Mother, she came up with a plan. No matter how unkindly Stella Ellis treated us, we'd go out of our way to be kind to her.

Mother went into action. She'd smile at Stella Ellis, ask how her day was going, and compliment her. "The best way to knock a chip off someone's shoulder is to pat them on the back" (anonymous). But Mother's interest wasn't feigned. She loved people, and Stella Ellis was a person with thoughts, problems, and dreams of her own. Little by little Mother showed her that she cared about those, and little by little Stella Ellis softened. As writer James Boswell (1740–95) noted, "We cannot tell the precise moment when friendship is formed. As in filling a vessel drop by drop, there is at last a drop which makes it run over; so in a series of kindnesses there is at last one which makes the heart run over."

I don't recall how long it took, but there came a time when Stella Ellis lit up whenever Mother walked into the cafe. She'd pay special attention to us, smile, chat, and even laugh. It was as if she'd come alive.

Lord, help me remember that kindness
is often what an unkind person needs most

May all my thoughts be pleasing to him,
for I rejoice in the LORD.

PSALM 104:34

"Kind hearts are the gardens; kind thoughts, the roots; kind words, the blossoms; kind deeds, the fruits" (from a nineteenth-century rhyme).

How are our thoughts like roots? Roots anchor plants in the ground; our thoughts connect us with God, and to the world. Roots absorb nutrients from the soil, the plant's life impacted by the soil's quality. Our minds absorb input that influences our thoughts, which give rise to our words and actions. Our life is impacted by the nature and quality of that input.

Roots exist in root systems. A fibrous root system is a mass of similar-size roots. If we take in only the ideas of this world, our thoughts will be like a fibrous root system, a confusing tangle of so-called wisdom.

Plants with a taproot system have one main root from which smaller roots emerge. To ensure we produce kindness, we need to establish a taproot thought system, with its one main root connected to God, "taking captive every thought to make it obedient to Christ" (2 Corinthians 10:5). Then, smaller thought-roots will grow from that taproot, blossoming into kind words, producing the fruit of kindness.

Lord, may my thoughts always be taprooted in you.

*Kind words are like honey—sweet to the soul
and healthy for the body.*

PROVERBS 16:24

I doubt any of us have escaped the at best deflating, at worst destructive, impact of unkind words. I've experienced words that caused some air to leak from my balloon, words that have popped it, and words that have ripped it to shreds. I've also felt the balloon-soaring pleasure of kind words sincerely spoken. Everyone enjoys, craves, and needs words like those. As Sharon Jaynes says in *The Power of a Woman's Words*:

> [Our tongues have the] huge potential for good or evil, to build up or to tear down, to empower or devour, to heal or to hurt. Our words can make or break a marriage, paralyze or propel a friend, sew together or tear apart a relationship, build up or bury a dream.

No wonder God says, "Do not let any unwholesome talk come out of your mouths, but only what is helpful for building others up according to their needs" (Ephesians 4:29 NIV84).

In the Bible's description of a virtuous woman, we read that "she openeth her mouth with wisdom and in her tongue is the law of kindness" (Proverbs 31:26 KJV). We can all enforce that law of kindness by being "done with . . . all unkind speech" (1 Peter 2:1). Often, "the kindest word in all the world is the unkind word, unsaid" (anonymous).

---

*Lord, I know how good kind words feel
and how badly unkind ones hurt.
May the law of kindness be enforced in my tongue.*

I will show you . . . by what I do.

JAMES 2:18

Sarah plopped onto the couch next to her husband and sipped her tea. "I feel bad for Janie Duncan. She's a single mom with four kids. She never has time to relax. Wouldn't it be nice if someone offered to watch her kids sometime and gave her a few hours for herself?"

"Yeah, that would really be nice. Maybe you should do it," her husband said.

"Well, it's not like I have a lot of time either," Sarah picked up a magazine and leafed through it. "I've got bridge club, my gardening, and my exercise class, and I've been thinking about volunteering at the hospital. . . . Oh well. It's a shame. Janie's so nice."

Like Sarah, I've sometimes thought about doing something kind but not done it. It's good to remember that: "People may doubt what you say, but they will always believe what you do" (Lewis Cass). When we describe someone as kind, it's because of what we've seen them *do*. Talk *is* cheap: "Suppose you see a brother or sister who has not food or clothing and you say, 'Good-bye and have a good day; stay warm and eat well'—but then you don't give that person any food or clothing. What good does that do?" (James 2:15–16).

Kind thoughts without action don't make us kind people. As writer François de La Rochefoucauld (1613–80) observed: "Thinkers think and doers do. But until the thinkers do and the doers think, progress will be just another word in the already overburdened vocabulary of the talkers who talk."

Lord, help me back up my kind thoughts with action.

Your kindness has often refreshed the hearts of God's people.

PHILEMON 1:7, 10

When our son, Kirk, was ten, he took piano lessons—and enjoyed them. One day, when his best friend was over, Kirk played a song he'd just learned. His friend made fun of the fact he played the piano. Our son never touched the piano again.

Kirk wasn't going to become a concert pianist. Yet I can't help but wonder what difference a kind comment would have made, or ponder the potential loss if Beethoven or Mozart had been the recipient of the same type of unkind remark. Our words and actions—kind or unkind—have great impact.

Loren Eiseley, in his story "The Star Thrower," tells of two men walking along a beach littered with starfish. One of the men repeatedly picks up starfish and throws them into the ocean. His friend asks, "Why are you doing that?"

"The sun's up, and the tide's going out. If I don't throw them in, they'll die."

"But," his friend protested, "there are miles of beach and starfish along every mile. You can't possibly make a difference."

The first man picked up another starfish, threw it into the ocean, and said, "I made a difference to that one!"

You and I can make a difference to the starfish in our lives. Professor and author Leo Buscaglia agrees: "Too often we underestimate the power of a touch, a smile, a kind word, a listening ear, an honest compliment, or the smallest act of caring, all of which have the potential to turn a life around."

Lord, may I never forget that my kindness and unkindness— to even one person—makes a difference.

You have been so gracious to me . . .
and you have shown such great kindness.
Genesis 19:19

My grandpa enjoyed stamp collecting. When I was eight, he took me to a stamp auction. Clutching my hard-earned $2.50, I studied the items up for bid, setting my sights on a well-worn, partially-filled album. I was mesmerized by its array of stamps from around the world. I could hardly contain my excitement as I imagined owning that exotic treasure.

I fidgeted through bidding on items far beyond my means, waiting for *my* album. Finally, the moment came. Grandpa had given me tips, so when the bidding started at 25¢ I knew not to jump in. At 50¢, trying to hide my eagerness, I raised my hand. 75¢ . . . my heart pounded. . . . $1 . . . I felt quite rich participating in such lofty bidding. . . . $2 . . . I swallowed hard. At $2.50 I raised my hand for the last time and silently prayed the gavel would come down. $3 . . . $3.50 . . . my heart sank. When the gavel pounded at $3.75, I was crushed.

As Grandpa and I were leaving, I felt a hand on my shoulder. A large pepper-haired man was smiling down at me. "Here," he said, handing me "my" album. "I bought this for you."

I was speechless. I didn't know this man, yet he'd given me an amazing gift. Actually, he gave me two gifts: the album . . . and a priceless lesson in kindness. I still have both.

Lord, may I take every opportunity to give kindness,
for it's a gift that can last forever.

Your kindness will reward you,
but your cruelty will destroy you.

PROVERBS 11:17

When I was four, a nine-year-old neighbor pushed me into a stone wall, breaking my nose. All she said was "I hope it happens again." My crookedly-healed nose and her mean words are still with me.

When I was in sixth grade, my parents gave me a turquoise wool pleated skirt and matching striped sweater for Christmas. I could hardly wait to wear them to school. When I did, my teacher told me never to wear them again because the school had plenty of heat and I didn't need such a warm outfit. I was floored. Later that year she told me a blouse I had on was not a flattering color. I had really liked it . . . until then.

What makes some people mean? King Saul repaid David's kindness by hurling a spear at him (1 Samuel 18:10–12). Nabal, husband of Abigail, "was surly and mean in his dealings" and refused to help David (1 Samuel 25:3–11). Did these people realize they were being nasty? Or did they not even think about it?

I don't know what became of my neighbor or that teacher. I do know Saul took his own life (1 Samuel 31:3–5), and Nabal had a heart attack and died (1 Samuel 25:37–38). I'm certain none of them was happy. It's true that hurting people hurt people. Tough as it may be—kindness includes understanding that people's unkindness is caused by their own internal pain.

Lord, help me not to take someone's unkindness personally.
May I simply turn the hurt and the person over to you.

*The LORD bless you. . . . This kindness is greater
than that which you showed earlier.*

RUTH 3:10 NIV84

During a difficult time in my life, my sister, Judy, sent me an Ephesians 6:10–20 care package. Verse 11 was the theme verse: "Put on the full armor of God, so that you can take your stand against the devil's schemes" (NIV84). Her package included a belt (of truth), a dress (breastplate of righteousness), sandals (ready feet), a bracelet (shield of faith), a baseball hat (helmet of salvation), and a prayer book (sword of the Spirit).

As Mother Teresa observed, "In this life we cannot do great things. We can only do small things with great love." Small kindnesses done with large love have a big impact. Judy's care package gave me a much-needed boost.

Another time, when I was having back issues, a friend sent me a darling card and a thick magazine. Her kindness warmed my heart and, in its own way, eased my discomfort. "Sometimes someone says something really small, and it just fits right into this empty place in your heart" (*My So-Called Life* TV show).

The apostle Paul expressed his appreciation for the Philippians' financial gift. Individual contributions were likely small, yet given with love and pooled together, those funds supported Paul in his time of need. He said, "You sent me aid again and again when I was in need. . . . The gifts you sent . . . are a fragrant offering . . . pleasing to God" (Philippians 4:16, 18).

---

*Lord, remind me I can do much good
through small kindnesses done with great love.*

Always be eager to practice hospitality.

ROMANS 12:13

What makes you feel welcome? For me, it's the little touches, those small kindnesses that say, "I'm glad you're here." It may be fresh flowers, nuts in a bowl, or a table set with best dishes and specially folded napkins.

The biblical definition of hospitality comes from the New Testament Greek *philos*, "loving," and *xenos*, "a stranger." In biblical times, travel was limited to walking or riding animals. Even distances short by today's standards necessitated overnight stays. Inns were few, so travelers often relied on the hospitality of strangers for food and rest. The Bible offered this practical instruction: "Cheerfully share your home with those who need a meal or a place to stay" (1 Peter 4:9).

Today, efficient travel and a proliferation of commercial accommodations mean we're rarely called upon to provide strangers with bed and board. But we can still practice the kindness of hospitality to friends and family who visit.

I've experienced all levels of hospitality—as well as its absence. What a treat when an obvious effort is made to show my visit is wanted. Hospitality says "Welcome! I'm so happy you're here."

Lord, may I give every guest the kindness
of showing them how very welcome they are.

When all goes well with you,
remember me and show me kindness.
GENESIS 40:14

I have a thing about plastic bags. Simply put, I hate to waste them. So it makes me crazy when I take a small purchase to a store clerk who automatically starts to put it in a plastic bag. I say, "No, thanks. I don't want to waste a bag." Then the clerk wads up the bag and throws it in the trash. What part of not wanting to waste a bag did they not understand?

As stewards of this planet, we're wise to be careful about the impact of our consumerism, but we can't (and don't want to) totally stop consuming. To lessen waste, packaging-free stores have appeared. More shoppers bring reusable bags to grocery stores. Recycling bins are popping up in public areas, and community recycling is becoming the norm. Other places ban plastic bags and cups as well as Styrofoam. I even heard of a restaurant in Japan that requires diners who don't finish their meal to contribute to a fishermen's fund. In Brazil, there's a Half for Happiness Campaign. Half portions of products such as steak and salad are sold at full price, and the extra sale proceeds are donated to organizations that help alleviate malnutrition. Kinder consumerism still has a long way to go, but it's beginning to take hold.

Lord, help me remember that everything I buy has an impact.
Let me choose a kind one.

If you suffer for doing what is right,
God will reward you for it.

1 Peter 3:13

Kindness isn't always fun, easy, or painless. There's evil in this world, and the cost of kindness can be huge, as seen in the following story, published in the *Los Angeles Times*:

Jaquie Creazzo was paralyzed by a bullet when she tried to save a woman from an attacker. Her response? "Thankfully, I'm still alive. Being paralyzed is a small price to pay to get this person, if you want to call him a person, off the street."

On a freeway ramp, Jaquie had seen two parked cars. The look on the face of a woman standing by them had made her stop.

"I didn't have a choice," Jacquie remembers. "There was this need, and it was written all over her face." The woman jumped into Jaquie's car. As Jaquie drove, the woman told her that the man in the other car had run her off the road, dragged her from her car, and raped her.

The attacker caught up to the women. He shot Jaquie three times before she steered across a median and onto the front lawn of the police department. He got out of his car, pulled the other woman from Jaquie's car, and threw her to the ground. His eyes met Jaquie's.

"It was like a dead stare. . . . His eyes were dark, empty, cold."

The man carried the other woman to his car. It was the last time she was seen alive. Police arrested him within days, but Jaquie Creazzo would never walk again.

Lord, bless Jaquie Creazzo and all like her who are selflessly kind.

DAY 199

Make every effort to add to your faith . . . kindness.
2 Peter 1:7 niv84

Are you up for a challenge? Here's one:

1. Pick a relationship you have daily—your spouse, significant other, your children, a friend, or anyone you see most every day.
2. For one week, focus on being especially kind to them. Go above and beyond.
3. Ask God to help you.
4. Remember that kindness is grace (giving undeserved good) and mercy (not giving warranted retribution). Kindness is living by the Golden Rule without expectation of a return, putting others first with little, if any, concern about its impact on us.
5. If the person asks what you're up to, respond with something like "I just love you" or "I want you to know you're special to me." Don't explain the challenge then—or later.
6. At week's end, reflect on how it felt. How did the person react?
7. Is your extra kindness something you want to continue? Why or why not?

Lord, open my eyes to the joy of being kind.
May I give you all the glory.

*"Let him who boasts boast about this; that he understands
and knows me, that I am the Lord,
who exercises kindness, justice and righteousness on earth,
for in these I delight," declares the Lord.*

JEREMIAH 9:24 NIV84

I confess. When I first drafted yesterday's challenge, it included sharing with your chosen person what you've learned about kindness; asking that person to accept the challenge so both of you would be above-and-beyond kind to each other for a week; keeping a list of the kindnesses received; and discussing those lists and the challenge experience at week's end. Telling you what the challenge originally was, though, is not what I'm confessing. My confession is that I took the challenge . . . and failed miserably and quickly. Less than a day.

I told David, my husband, about the challenge. He knows I'm competitive, and that overshadowed everything for him. He pushed back: "You're just going to try to prove you're kinder to me than I am to you."

Did I mention he'd missed the point? Well, I nagged him into trying it anyway, and we ended up in an argument. Neither of us spoke to the other for a day. So much for my kindness challenge with my husband. So I looked for lessons in that experience . . . and I changed the challenge. I learned:

- Kindness can't be forced.
- It's best to be kind and ask nothing in return.
- Pointing out my kindness reduces its impact.
- I should have discussed all this with God first!

Lord, thank you for using my mistakes to teach me.

Never let loyalty and kindness leave you!
Tie them around your neck as a reminder.
Write them deep within your heart.

PROVERBS 3:3

Now that we've tasted how sweet kindness is, we can expand our focus. For one week, let's look for opportunities to be kind to as many people as possible. Let's aim high and include everyone we see each day—those we know and those we don't, as well as anyone God puts on our heart. For each one, ask yourself and God, "What can I do for or say to that person as an act of kindness?" Then do it or say it.

This is probably a tall order, given our busy days. But it's only a week. Then we can assess and decide what to do going forward. But wouldn't it be fun if others could say of us, "She was always doing kind things for others" (Acts 9:36)? I'm ready to give it a try.

Let me be a little kinder
Let me be a little blinder
To the faults of those about me
Let me praise a little more.
Let me be when I am weary
Just a little bit more cheery . . .
Let me think more of my neighbor
And a little less of me (Edgar Guest)

Holy Spirit, fill my mind and heart with kindnesses—
and help me do them!

There is no faithfulness, no kindness,
no knowledge of God in your land.

HOSEA 4:1

This verse from Hosea expresses how I sometimes feel. The world is full of people who reject or ignore God. This fact, as well as today's widespread hatred, division, violence, conflict, entitlement, and self-centeredness, is distressing.

The psalmist's words apply today:

The wicked are stringing their bows
and fitting their arrows on the bowstrings.
They shoot from the shadows
At those whose hearts are right.
The foundations of law and order have collapsed.
What can the righteous do? (Psalm 11:2–3)

Sin is rampant in this world, but there's also a lot of goodness and kindness. We just need to look for it.

Consider the amazing kindnesses displayed during and after 9/11. Look at people's overflowing generosity in the wake of disaster. Search the news for heartwarming stories of kindness. They're there!

Instead of an ostrich's head-in-the-ground approach to the news, we can keep our antenna up for the kindness that abounds in this world gone sideways. By storing it in our hearts, we can buffer the unkindness that vies for attention. Thankfully, "the everyday kindness of the back roads more than makes up for the acts of greed in the headlines" (Charles Kuralt).

Lord, help me notice the kindness.

May kindness and faithfulness be with you.

2 SAMUEL 15:20

So I did what I challenged you to do. How did my week of kindness go?

I gave up a parking space, asked store clerks about their day, complimented people, gave away my store coupons, let someone go ahead of me in a checkout line, smiled at everyone, and held doors open. Not an impressive list, I know.

I asked myself, "Should I be doing bigger things, like volunteering in a nursing home or giving a large donation to charity?" My answer was yes and no. It's great to do bigger things, but we're talking here about everyday kindness, about making kindness a priority in our normal day. And, I realized, little things make a difference.

Who's to say my smile didn't brighten the day of someone feeling low, my compliment didn't boost another's sagging self-confidence, my attention to a store clerk didn't come when they were convinced no one cared, that giving up that parking space didn't lessen someone's stress? Not to mention how much my husband enjoyed my bringing him a snack, doing chores that are normally his, and, because his love language is service, seeing how much I care.

As for me, most important was my mind-set change. Instead of focusing on myself and my agenda, I was other-directed, searching for ways to be kind. It felt good.

Lord, send me more opportunities to be kind.
Help me recognize and act on them.

LOVE

God is love.
Whoever lives in love lives in God,
and God in him.

1 JOHN 4:16

Dear Lord,
It's time to focus on your fruit of love. Where do I even start? The immensity of these next forty days overwhelms me, for my goal is to learn to love as you love. Your love is infinite. I can't even begin to comprehend its magnitude. You love extravagantly, lavishly. It's incredible to think I can love that way, too, if I let you lead me. My attempts at love appear so small in comparison.

You've said the two greatest commandments are to love you with all my heart, mind, soul, and strength and to love my neighbor as myself. So, it looks like I begin with you, God. You are love. Help me understand what that means. Make me aware of evidence of your love in every aspect of my life. Show me what loving you with all my heart, mind, soul, and strength entails. And who is my neighbor? How do I love them as you want me to? I love you, Lord, but I want to love you even more—not just in thought, but in word and deed, in every action of my life.

Love seems so complex and complicated, yet it's also simple and pure. Thank you for your gift of love.
Amen.

God is love.

1 JOHN 4:16

To understand the fruit of love, we look to God, for God is love. This means that trying to define this fruit is trying to describe God. It's more than minds can fathom. Without God, we can't truly love. We're too self-centered, too sinfully inclined. "Love comes from God" (1 John 4:7). We love because God first loved us (1 John 4:19). "Whoever lives in love lives in God, and God in him" (1 John 4:16).

Through God's example we're shown how to love. Through his Spirit, we have the power to do it.

- To understand love, look to God.
- To be able to love, turn to God.
- To live in love, abide in God.

Since God is love, if we act contrary to love, we're acting apart from God, separating ourselves from him. That's why, after an initial flash of pleasure, we feel dreadful and empty when we don't act in love.

God created us to live in relationship with him; apart from him, we have no good thing (Psalm 16:2 NIV84). Apart from him, we cannot truly love.

Remind me, Lord, that whenever I question if I'm acting in love, all I need to ask is what you would do.

Love comes from God. Everyone who loves
has been born of God and knows God.
Whoever does not love does not know God,
because God is love.

1 JOHN 4:7–8 NIV84

I love pizza. I love coffee. I love my dog. I love shopping. I love that movie, that book. I love your new dress. I love that color on you. I love my family. I love you. I love God.

The word *love* is ubiquitous. It's used about pretty much everything. We say we love cupcakes and shoes, sayings and ideas. *Love* is probably one of the most used and *mis*used words in the English language. It's uttered millions of times every day to mean everything from barely anything to absolutely everything.

The fruit of love means something far different and more profound than our constant use of the word *love* suggests. It defies simple definition. Even forty days of focus will only scratch its surface. That's why we need God's power to produce this fruit.

It's fine and fun to "love" a lot of things and people. But it's crucial to understand what the fruit of love is and what it is not. The fruit of love doesn't come naturally or easily. It may not be fun. It may be costly. Real love comes only from God and through him.

Lord, help me understand the difference between
the love you teach, and the love taught by the world.
Through your Spirit, enable me to love as you love.

If you love those who love you, what credit is that to you?
Even sinners love those that love them.

LUKE 6:32 NIV84

A friend confided, "I don't love my husband anymore. He's no fun. He's cross most of the time. I don't even *like* him. How can I *love* him?"

The answer is simple in theory, difficult in practice. It is possible to love someone we don't like, because love is action, not necessarily feeling. If we only love those we like, we're not loving God's way. I doubt God likes us when we sin. But he loves us. "God showed his great love for us by sending Christ to die for us while we were still sinners" (Romans 5:8). God's love is rooted in who he is; it's not a response to who we are.

When we like someone, it's because we enjoy them. Liking is "me" centered. It asks "How does _____ make me feel?" We like those who cause us to feel happy. The love God teaches is being loving even when it's really, really hard. The more challenging love is, the more it's God's love we're giving.

It's been said God's intention for marriage may not be so much to make us happy, as to make us holy. I'd say the same about love: The more our love depends on who we are, not on who another is, the more Christlike our character. Like is self-directed feeling. Love is other-directed action. My friend may not like her husband. But with God's help, she can love him.

Lord, it's hard to love people I don't like. Please help me.

In all these things we are more than conquerors
through him who loved us.
ROMANS 8:37 NIV84

Feelings can overtake us. We can clench our fists, grit our teeth, scrunch our eyes, and try with all our might to get rid of them, but we can't will them away. When we want to act with love but our feelings are yelling, "No! I don't want to!" we may not be able to stop their uproar, but we can ignore it, and act with love by:

- *Turning to God:* Our emotions are powerful. God is more powerful. "Watch out for attacks from Satan. . . . Stand firm. . . . Trust the LORD" (1 Peter 5:8–9 TLB).
- *Refocusing our thoughts:* Our thoughts impact our emotions. Choose to "fix your thoughts on what is true and good and right" (Philippians 4:8 TLB).
- *Choosing self-control:* We don't have to act how we feel. That's what this fruit is for. "In your anger do not sin" (Ephesians 4:26 NIV84).

Acting with love when we don't feel love is like swimming upstream. It can be done, but it takes strength and endurance. When we don't have enough of our own, we can ask God for what we need. The more we practice swimming against the current of our emotions, the stronger we become, and the easier it will be the next time our emotions surge.

Lord, help me conquer my feelings with love.

What is causing the quarrels and fights among you?

JAMES 4:1

Back to my friend who no longer likes her husband. She called and told me they had a huge fight. "I told him all the things he does that I can't stand, so he could apologize."

"Did he?" I asked.

"No! Now he's not even talking to me."

She further illuminated her method to elicit her husband's repentance. She'd cried, yelled, and barraged him with a litany of his shortcomings.

Acting with love when we don't feel love—when we don't feel "like"—doesn't mean never mentioning what's bothering us. But if we want any chance of results, rapid artillery fire of our dissatisfactions isn't the answer. What if my friend had tried a different and biblically-based approach? Instead of lambasting her husband, she could have given him a PEP talk.

My suggested PEP talk is based on **P**hilippians 4:8; **E**phesians 4:15; and **P**hilippians 4:8. Ask for God's help, then tell the person some things about them that are right or worthy of praise—and yes, there are some (Philippians 4:8). Then, as Ephesians 4:15 says, "Speak the truth in love." The "in love" part is just as important as the "truth" portion. Say what's troubling you, but say it with self-control, patience, gentleness, and kindness. Follow that with more about what *is* good and admirable (back to Philippians 4:8).

A PEP talk yields better results than an emotional tirade, however justified and cathartic a tirade may feel.

Lord, when I want to give someone a piece of my mind,
help me give them a PEP talk instead.

We love because [God] first loved us.

1 JOHN 4:19 NIV84

When we consistently love without feeling love, two interesting—and delightful—things may happen. First, we may find ourselves feeling love. Second, the person we didn't feel love toward may become more lovable. Acting with love can beget love.

In *Woman Power*, Dr. Laura Schlessinger told of a woman who acknowledged that her behavior had been destroying her marriage. When she started *acting* with love, regardless of her feelings, changes occurred. She said, "It is MAGIC! The feelings of love and respect for my husband have grown. . . . I feel closer to him. . . . He is being more caring, more attentive, more fun." Her choice to act with kindness, selflessness, and thoughtfulness had changed her feelings and transformed their relationship.

Humans respond to love. God made us to want love, crave it, need it. The more love we receive, the more love we're able to give. The more love we give, the more love we receive. It's a beautiful, God-made, nonvicious circle.

How do we get that circle started when we don't feel loved? The answer lies in the Person hanging on a rugged cross on the top of a barren hill. He loves us enough to die for us, and God loves us so much he gave us his only son to do exactly that. Paul says, "May you have the power to understand how wide, how long, how high, and how deep his love is" (Ephesians 3:17–18). That's where it all begins. With God's love for us. We can receive that love, then give it away. The circle has begun.

Lord, may I be part of your circle of love.

DAY 210

*How great is the love the Father has lavished on us,
that we should be called children of God!
And that is what we are!*

1 JOHN 3:1 NIV84

Lavish. I love that word. That is what God's love for us is—abundant, rich, deep, extravagant. The Bible is the story of God's love for mankind. His love for us is completely undeserved. In fact, God's love is characterized by many "uns":

- *Unearned:* "It is by grace you have been saved, through faith." (Ephesians 2:8 NIV84)
- *Unconditional:* "Nothing can ever separate us from God's love." (Romans 8:38–39)
- *Unselfish:* "Jesus . . . being in very nature God . . . made himself nothing by taking the very nature of a servant." (Philippians 2:5–7 NIV84)
- *Unrelenting:* "The Lord . . . is patient with you, not wanting anyone to perish, but everyone to come to repentance." (2 Peter 3:9 NIV84)
- *Unfailing:* "I trust in your unfailing love; my heart rejoices in your salvation." (Psalm 13:5 NIV84)

God loves us with an everlasting love (Jeremiah 31:3 NIV84). His love is unmerited, but it is ours.

Thank you, God, for loving me.

*Three things will last forever—faith, hope, and love—
and the greatest of these is love.*

1 CORINTHIANS 13:13

Now back to the *I love you* and *I love chocolate* dilemma. The English language lacks precision when it comes to the word love. The ancient Greeks had four words for *love*:

- *Eros*—love associated with sensuality, physical desire, romance and emotion.
- *Storge*— instinctual love in family relationships.
- *Philia*—affection-based love found in friendships.
- *Agape*—unconditional love based on an act of the will.

Only *philia* (e.g., 1 Samuel 18:1) and *agape* (e.g., John 3:16) actually appear in the Bible, but Scripture contains illustrations of all four. We find *eros* in the Song of Solomon, and *storge* in Genesis. *Agape* love, however, permeates the Bible. It's the only form of love not related to emotions. *Agape* is action, what we do, what we say, not necessarily what we feel. It's the love Jesus commands: "Love each other as I have loved you" (John 15:12 NIV84).

Sadly, the world focuses on every form of love except *agape*. If you don't feel love, don't give it. If you're no longer "in love," find someone new. The most beautiful, unselfish . . . and difficult love is too often ignored, without doubt because it's so demanding.

Lord, I need your strength to love as you love.

Greater love has no one than this,
that he lay down his life for his friends.

JOHN 15:13 NIV84

Jesus established the consummate bar for love when he said, "there is no greater love than to lay down one's life for one's friends." Then he met that standard (1 John 3:16).

That doesn't mean we must die for someone to demonstrate we truly love them. We lay down our lives when we put our needs and wants aside and address those of others first. Instead of thinking, "What's in it for me?" or "What do I want?" we ask what's best for the one we love. For Jesus, what was best for mankind was paying for our sins by dying on our behalf in order to allow us an eternal relationship with God. In sending his Son, God answered "What's best for them?" with "My Son's life for theirs."

To love as God, as Jesus, loved, we can daily ask and answer the question, "What's best for [the other person]?" We don't always know what's best, but God does. Partnering with him through prayer and paying attention to his Spirit's leading, we can determine how best to love another. "This is my prayer; that your love may abound more and more in knowledge and depth of insight, so that you may be able to discern what is best" (Philippians 1:9 NIV84).

Thank you, Jesus, for putting my need for forgiveness
above yourself.

Let us not love with words or tongue
but with actions and in truth.

1 JOHN 3:18 NIV84

I admit, I sometimes get caught up watching a certain dating reality show. Every season I wonder how so many people can fall in love with the same person so quickly—and how that person can so rapidly choose a life mate. The brevity of most of the relationships generated by the show tells me my skepticism is not misplaced.

In one season, the man had been divorced. Explaining he wanted his next marriage to last, he said he wasn't going to say, "I love you" until he was certain the words were true. Good for him! But many viewers were upset that he still hadn't said those three magic words when the season ended. What a vivid example of the world's shallow approach to "love." How many times is "I love you" spoken much too casually? If those words were taken more seriously, fewer hearts would break.

It's easy to say, "I love you." It's challenging to live that love. Words of love are meaningless without love put into action. As with faith, what good is it if you say you love but don't show it by your actions? (See James 2:14.)

God planned that lasting relationships would include *agape* love—commitment, putting the other first, loving without condition or expectation. That's a tall order, one that many don't consider before they say, "I love you."

Lord, let me not love with my words
unless I can love with my life.

Let us continue to love one another, for love comes from God.
Anyone who loves is a child of God and knows God.

1 JOHN 4:7–8

It's time to pause and reflect on what we've covered and where we stand. Here's some food for thought:

- To understand love, do I look to God?
- To be able to love, do I turn to God?
- To live in love, do I abide in God?
- Do I love even when I don't feel like it?
- Do I fix my thoughts on what is good about the other person?
- Are my actions defined by how I feel or by what I know God wants?
- When I'm upset, do I speak the truth in love, beginning and ending with something positive?
- Do I acknowledge, accept, and revel in God's love for me?
- Is my love for others unconditional, unselfish, unrelenting, unfailing, and/or given even when unearned?
- When I love, do I put the interests of the other person before my own?
- Am I careless or careful about what my "I love you" means?

Lord, I want to live your fruit of love.
Please help me where I'm lacking.

Love the LORD your God with all your heart
and with all your soul and with all your mind
and with all your strength.

MARK 12:30 NIV84

Jesus said the most vital of all God's commandments is to love God with all our heart, soul, mind, and strength. That's a lot of love. What does it mean to love like that?

- *All our heart*: Our heart is what truly matters to us. It holds our priorities and passions.
- *All our soul:* Our soul is who we are, our essence, and the part of us that will live forever with God.
- *All our mind:* Our mind is "the seat of reflective consciousness . . . perception and understanding." (*Vine's Expository Dictionary*) Our mind is comprised of our thoughts and intellect.
- *All our strength:* Our strength means our power, our energy.

We're to love God with our entire being, with everything we are, with complete dedication. We're to hold nothing back. We're to give God our all, all the time.

I love you, Lord. May it always be with all my heart,
soul, mind, and strength.

You shall love your neighbor as yourself.
MATTHEW 19:19 ESV

Trying to remember everything the Bible tells us to do is nearly impossible. But God uncomplicated it.

In Matthew 22:37–40, Jesus gave us two commandments that encompass all the rest. We're to love God with all that we are, and we're to love our neighbors as much as we love ourselves. Sounds easy. Obey two commandments and we'll be good. The problem is, those two commandments are immense. Yesterday we looked at the first; today we turn to the second.

Jesus identified our neighbor when he told the story of the Good Samaritan (Luke 10:29–37). There, the only person who helped an injured Jewish man was from Samaria, whose people were notoriously hostile to the Jews. Our neighbor thus includes all who are in need, even those we may disdain. It's everyone with whom we come in contact. We're to love them as we love ourselves and treat them the way we want to be treated (Matthew 7:12). If you love your neighbor as much as you love yourself, you will not want to harm him. All Ten Commandments are wrapped up in this one (Romans 13:8–9 TLB).

Lord, you've said to love each other as you have loved us.
I can do that only through your strength.
I ask for that now.

This is love for God: to obey his commands.
1 JOHN 5:3 NIV84

We show our love for God by doing what he says, by loving
and serving him (Deuteronomy 10:12 NIV84), by acting with
justice, loving mercy, and walking humbly with him (Micah 6:8
NIV84). God does not view meaningless ritual as love.

> Stop bringing meaningless offerings! Your incense is
> detestable to me. . . . Your New Moon feasts and your
> appointed festivals I hate with all my being. They have
> become a burden to me. . . . Stop doing wrong. Learn
> to do right! (Isaiah 1:13–14, 16–17 NIV84)

> Sacrifice and offering you did not desire. . . . Then I
> said, "Here I am. . . . I desire to do your will, my God;
> your law is within my heart." (Psalm 40:6–8 NIV84)

> I want you to show love, not offer sacrifices. I want you
> to know me more than I want burnt offerings. (Hosea
> 6:6; see also Matthew 9:13)

> The Lord is more pleased when we do what is right and
> just than when we offer him sacrifices. (Proverbs 21:3;
> see also 1 Samuel 15:22)

When God says something once we should listen. When he
says it over and over . . .

Thank you for reminding me, Lord,
that the love that counts is action love.

LOVE

I have set before you life and death,
blessings and curses. Now choose life.
DEUTERONOMY 30:19 NIV84

The Bible contains 1,189 chapters and 31,102 verses, but its essence can be summarized in three passages about love:

- "'Love the LORD your God with all your heart and with all your soul and with all your mind.' This is the first and greatest commandment. And the second is like it. 'Love your neighbor as yourself.'" (Matthew 22:37–39 NIV84)
- "I set before you today life and prosperity, death and destruction. For I command you today to love the Lord your God, to walk in obedience to him, and to keep his commands, decrees and laws; then you will live and increase, and the Lord your God will bless you. . . . But if your heart turns away and you are not obedient, and if you are drawn away to bow down to other gods and worship them, I declare to you this day that you will certainly be destroyed." (Deuteronomy 30:15–18 NIV84)
- "For God so loved the world that he gave his one and only Son, that whoever believes in him shall not perish but have eternal life." (John 3:16 NIV84)

That is God's message in a nutshell: Love. Obey. Believe. This brings life and blessings. On the contrary, failure to love, disobedience, and unbelief bring curses and death.

The choice is ours.

Lord God, I choose love and life.

Do everything in love.

1 CORINTHIANS 16:14 NIV84

Eileen's husband never forgets their anniversary or her birthday. He acknowledges each with a card, gift, or flowers. He works hard and provides well. Yet Eileen speaks of her marriage as being lonely and empty. Why? She feels unloved. Though her husband does some nice things, his manner toward her is generally impatient, unkind, disinterested, or critical. Eileen is learning in her marriage that, whatever we do, if we don't have love, we are nothing (1 Corinthians 13:1–3 NIV84).

Yes, God's love is a doing love, not necessarily a feeling love. But if our actions are loving, yet the way we do them and our attitude are not loving, the deeds count for nothing. Loving as God loves means actions accompanied by patience, kindness, unselfishness; not being begrudging or boasting; having no arrogance or rudeness; no insistence on our own way; not being irritable, easily angered, or resentful; not holding grudges; and not enjoying things we know are wrong. It means rejoicing with truth, loyalty no matter the cost, believing the best, defending, always trusting and hoping, and never giving up (see 1 Corinthians 13:4–7).

Love is everything to God. He is love. No wonder he speaks about it in absolutes. Without love we're *nothing*. Love *always* displays the listed qualities. We're to do *everything* with love (1 Corinthians 16:14). What we do is important. Just as essential is how we do it.

Lord, help me to do everything with love.

Love is patient and kind.
1 CORINTHIANS 13:4

Love is patient. Patience is:

- accepting that life isn't always how we want it to be
- keeping on, no matter what
- doing what we should, and trusting the rest to God

Love is kind. Kindness is:

- grace (giving undeserved good) and mercy (not giving justified retribution)
- living by the Golden Rule
- putting others first without expecting anything in return

The bricks of patience and kindness are essential to the house of love God wants us to build. "The wise woman builds her house, but with her own hands the foolish one tears hers down" (Proverbs 14:1 NIV84). It's up to us: "Everyone who hears these words of mine and puts them into practice is like a wise man who built his house on the rock. The rain came down, the streams rose, and the winds blew and beat against that house; yet it did not fall because it had its foundation on the rock" (Matthew 7:24–25 NIV84).

---

*Lord, help me build a house of love according
to your specifications, the only ones
that will allow it to withstand the storms of life.*

Anger is cruel, and wrath is like a flood,
but jealousy is even more dangerous.

PROVERBS 27:4

Jealous Man Kills Brother . . . Ruler Seeks Death of Subordinate
Seen as Threat to His Authority . . . Jealous Siblings Frame Brother
. . . Jealous Husband Attacks Wife's Alleged Lover . . . Despot Seeks to
Expand Empire by Destroying Christians.

Recent news headlines? No, these stories occurred thousands of years ago. Adam and Eve's son Cain, envious of God's response to his brother Abel's offering, killed Abel (Genesis 4:1–8). King Saul became jealous of David's achievements and sought to have David killed (1 Samuel 16–31). Joseph's brothers, jealous of their father's love for him, sold him into slavery (Genesis 37:3–35). Proverbs 6:34 states, a "woman's jealous husband will be furious, and he will show no mercy when he takes revenge." Satan's jealousy of God and his resultant attempts to destroy God's people permeate the Bible. Jealousy is nothing new.

In Noah Webster's 1828 dictionary, he defined *jealousy* as "the uneasiness which arises from the fear that another does or will enjoy some advantage which we desire for ourselves."

Jealousy can destroy relationships. Real love is not jealous (1 Corinthians 13:4 TLB). The apostle James wrote, "Wherever there is jealousy . . . you will find disorder and evil of every kind" (James 3:16). When jealousy threatens, turn it over to God.

Lord, if ever I become jealous,
remind me that jealousy is love's enemy.

Love is not boastful or proud.

1 CORINTHIANS 13:4–5

No one is impressed by braggarts, by those who believe they're superior, who flaunt who they know, what they own, what they've done, where they've been. People like that are generally insecure, seeking human approval. Boasting and pride focus on self. Neither spells love. We are told:

> Don't let the wise boast in their wisdom, or the powerful boast in their power, or the rich boast in their riches. But those who wish to boast should boast in this alone: that they truly know me and understand that I am the LORD who demonstrates unfailing love. (Jeremiah 9:23–24)

The apostle Paul said, "May I never boast about anything except the cross of our Lord Jesus Christ" (Galatians 6:14). Boasting in the Lord puts us in our proper place: at the foot of that cross.

Of everyone who's ever lived, Jesus had the most to boast about. Yet, he was the most loving, and the least proud and boastful person ever to walk the earth. "Though he was God, [Jesus] did not think of equality with God as something to cling to. Instead, he gave up his divine privileges. . . . He humbled himself in obedience to God and died a criminal's death on a cross" (Philippians 2:6–8).

Jesus looked only to his heavenly Father for approval. We're to do the same (Galatians 1:10).

Lord, may I never boast except in you.

Your love has given me great joy.
PHILEMON 1:7 NIV84

Dick Hoyt's son Rick was born with cerebral palsy. Doctors recommended institutionalizing him. His parents refused. Unable to talk, Rick learned to communicate by computer. When he was seventeen, he asked his father to run a five-mile race with him, a fundraiser to benefit a paralyzed friend. Dick Hoyt wasn't a runner, yet he pushed Rick in a wheelchair for the race.

After the race, Rick typed, "Dad, when I'm running, it feels like I'm not handicapped." That was all Dick Hoyt needed to know. He began training and, with Rick, regularly competing in endurance events, pushing his son in a wheelchair for the runs.

As of March 2016, when Dick was 73 years old and Rick 54, they had completed together 257 triathlons, including 6 IRONMEN and 7 half IRONMEN, 22 duathlons, 72 marathons, including 32 Boston Marathons, 97 half marathons, and 681 other races of varying lengths. Their total events as of that date were 1,130. (See "Racing History" at TeamHoyt.com.)

Through his love for Rick, Dick Hoyt shows the world God's selfless love. "Whoever lives in love, lives in God, and God in him" (1 John 4:16). May this father and son be an inspiration to us all.

Lord God, thank you for the blessed joy of unselfish love.

*Everyone should be quick to listen,
slow to speak, and slow to become angry.*

James 1:19 niv84

The Bible says that love isn't touchy or irritable (1 Corinthians 13:5 amp). The Bible also says love isn't easily angered. But it doesn't say love is never angered. God is love, and God gets angry. But he doesn't get angry over the inconsequential stuff, only big things—like lack of faithfulness to him and his ways, rejection of his Son, and failure to trust him. I shudder at what my life would be like if God were easily angered, if he was touchy or irritable, because I'm sure I give him continual cause. Thankfully, "The Lord is . . . slow to anger, abounding in love" (Psalm 103:8 niv84).

His Word tells us how to deal with our anger. We're to use his fruit of self-control:

When angry, do not sin; do not ever let your wrath (your exasperation, your fury or indignation) last until the sun goes down. Leave no [such] room or foothold for the devil [give no opportunity to him]. (Ephesians 4:26–27 amp)

Satan uses little annoyances to get to us. As he did with Eve, Satan points out what we don't have. If we listen to him, we're following the enemy's way, not the way of God's love. When we live the fruit of love, little annoyances won't seem important.

Lord, remind me that love doesn't swat at the gnats of life.

Love keeps no record of wrongs.

1 CORINTHIANS 13:5 NIV84

How would you like to drag a huge bag of garbage everywhere, with it growing larger, heavier, its stench increasing daily? Would you choose to carry it?

Most of us do carry such a burden inside our mind and heart. When we feel wronged, we refuse to let go of the offense. We drudge and trudge with our sludge of grudge.

Love carries no garbage bag. It discards every transgression, or forgives it and hands it to God. He readily accepts our rubbish, but he doesn't keep it. God tells us he blots out transgressions for his own sake (Isaiah 43:25). He recognizes how oppressive they are to carry. So, why do we lug around our refuge of hurts? Love "does not hold grudges" (1 Corinthians 13:5 TLB). God says to give him our burdens (Psalm 55:22; 1 Peter 5:7). Yet "we humans tend to remember what God says to forget and to forget what God says to remember" (Dr. Del Tackett of Focus on the Family's *The Truth Project*). We can help reverse that irony by getting rid of our garbage bag.

Lord, here's my garbage bag.
When I'm wronged, help me forget,
or forgive and turn it over to you.

Truth is gone, and anyone who renounces evil is attacked.
ISAIAH 59:15

God is not ambiguous: the distinction between good and evil is as clear as that between black and white. Yet we humans are blurring the two, living in a frightening shade of gray as we claim truth is whatever we believe it to be, that truth for one person may not be truth for another. This subjective, personal truth masquerades under the misnomers of *tolerance* and *love*.

Given man's sinful nature, holders of this subjective truth can eventually come to embrace evil, labeling themselves broad-minded and nonjudgmental. The world renounces truth and delights in evil. God "does not delight in evil but rejoices with the truth" (1 Corinthians 13:6 NIV84). The Bible warns:

> Don't you realize that making friends with God's enemies—the evil pleasures of this world—makes you an enemy of God? I say it again, that if your aim is to enjoy the evil pleasure of the unsaved world, you cannot also be a friend of God. (James 4:4 TLB)

Jesus frequently said "I tell you the truth. . . ." No wonder; he is "the way and the truth and the life" (John 14:6). The world has "exchanged the truth of God for a lie" (Romans 1:25 NIV84). That lie calls evil good and good evil. Isaiah 5:20, written over 2,700 years ago, says "what sorrow" there is for those who do exactly that.

Lord, if I ever begin to blend the black and white of your truth into the gray of the world's . . . please stop me.

His banner over me is love.

Song of Solomon 2:4 niv84

Reading that love "always protects" and "always perseveres" (1 Corinthians 13:7 niv84), I envision Superman fighting off bad guys. Some bad guys, like physical dangers, are obvious. Others, like unkindness, criticism, and disrespect, can be insidious. Yet they can damage a person's heart and soul. Love is alert to what could injure, not just physically, but emotionally and spiritually as well.

Sometimes love means keeping our mouth closed. Sometimes it means opening it. Love considers beforehand whether words or actions might devalue a person. If they could, love protects through restraint. If others mistreat, whether through carelessness or intent, love steps in to stop it. If imprudent or dangerous behavior is imminent, love intervenes.

We can try to be superheroes swooping in where blatant peril threatens, but just as important is defending the sensitivities of another.

Lord, fill me with love that keeps me alert to what can harm and diligent to protect against it.

Find rest, O my soul, in God alone;
my hope comes from him.
PSALM 62:5 NIV84

Have you ever tried to love a difficult person, someone you find quite unlovable? You give and give. They take and take. We can't force others to change. Yet hope fuels our efforts to continue loving them because love "always hopes" (1 Corinthians 13:7 NIV84). Hope believes that something we want is possible. Hope sees a thin line of light at the bottom of a seemingly closed door, and believes God may someday unlock that door, throw it wide open, and let the light pour in.

We can always have hope because "with God everything is possible" (Matthew 19:26). He gives us strength to continue loving. "Those who hope in the Lord will renew their strength" (Isaiah 40:31 NIV84).

God calls us to love unconditionally, expecting nothing in return. This is hard when the person we're trying to love is, shall we say, challenging. Love hopes and believes good is there, and trusts God for if and when it will be revealed. Meanwhile, love "never loses faith": it is "ever ready to believe the best of every person; its hopes are fadeless under all circumstances" (1 Corinthians 13:7 AMP). Though we can't change an unlovable person, maybe—just maybe—God will. Our love for that person may be part of God's plan to do exactly that.

Thank you, Lord, for the hope in love.

Whatever you do, work at it with all your heart
as working for the Lord, not for men.

<small>COLOSSIANS 3:23 NIV84</small>

Maria, in *The Sound of Music*, chose "raindrops on roses and whiskers on kittens" as some of her favorite things. My list of favorite things includes a great massage. It's easy to find a good massage; it's difficult to find a great one.

My massage therapist, Morgan, gives great massages. Why? She's well trained, polite, and professional, but most therapists are. I believe what makes Morgan's massages great is that she puts 1 Corinthians 13 love into her work. She accepts her clients as we are. She places our comfort ahead of her own fatigue. Morgan is patient and kind, doesn't complain or boast of her skill, and is never rude or irritable. She puts her heart into her job. And what is in her heart? I learned when I asked why she chose this career. Her mother has multiple sclerosis, and Morgan learned massage to help relieve her mother's symptoms.

The love that motivated Morgan to pursue this skill permeates her work. She's booked solid. No wonder. Love makes all the difference.

Lord, whatever work I do, help me do it with love.

Love endures through every circumstance.

1 CORINTHIANS 13:7

A drunk driver slammed into a car carrying seven-year-old Mikey Cortez and several members of his family. One of Mikey's brothers and four other relatives died. It was uncertain whether Mikey would live. His father promised God that if Mikey survived, whatever his condition, he and his family would always be there for him. Mikey lived, but brain damage left him in a persistent vegetative state. His father kept his promise of love.

Mikey was never again able to bathe, dress, feed himself, walk, or talk. For the next thirty-one years, his parents and family cared for him and included him in every activity they could. They gave him as full and normal a life as possible. When Mikey's kidneys failed, his family learned dialysis and administered it at home. One day shy of his thirty-ninth birthday, Mikey died. His family was at his side.

As this account—reported by John Rogers of the Associated Press—shows, the Cortez family lived what the apostle Paul described: "Love bears up under anything and everything that comes. . . . It endures everything without weakening" (1 Corinthians 13:7 AMP). The Cortez family poured love into their son's life. Lavish, extravagant love. God's love.

———————————

Thank you for the inspiration of those who truly live your love.
Help me learn to love like that.

I trust in God's unfailing love forever and ever.
PSALM 52:8 NIV84

I have a tough time getting my mind around eternity. After a few minutes of trying to imagine life, God, and space, continuing on and on and on and on . . . my brain protests. "Such knowledge is too wonderful for me, too lofty for me to attain" (Psalm 139:6 NIV84).

Jesus came to give us eternal life. He commands us to love, for love is something we'll need, experience, and do for eternity. "Love will last forever" (1 Corinthians 13:8). Maybe that's why it's so important we get love right.

God has placed in our souls a permanent hunger for love as well as the ability, through him, to love and be loved for eternity. We can try to comprehend this until our minds ache, but we will never completely understand, until we meet God face to face (1 Corinthians 13:9–10).

Love for eternity—Lord, it's too wonderful
for me to understand. But someday I will, when I meet you
face to face and experience it on and on and on . . .

My lover is mine, and I am his.

SONG OF SONGS 2:16

God could have made the world monochromatic. He gave us dazzling color. He could have provided a single food source. He provided infinite delectable tastes. God could have created only barren landscapes. He gifted us with breathtaking panoramas. God could have made love all duty and no fun. He has allowed us indescribable pleasures.

God delights in our delight, as is evident in the sensual Song of Songs, an illustration of married love the way he intended it to be. The words express loyalty, devotion, mutual appreciation, and exclusivity. We read of the ecstasy achievable when love is not awakened until the time is right (Song of Songs 2:7). Married love, as God planned it, is beautiful, powerful, saturated with satisfaction, burgeoning with deep contentment. "Many waters cannot quench love, nor can rivers drown it" (8:6–7).

In stark contrast, God says that those who abuse sensual love will "be lost because of [their] great foolishness" (Proverbs 5:23). He also tells us, "Drink water from your own well—share your love only with your [spouse]. Why spill the water of your springs in the streets, having sex with just anyone? You should reserve it for yourselves. Never share it with strangers" (Proverbs 5:15–17). Scripture shows God's way for married love— and what a joyful love that can be.

I see what you have made, God, and it is good, very good.

A man leaves his father and mother and is joined to his wife,
and the two are united into one.

GENESIS 2:24

Wedding vows vary, but most pledge love "until death do us part." Some couples become so united in love that one passes away within a short time of the other. The strength and beauty of their love inspires, as these stories from myasd.com show:

- Gordon and Norma Yeager were in a car accident after being married seventy-two years. Together in one hospital room, Gordon's breathing ceased, but monitors showed his heart continued beating until Norma passed an hour later.
- When Ed Hale met Floreen, it was love at first sight. An accident had left Floreen unable to walk. Ed cared for her through sixty years of marriage. He promised her he wouldn't die first. When Ed became gravely ill, Floreen's heart failed. In a bed by hers, Ed held her hand and died thirty-six hours after she did.
- After sixty-four years of marriage, Frank and Eleanor Turner suffered almost simultaneous strokes. They held hands until Eleanor was moved to a hospice. Frank passed away, unaware Eleanor had died just hours earlier.
- James and Marjorie Landis were married sixty-five years when Marjorie died. James died of a heart attack eighty-eight minutes later.

Lord, thank you for inspiring bonds of love.

How great is the love the Father has lavished on us,
that we should be called children of God!
And that is what we are!

1 JOHN 3:1 NIV84

Trying to grasp the depth of God's love for me, I think of my love for my children, a love so profound and intense that words fail. We are God's children. Our love for our children can help us understand God's love for us:

- "Come to me" (Matthew 11:28). "This is the way; walk in it" (Isaiah 30:21 NIV84). I yearn for my children to turn to me, to follow my guidance.
- "The Lord corrects those he loves" (Proverbs 3:12). I never liked disciplining my kids, but I did so, out of love.
- "Whenever you face trials . . . the testing . . . develops perseverance . . . so that you may be mature and complete" (James 1:2–4 NIV84). I've let my children make mistakes, so they could learn.
- "Nothing in all creation will ever be able to separate us from the love of God" (Romans 8:39). Nothing could ever keep me from loving my children.

We've all been on one end or the other (or both) of parenting. We can comprehend God's love through a parent's eyes.

Lord, thank you for teaching me—through my children—
that I can trust in your love.

*Better a meal of vegetables where there is love
than a fattened calf with hatred.*

PROVERBS 15:17 NIV84

"What a person desires is unfailing love" (Proverbs 19:22 NIV84). Isn't it beautiful that what we desire and who God is are identical? We need love. God is love. We therefore need God.

Realizing that God and love are synonymous is revealing. As you read these statements—some from the Bible—substitute the word *God* wherever you see *love*: "Whoever pursues righteousness and unfailing love will find life" (Proverbs 21:21). Without love, we're nothing (1 Corinthians 13:1–2). Love makes us more than conquerors (Romans 8:37). Love brings joy. Love energizes, motivates, strengthens, and empowers. Love helps smooth even the roughest times. Without love, even the best times feel lonely. With love we're rich even if we're poor materially. If we have everything money can buy and don't have love, we're destitute.

In every person's heart and soul are empty spots. Some of us try to fill them with possessions, addictions, worldly pleasures, self-love, and infatuations. But only God's love can fill those spaces. Only God's love truly satisfies.

———————————

Lord, I need love. I need you.

Be imitators of God, therefore, as dearly loved children
and live a life of love, just as Christ loved us.

EPHESIANS 5:8

I noticed them on the first day of our five-week cruise: a man and his wife were pushing the wheelchair of a severely handicapped woman in her midtwenties. Our ship wasn't large, and I saw this family nearly every day.

On one tour, to a sloth rescue center in Costa Rica, the young woman, who was blind, was allowed to pet a sloth, something other visitors weren't permitted. She grinned and said, "It's soft like a kitten."

Next came a canoe ride. The couple lifted her into the small boat, and off they all went for a jungle tour. I saw them at dinners, participating in shipboard games, at the pool, in the hot tub, at all the evening shows. The parents included their daughter in everything they did. They spared no expense, no experience, no act of love.

Based upon apparent nationalities, this young woman had been adopted. These parents had chosen to take on this challenging responsibility of care. By the looks on their faces, they and their daughter were enjoying every minute.

But what brought tears to my eyes were Sundays. Few attended the onboard church services. Yet each week, there in the front row, singing hymns of thanksgiving and praise, were that couple and their daughter—God's love personified.

Lord, bless this precious family.
Thank you for their beautiful example of love.

In this world you will have trouble.
But take heart! I have overcome the world.

JOHN 16:33 NIV84

You will get no course map to inspect. There is fire, mud, water, barbed wire, and occasionally Hell on Earth. There will be obstacles to catch you off guard. Curve balls, so to speak. Get over it. We're here to rip you from your comfort zone.

This is a course description from an event called Spartan Race. Ready to sign up?

There's a similar race we run each day. It's called life. Satan fills it with obstacles to catch us off guard and cause Hell on Earth. Satan's obstacles include people who offer the opposites of love. They're impatient, unkind, jealous, haughty, selfish, and rude. Some hold grudges, enjoy wrong, reject truth, are disloyal, cause hurt, and give up when things are tough. Each can be an obstacle in our attempt to live love.

Obstacle courses have long been part of military training. Maneuvering with God's love through Satan's obstacles strengthens us for life's battles against the "powers in this dark world" (Ephesians 6:12). One day we'll be able to say, "I have fought the good fight, I have finished the race, and I have remained faithful" (2 Timothy 4:7).

Lord, help me leap the hurdles of life
with the power of your love.

He was despised and rejected—a man of sorrow,
acquainted with deepest grief.
We turned our backs on him and looked the other way.

ISAIAH 53:3

A plaque in my home reads, "Dance as if no one is watching. Sing as if no one is listening. Love as if you've never been hurt." I've never had trouble with the first two. It's the last I struggle with. When someone hurts me, my first inclination is to either strike back verbally or withdraw emotionally. How can I love a person who has wounded my heart?

We're made in God's image. He has feelings; we have feelings. He feels hurt; we feel hurt. Jesus showed us how to react to hurt (John 13:15). He was ignored, scorned, ridiculed, cursed, beaten, and spat upon. Those he came to save rejected him, framed him, crucified him. Even today he's disregarded, taken for granted, or forgotten. What about God the Father? God's children have disobeyed and rejected him, again and again. And the Holy Spirit? He's been repeatedly grieved.

Regardless of how many times he's been hurt, God loves us with an unfailing and everlasting love (Jeremiah 31:3). To love similarly requires what can be obtained only through the Holy Spirit: the fruit of love. When we're hurt, we need it more than ever.

Lord, one of the hardest things you ask of me
is to love like I've never been hurt.
Give me the strength to love that much.

People judge by outward appearance,
but the Lord looks at the heart.

1 SAMUEL 16:7

Beachcombing in New Zealand, I saw a glimmer in the sand. I picked it up. Traces of turquoise sparkled from among drab white and gray. It was a shell from a pāua, a species of abalone indigenous to New Zealand. Pāua cluster in colonies beneath the sea.

Covered with lime deposits and barnacles, each pāua resembles bumpy concrete. Only when someone goes beneath this coarse exterior does the pāua's true splendor emerge. After the shell's outer crust is removed, polishing reveals a dazzling array of iridescent color. It was there all the time. It just needed to be brought to the surface.

When I hold my pāua in the daylight, the sun highlights luminous patches of blue and green where the shell's covering was washed away or chipped off. Could I be missing someone's inner beauty by not recognizing their protective façade for what it is—and not even considering what's beneath it? "As a face is reflected in water, so the heart reflects the real person" (Proverbs 29:19). When I'm struggling to act with love toward someone, I think of the pāua shell. It reminds me to follow God's example, to ignore their exterior and ponder their heart. There may be a lot there to love.

Lord, teach me to look for and see the beauty
hidden inside others' hearts.

*I was filled with delight day after day,
rejoicing always in his presence, rejoicing
in his whole world and delighting in mankind.*

PROVERBS 8:30 NIV84

Love can take effort and be difficult. But we need not walk in love's garden and look only at the ground. Love's soil brings blooms of splendor. Yes, we're to love even if the feeling of love is absent. But when love and the feeling of love coincide, the experience is delicious, even dazzling!

Love truly is delightful. From our first school-age crush, to loving ice cream, the color blue, or an engrossing book, to lifelong love, the feelings can be fun, satisfying, fulfilling, and grand. When we love something because it makes us feel beautiful and special, wonderful! If we love coffee and can't imagine a day without it, terrific! If we're head over heels in love, enjoy! If we overflow with parental love, what a blessing! If we bask in the strong love of friends, what a gift! If we feel love toward God as we gaze at his wonders in this amazing world, fabulous!

Let's never hesitate to jump in wholeheartedly and enjoy feeling love for our life and all it includes. For that, too, is what God wants for us: "However many years a man may live, let him enjoy them all" (Ecclesiastes 11:8 NIV84).

---

*As long as I put you first in my life, God,
I can love with abandon.
Thank you for all you have put in my life to love.*

*Let each man of you without exception love his wife
as being in a sense his very own self; and let the wife see
that she respects and reverences her husband, that she notices him,
regards him, honors him, prefers him, venerates,
and esteems him; and that she defers to him, praises him,
and loves and admires him exceedingly.*

EPHESIANS 5:33 AMP

Imagine a list of every possible emotion, from the most wonderful to the most painful. Marriage offers them all. It's the relationship which, ideally, encompasses every form of love—unconditional, romantic, sexual, friendship, and instinctual. Different times, stages, and even days may bring to the forefront one kind of love more than another. The most rewarding marriages blend them all. The less satisfying lack or are weak in one or more. But if God's unconditional 1 Corinthians 13 fruit of love is missing, a marriage will fail. It may exist, but only as an empty shell.

Most wedding vows contain a promise to love for better or for worse, for there will indeed be better and worse. 1 Corinthians 13 love is the only love that will uphold a marriage through its myriad emotions and inevitable tough times. Every kind of love within a marriage may wax and wane, but without the fruit of love, a marriage is but a house of cards.

*Lord, thank you for marriage, a relationship so close,
deep and long that in it we experience every emotion.
Fill me and my spouse with your fruit of love,
for we need it to carry us through our ups and downs.*

Whatever you have learned or received or heard from me,
or seen in me—put it into practice.
And the God of peace will be with you.
PHILIPPIANS 4:9 NIV84

My car recently reached its one hundred thousand–mile milestone. Hoping to get another one hundred thousand miles from it, I took it in for its checkup and maintenance work. The best way to ensure a smoothly functioning, long-lasting vehicle is regular checkups. We do this for our cars and our bodies. Why not do it for our relationships? Regular maintenance, repair, or prevention will keep them running.

We can use 1 Corinthians 13 as a starting point for a relationship checkup:

- Am I patient? . . . Am I kind?
- Am I boastful, proud? . . . Rude? . . . Focused on self?
- Am I irritable, touchy, easily angered, holding grudges?
- Do I close my eyes to the truth about myself?
- Do I protect my marriage from physical, emotional, and spiritual harm?
- Am I treating my spouse the way I want to be treated?

The best relationship-repair specialist is God. He provides the tools and expertise required. All we need do is ask.

Lord, remind me to do regular relationship love-checkups
and tune-ups—and not wait till one hundred thousand miles.

When I consider your heavens,
the work of your fingers, the moon and the stars . . .
what is man that you are mindful of him?

Psalm 8:3–4 niv84

I stood on the balcony of our cruise ship cabin. The only sound was the sea's rush as the vessel pushed through the Pacific Ocean expanse. I breathed deeply of the night sky. Countless star sparkles punctuated the haze of the Milky Way. At horizon's edge, the four star-points of the Southern Cross spoke of the One who created the beauty surrounding me. I was mesmerized by the immensity of the universe of which I'm but an infinitesimal part, a fleeting speck in immeasurable time. Yet I matter to God! I'm but one of billions, yet he cares for me as if I filled the universe on my own.

As a breeze whispered, I tried to grasp the incomprehensible truth that God knows I'm here, that I can talk with him. I marveled that he is with me always, concerned about my life, answers my prayers, and delights in delighting me. And I wondered why. When God has all creation, past, present, and future, why does he bother with me?

Because he is Love. Because he is who he is. Because he is I AM, I am. I don't fully comprehend, but, in the vastness of that tranquil night I experienced my Creator and his love.

Almighty God, thank you that my soul
is part of the progression of eternity
that you in your love have created.

GOODNESS

*The Kingdom of God is not a matter of what we eat or drink,
but of living a life of goodness and peace
and joy in the Holy Spirit.*

ROMANS 14:17

Dear Lord,
*You began this earth with goodness and have promised you'll end
it with goodness. Meanwhile, we humans have tainted it with sin.
I'm no exception.*

*I want to live a life of goodness, yet much within and without
tempts me to fail. The forces of evil try to get the best of me. Help
me defeat them with goodness, for goodness is something Satan cannot tolerate.*

*You, God, are absolute goodness. You've offered it to me as a
fruit of your Spirit. What a gift! Yet frequently, when I've reached
for it, it's slipped from my hands because they're too full of the things
of this world. Other times I've dropped this gift to pick up something Satan has held out, not recognizing until too late it was
from him.*

*You've created a world of abundant goodness. Yet I have fallen
for Satan's schemes and sullied your masterpiece—just as generations before me have. Help me notice, appreciate, and foster the
goodness you pour out on your world. Use me to combat the darkness that tries to, but never will, extinguish your light.*

*Your plan is one of goodness, God. It includes my life overflow-
ing with that fruit. Oh, that it would be so. Teach me, lead me,
walk with me.*

Amen.

He has showed you, O man, what is good.
And what does the Lord require of you?
To act justly, and to love mercy
and to walk humbly with your God.

MICAH 6:8 NIV84

Webster's defines *good* as being "of somewhat high but not excellent quality." I'm certain that's not God's definition that he had in mind when he said he has shown us what it means to be good. He wants us to be excellent. In fact, he wants us to be perfect (see Matthew 5:48).

We aren't able to be perfect in our own power. Our goodness comes only from and through Jesus who "by one sacrifice has made perfect forever those who are being made holy" (Hebrews 10:14).

In our culture, goodness and what's considered good have become subjective. But the fruit of goodness is not a matter of opinion. It's doing what pleases God. It's what our character and actions become filled with when we follow him. Goodness is defined by God, not man. If we ask, the Holy Spirit will define goodness for us as we go through each day (see Proverbs 4:20).

Lord, I can only achieve true goodness if I seek,
listen to, and follow your Spirit's leading.
Help me to do that always.

You are good and do only good; teach me your decrees.

PSALM 119:68

God is 100 percent goodness, so he always acts with pure goodness. He "causes everything to work together for the good of those who love God and are called according to his purpose" (Romans 8:28).

The purity of God's goodness cannot coexist with sin. It's like trying to mix oil and water. To know God, we must be washed clean by Christ's blood (John 14:6). Once we accept Christ as our Savior, God enables us to shine with his goodness:

> His divine power has given us everything we need for life and godliness through our knowledge of him who called us by his own glory and goodness. Through these he has given us his very great and precious promises, so that through them you may participate in the divine nature. (2 Peter 1:3–4 NIV84)

Even so, our goodness compared to his is like a candle flame to the sun. God's goodness is so glorious that even attempting to comprehend it is like trying to stare directly into that blazing star. God said to Moses, "I will make all my goodness pass before you. . . . But you may not look directly at my face, for no one may see me and live" (Exodus 33:19–20).

Thank you, God, that no matter what happens,
you, in your goodness, will use it for good.

[Jesus] never sinned, nor ever deceived anyone.
He did not retaliate when he was insulted,
nor threaten revenge when he suffered.
He left his case in the hands of God.

1 PETER 2:22–23

Have you wondered why Jesus never sinned? The obvious answer: Jesus is the Son of God; Jesus is in fact God. Yet Jesus was also a man (1 Timothy 2:5). Like all men, Jesus was tempted to turn from God's ways, to make decisions according to his own wants and needs (Matthew 4:1–11). How did Jesus keep the human part of him from sinning?

Jesus was victorious over every temptation because he did only God's will. When Satan tempted Jesus in the wilderness, Jesus responded every time with "It is written . . ." (Matthew 4:4, 7, 10 NIV84), and he obeyed God. Jesus made it clear: "I do nothing on my own, but say only what the Father taught me. The one who sent me is with me; he has not left me alone, for I always do what pleases him" (John 8:28–29).

That is the secret of living the fruit of goodness: doing only what pleases God. That requires a continual, intimate relationship with him. Jesus had that kind of relationship: "The Father is in me and I am in the Father" (John 10:38). Jesus always consulted God first; he spent much time in prayer (Luke 6:12; Matthew 14:23). He calls us to do the same.

Lord, help me to do only what pleases you.

From now on all generations will call me blessed.

LUKE 1:48

The Bible doesn't give much detail about Mary, the mother of Jesus. But it's clear she was filled with goodness.

When Mary was engaged to Joseph, an angel told her she would bear God's Son. A lesser woman would have panicked. Mary replied, "I am the LORD's servant. May it be to me as you have said" (Luke 1:38 NIV84).

On the eve of Mary's delivery, she rode a donkey for ninety miles—from Nazareth to Bethlehem. Her response could have been, "Are you kidding?! I'm big as a house and you want me to get on that thing and ride all that way?" No, she patiently went, only to find she had to give birth in a stable.

She didn't berate Joseph with "What! You didn't plan ahead and arrange a decent room for us?!" Even after the arduous donkey ride, uncomfortable delivery room, and shepherds' staring faces, an exhausted Mary didn't spew out unkind words. She quietly treasured and pondered in her heart what she'd experienced (Luke 2:19).

When Jesus was twelve, he went with his parents to Jerusalem. Unbeknownst to them, he stayed behind when they left. They discovered he was missing, journeyed back, and found him in discussions with temple teachers. Mary admonished, but didn't punish, him. Again, she just treasured the event in her heart (Luke 2:51 NIV84).

Why was Mary able to react with such goodness? The answer lies in her song: "My soul glorifies the Lord and my spirit rejoices in God my Savior" (Luke 1:47 NIV84).

Lord, may I follow Mary's example.

Guard the good deposit [of sound teaching]
that was entrusted to you—guard it with the help
of the Holy Spirit who lives in us.

2 TIMOTHY 1:14

"Could you please get that one for me?" I pointed to my tan suitcase.

"Sure," the burly man said, lifting it from the baggage claim carousel.

My back is temperamental. If I push it too far, it protests. I know my limits, and I'm not shy about asking for help lifting, be it luggage, bags of dog food, or anything else that might set off my back's complaining.

I wish I were as quick to ask for help in nonphysical areas of my life. Many moments test my emotional and coping limits. I need God's help. When I don't turn to him, I can injure my day, my relationships, and even my life and the lives of those I care about.

God knows that, left to our own devices, we won't always choose goodness. He offers his help (Romans 8:26). "'Not by might nor by power, but by my Spirit,' says the Lord Almighty" (Zechariah 4:6 NIV84). I just need to remember to ask.

Just as I protect my unpredictable back, Lord,
help me protect goodness by asking for your help
when I approach my emotional limits.

GOODNESS

Produce fruit in keeping with repentance.
Matthew 3:8 niv84

Why does human "badness," sinfulness, permeate the Bible? Perhaps to help us realize how greatly we need God and how deeply he wants us. Could our attaining goodness be crucial to God because it's the only way we can be with him for eternity?

For that is what he craves. God's love for us is intense, fierce. His entire focus is to bring us into a forever relationship with him: "'Even now,' declares the Lord, 'return to me with all your heart'" (Joel 2:12 niv84).

God "does not want anyone to be destroyed, but wants everyone to repent" (2 Peter 3:9). He says to "seek good, not evil, that you may live. Then the Lord Almighty will be with you" (Amos 5:14 niv84).

God is pure goodness. We can have a relationship with him only when we achieve goodness. "Our righteousness [goodness] . . . comes through faith in Jesus Christ to all who believe" (Romans 3:22 niv84). We can never achieve it through our works. But, we can, through our works, show our faith (James 2:18).

Father, I repent, and, with thanksgiving, return
to your arms. May I, through your fruit in my life,
show the world I'm yours.

Do not forget to do good.

HEBREWS 13:16 NIV84

It's easy to *want* to live the good God teaches. It's also easy to *not* live it, to do whatever we feel like doing. Christian beliefs don't guarantee goodness in our actions. That requires following the guidance of God's Spirit.

According to BibleHub.com, the New Testament's *goodness* is derived from two Greek words: *agathosune*, the personal quality of intrinsic goodness, and *chrestotes*, goodness that expresses itself in deeds. God's fruit of goodness includes both—inner character and outer action, being and doing.

The apostle James talked about this duality as it relates to faith: "Faith by itself isn't enough. Unless it produces good deeds, it is dead and useless" (James 2:17). Similarly, wanting to be a good person isn't enough. Goodness requires *doing* what God instructs. Conversely, as with faith, simply doing good things is not sufficient. Doing good for selfish reasons isn't goodness.

---

*Lord, help me to have a character of goodness
and to live it, all for you.*

God is working in you, giving you the desire
and the power to do what pleases him.

PHILIPPIANS 2:13

Goodness is thinking, doing, and speaking what pleases God. It requires accepting Christ as Savior, so that God's Spirit lives in us. Even then, we don't suddenly live constant goodness. Like Paul, we "press on to take hold of that for which Christ Jesus took hold of [us]" (Philippians 3:12 NIV84). God is shaping us into who he wants us to be: "we are the clay, [he is] the potter" (Isaiah 64:8 NIV84).

Living the fruit of goodness is a journey, not a moment of magical transformation. Our road to goodness, which can be quite bumpy, can be divided into three parts:

1. *Life is all about me.* At the beginning, we don't know God. Ruled by our sinful nature, we've no desire to live differently from how we always have.
2. *I want to, but I don't always.* God calls, and our hearts respond. We acknowledge Christ as our Savior and receive God's Spirit. Wanting to do God's will, we often don't.
3. *Life is all about God.* We want to do what God desires us to do—and we do it more and more.

It's during this third part of the journey that God's fruit of goodness ripens to its glorious best.

Thank you, Lord, for placing me on the road to goodness.
May I come nearer each day to my destination.

The fool says in his heart, "There is no God."
PSALM 14:1 NIV84

On a trip to Holland, I joined fellow travelers on a curiosity visit to Amsterdam's red-light district. Inching along the narrow people-packed alleyways, I peeked into glass doors of beckoning young women. It seemed surreal . . . and frightening. . . a picture of life without God:

> They wouldn't worship [God] or give him thanks. . . .
> As a result, their minds became dark and confused. . . .
> Instead of worshipping the glorious, ever-living God,
> they worshipped idols. Their lives became full of every
> kind of wickedness. (Romans 1:21–23, 29)

Life without God offers short-term pleasures, long-term emptiness at best, and much worse eternally. Amsterdam is one example. More insidious is today's call—coming from many directions—to put oneself and one's own needs first, a call to worship oneself. When I googled "looking out for number one," I got almost half a billion sites. Judging from the ones I skimmed, "number one" in those articles is self, not God.

It's tempting to put ourselves first. But God knows self-absorption is a dead end. He draws us from the depths of "it's all about me" and places us on the road to goodness. Thus begins the transformation of a saved human being into the image of Christ.

God, show me the self-centered ways I'm living
so I stay with you on this road to goodness.

I long to obey your commandments!
Renew my life with your goodness.

PSALM 119:40

I confess: I used to be an addict. A sugar addict. I "needed" my chocolate fix. I knew sugar wasn't good for me. I could see and feel its negative impact on my body. I wanted to stop consuming it . . . tomorrow.

Satisfying my sugar cravings was a lot like satisfying many impulses. In those moments, we do what we want to do. It feels good at the time, even when we know we'll be sorry later. But with "a change of heart produced by God's Spirit," we begin to care that we're not doing what's best (Romans 2:29). We think, "*I want to do what is right, but I don't do it. . . . I want to do what is good, but I don't. I don't want to do what is wrong, but I do it anyway*" (Romans 7:15, 18–19).

"Lord, if you kept a record of our sins, who . . . could ever survive? But you offer forgiveness" (Psalm 130:3–4). We're grateful, and don't want to fall short anymore. We want to live a life of goodness—for God. The problems come when we try to do it without him. We're to "Let the Holy Spirit guide your lives. Then you won't be doing what your sinful nature craves" (Galatians 5:16).

God offers his hand. When we fall, he will pick us up, dust us off, and set us back on the road to goodness. All we need do is ask.

———————————

Lord, when sin tempts, may I reach for your hand,
take hold of it, and never let go.

A good person produces good things
from the treasury of a good heart.

MATTHEW 12:35

I don't crave sugar anymore. Now fresh fruit appeals to me more than sweets do.

How did I lose my taste for sugar? I started putting my health first. I filled myself with the goodness of fresh and nutritious food. Soon I didn't want the bad stuff anymore. Initially it was hard to resist old habits, but it became easier. Short-term denial netted long-term benefits. I had tasted what I *should* be eating, and it was good!

When we continually put God first, our old ways lose their appeal. We "taste and see that the Lord is good" (Psalm 34:8) and discover that nothing feels as good as goodness. To glorify him, we choose more and more often to "do what is good and run from evil so that we may live!" (Amos 5:14–15).

That doesn't mean we're perfect: "If we claim we have no sin, we are only fooling ourselves and not living in the truth" (1 John 1:8). We still make mistakes; we still sin. But we do so less often. When we do make them, we tell God we're sorry and move on . . . with him. And that is good. Very good.

Oh that someday you can say to me Lord,
"Many daughters have done virtuously, nobly,
and well with the strength of character that is steadfast
in goodness, but you excel them all."

[PROVERBS 31:29 AMP]

Teach me to do your will, for you are my God;
may your good Spirit lead me on level ground.

PSALM 143:10 NIV84

It's all about me. . . . I want to, but I don't. . . . It's all about God.
Today let's ask:

- Where am I on the road to goodness?
- What causes me to take wrong turns?
- Do I put myself or God—my way or God's way—first?
- Am I trying to walk the road alone? Do I ask God for help?
- What are three specific things I will do to move closer to where I want to be?

Lead me, Lord.

The godliness of good people rescues them.

PROVERBS 11:6

In *The Wizard of Oz*, Dorothy wondered what she'd encounter along the Yellow Brick Road. When she learned it included "lions and tigers and bears," she said, "Oh my!"

I've felt that way, too, as I travel the road to goodness: I hear about holiness, godliness, righteousness, sanctification, transformation. Oh my! Goodness is daunting enough, but all those other things too? What do they mean?

1. *Holiness* is being set apart for God, choosing us: "to be holy and without fault in his eyes" (Ephesians 1:4).
2. *Sanctification* is a process. The Holy Spirit's lifelong work in us helps us defeat sin and makes us more like Jesus.
3. *Righteousness* is God's declaration that we are right with him. When we acknowledge Christ's death paid for our sins, God sees us as righteous. That doesn't mean we'll never sin again. It means Christ has already paid the price.
4. *Godliness* means living to honor and glorify God.
5. *Transformation* means change: "The Lord . . . makes us more and more like him as we are changed into his glorious image" (2 Corinthians 3:18).

Are these five aspects of our faith walk interrelated? Yes. Confusing? Perhaps. Impossible? Not with God.

Thank you, Lord, that nothing—not even the transformation of my heart and character—is impossible for you.

God, who began the good work within you,
will continue his work until it is finally finished
on the day when Christ Jesus returns.

PHILIPPIANS 1:6

My fruit production was on the upswing. I was learning to hold my tongue, respond instead of react, keep silent when annoyed, let go of the unimportant, and turn the important over to God. But then my husband got grouchy. People I care about were facing stressful situations. I felt tired and unappreciated. My husband said something that offended me. I'm not trying to make excuses. It's just that the perfect storm hit. Words I later regretted flowed from my mouth.

I wanted to produce a fruit orchard for God, but my words had just wiped out a few trees. "I said, 'I will watch my ways and keep my tongue from sin; I will put a muzzle on my mouth.' . . . [But] my heart grew hot within me. . . . Then I spoke" (Psalm 39:1, 3 NIV84).

I felt terrible. I'd let God down. In his goodness he reminded me there is "no condemnation for those who are in Christ" (Romans 8:1), that "only God is truly good" (Mark 10:18), and that "not a single person on earth is always good and never sins" (Ecclesiastes 7:20). That's why we have a Savior.

After taking a wrong turn off the road to goodness, "stop at the crossroads and look around. Ask for the old, godly way, and walk in it. . . . You will find rest for your souls" (Jeremiah 6:16).

Thank you, God, for giving me sunshine after my storm.

Do not be afraid . . . for the battle is not yours, but God's.

2 CHRONICLES 20:15

We have an enemy. He wants to destroy all our relationships, including our relationship with God. He wants to prevent our growth in goodness. He delights when we're impatient, when we're harsh rather than gentle, when we lose self-control. He'd love to uproot our entire fruit orchard and tries to, every chance he gets. Our enemy is Satan, the opposite of goodness.

Our military would never go into battle without a plan. They study the enemy. They learn its ways. When it attacks, they're ready. The question is not whether Satan will attack. It's when. We need to be prepared.

God has provided a foolproof battle plan for Satan's attacks. It's found in 2 Chronicles 20:1–30, Ephesians 6:10–18, and 1 Peter 5:9:

- Put on the full armor of God (more on this tomorrow).
- Turn to and focus on him.
- Remember what God has done in the past, and thank him.
- Tell him the situation, acknowledging your weakness and his power. Ask for his help. Listen for his guidance.
- Worship him and praise him.
- Obey him.
- Trust him and stand firm, continuing in praise and worship.

Thank you for providing a battle plan Lord,
and for reminding me the battle is yours.

Put on the full armor of God so that you can take your stand against the devil's schemes.

EPHESIANS 6:11 NIV84

When he was three, my grandson, Wyatt, was fascinated by knights. He'd put on plastic armor and pretend to do battle. When he donned his helmet, held his shield, and brandished his rubber sword, he felt unconquerable. Wyatt's enemy was imagined. Ours is real. When he wore his play armor, Wyatt *felt* invincible in his play armor. We can be truly invincible in the armor God provides.

Throughout history, soldiers have donned armor and charged into battle. God's instructions are different. He doesn't tell us to put on his armor and fight. He tells us to put it on and "stand" (Ephesians 6:13–14). The battle is his. We're to stand, wearing the belt of truth, the breastplate of righteousness, the shoes of the gospel, the shield of faith, and the helmet of salvation as we hold the sword of the Spirit, God's Word (vv. 14–17). Then, we're to pray, focusing on God, trusting him to battle for us as his armor protects us from "the devil's schemes" (v. 11).

We'll have no reason to fear, for God goes with us to fight for us against our enemies to give us victory (Deuteronomy 20:3–4 NIV84).

Lord, may I stand firm against Satan's attacks, dressed in your armor.

Do not give the devil a foothold.

Ephesians 4:27 niv84

I've watched my kids scale rock climbing walls and been amazed at how those tiny footholds allow them to climb to the top. Even the slightest resting spot for their toes provides the boost they need to advance. Once they have a foothold, they move quickly.

The Bible cautions us not to give the devil a foothold. God knows how subtle and seductive Satan can be. We may hesitate to say or do something we know isn't what God wants, decide it's not such a big deal, and say or do it anyway. Next time, we hesitate less . . . but one of those next times, we transgress without pause. Before long, disobedience to God's Word becomes a habit. Seemingly small things, like unkind words, can swiftly become large things, like broken relationships and a hostile character.

For most of us it's not the big sins that tempt. It's those we convince ourselves are insignificant. But each seemingly minor indiscretion can lead to more and larger ones. One stray seed from a noxious plant can rapidly spread and become a field of weeds. That's why God tells us to nip our weeds in the bud.

When we refuse to give Satan footholds—like "unwholesome talk . . . bitterness, rage and anger . . . along with every form of malice" (Ephesians 4:29, 31 niv84), he can't even get started.

Lord, Remind me there's no wrong behavior that's all right.

Stay alert! Watch out for your great enemy the devil.
He prowls around like a roaring lion,
looking for someone to devour.

1 PETER 5:8

Our son, a former military officer, speaks of SA. That's a military term for "situational awareness," knowing what's going on around you. It's essential on the battlefield where poor SA can mean injury or death. SA can make the difference between winning and losing a battle or even a war.

Situational awareness can do the same in our lives. Satan can be overt, or subtle. Staying alert and watching out for him is essential for a life of goodness. Weak SA regarding our enemy the devil can result in emotional injury to ourselves and others. It can cause spiritual death. Our SA can mean the difference between winning and losing our battles against Satan.

Although we didn't know the term at the time, my husband and I taught SA to our kids when they were learning to drive. We'd ask, "What color is the car behind you? What did the sign you just passed say? How fast are you driving right now?" Their driving SA remains top-notch and has likely helped them avoid collisions, injury, and worse. Similarly, we can ask SA questions about what's occurring in our lives: "Where, who, are these thoughts coming from? Why am I feeling stress when all is good? Is Satan scheming here?" We can know when to call on "the Lord of Heaven's Armies" to bring us victory (Zechariah 4:6).

Lord, please grant me spiritual SA
so I'll be alert to Satan's lies and schemes.

Search me O God, and know my heart. . . .
See if there is any offensive way in me,
and lead me in the way everlasting.

PSALM 139:23–24

I marvel at God's patience. He has forgiven me more times than I can count.

Though I truly want to please God with all I say and do, I still get irritable, unkind, judgmental, and harsh. But God knows that my heart is to know and follow him. He sees I'm on the stretch of the road to goodness where I don't always do what's right, but I want to . . . for him. And God is good with that. He's "compassionate and merciful, slow to get angry and filled with unfailing love" (Psalm 103:8).

When our hearts are right, God's patience is great. But he has little tolerance for those whose hearts are in the wrong place even if they do right things. Some of Jesus's strongest words were to religious leaders who purported to act in goodness, but whose hearts were not with him: "Everything they do is done for men to see. . . . You snakes! You brood of vipers! How will you escape being condemned to hell?" (Matthew 23:5, 33 NIV84). King David sinned greatly. He suffered painful consequences, but because his heart was right, God forgave and blessed him. When our heart contains goodness, we may stumble, but we won't fall. Eventually, our actions will match our intent to follow God, for "A good person produces good things from the treasury of a good heart" (Matthew 12:35).

Lord, thank you for your patience with me.

I am sending you to them to open their eyes
and turn them from darkness to light,
and from the power of Satan to God.

ACTS 26:17–18 NIV84

Jesus said, "I am the light of the world. Whoever follows me will never walk in darkness, but will have the light of life" (John 8:12 NIV84) The apostle Paul wrote, "The fruit of the light consists in all goodness, righteousness and truth" (Ephesians 5:9 NIV84). We're called to produce this fruit, bringing God's light to others. By our lives we're to "show others the goodness of God, for he called you out of the darkness into his wonderful light" (1 Peter 2:9).

But can our little lights really overcome "fruitless deeds of darkness" (Ephesians 5:11 NIV84)? Imagine a pitch-dark room, no windows, no illumination from any source. Then a candle is lit. Can that thick darkness hide the candle's light? No, "the light shines in the darkness, and the darkness can never extinguish it" (John 1:5).

"God is light; in him there is no darkness at all" (1 John 1:5 NIV84). By lighting our candles of goodness, however small, we can share his light with others.

For once I was darkness, but now I am light in you Lord.
Help me live as a child of light.

[EPHESIANS 5:8 NIV84]

Look, I am making everything new!
REVELATION 21:5

I stood on the deck of our home and watched the sunrise. A shard of brilliance burgeoned into a coral sphere, flooding the eastern sky. The air was cool, barely stirring. A bevy of birds swooped, soared.

I thrill at this herald of a new day. No matter what has gone before, daybreak offers the chance to change what needs changing. It holds the hope of goodness.

God delights in the new. His Word speaks of our singing a new song, being given a new spirit, a new heart. He brings a new covenant, a new command, new life, and a new way. He makes us new creations and produces a new attitude in us. He gifts us with a new order, a new birth, and a new identity. God pledges a new heaven and a new earth. He offers the chance to change what needs changing. He holds out the hope of goodness. (Isaiah 43:1; Ezekiel 36:26; Psalm 40:3; 2 Corinthians 5:17; Luke 22:20; Romans 6:4.)

I'm relieved and thankful that God lets us start over. And if we don't get it right that time, he gives us yet another sunrise, day after day after day.

Thank you, Lord, that your mercies are fresh each morning. May each sunrise bring me closer to your goodness and mine.

Put off your old self . . . and put on the new self,
created to be like God in true righteousness and holiness.
EPHESIANS 4:22–24 NIV84

A snake's skin doesn't grow as its body does. To mature, the snake must repeatedly shed its skin. When it does, new skin takes its place:

> The entire skin normally comes off in one piece, a procedure that can be likened to removing a sock. This shedding is not without purpose: snakes replace their skins to allow for growth, as well as to remove parasites along with the old skin. (wisegeek.org)

The Bible says that to allow for growth in the Lord we must shed whatever could inhibit our spiritual maturation, along with any behavioral parasites. We're to "get rid of all bitterness, rage and anger, brawling, and slander along with every form of malice" (Ephesians 4:31 NIV84) and "put on [our] new nature" (Colossians 3:10).

These directives require conscious shedding of specific conduct and permit growth of our character. It's not enough to patch ourselves up with a little goodness here and a little goodness there. God wants each of us to become a new person (2 Corinthians 5:17). If wrongful action reinfests our life, we're to shed it again. Each time we do, we can grow in our walk with God.

When anything becomes a barrier
to my growth in you, Lord, help me shed it.

They will tremble in awe of the Lord and of his goodness.
HOSEA 3:5

Media bombards with news of violence, hatred, and conflict. Evil is alive and teeming in the world. Can goodness bloom in a garden overrun with weeds? Why does God permit weeds? Jesus told a parable about a man who planted wheat in his field, but in the dark of night, an enemy sowed weeds. The man's servants asked whether the weeds should be pulled:

> No . . . because while you are pulling the weeds, you may uproot the wheat with them. Let both grow together until the harvest. At that time I will tell the harvesters: First collect the weeds and tie them in bundles to be burned; then gather the wheat and bring it into my barn. (Matthew 13:29–30 NIV84)

The wicked will be destroyed. Evil will be overcome. No one but God knows when this will happen (Matthew 24:36). Until it does, evil will be a reality.

But we don't need to allow its presence to blind us to the existence of goodness. As I write, I'm gazing at a luminous sky. I just hung up from FaceTiming with our son and grandchildren. My husband is watching a TV special on the splendor of peacocks. All these proclaim God's goodness. We can open our eyes and hearts to it, letting it remind us that no matter what occurs in this complicated world, no evil can separate us from the goodness of God's love (Romans 8:38–39).

With all the evil which surrounds,
may I focus on your goodness Lord.

The earth is full of the goodness of the LORD.

PSALM 33:5 KJV

It's a modern-day scourge, it's international, and its eradication is challenging. *It* is terrorism, and it's evil personified. But God is in control. When he chooses to act, terrorism will be defeated. "The wicked plot against the godly. . . . But the LORD just laughs, for he sees their day of judgment coming (Psalm 37:12–13).

I know this is true. Yet, in light of today's headlines, I need to snuggle into the comforting goodness of God. He promises, "As a mother comforts her child, so will I comfort you" (Isaiah 66:13 NIV84).

Unsettled by the world's turmoil, I stood outside and gazed at serene clouds gracing a sapphire sky. Unsullied air caressed my face. Birdsong entranced. Tree leaves trembled. Flowers spoke colors. And I felt God's embrace.

God's goodness can be a blanket when the cold winds of evil swirl. Every tree, plant, flower, bird, insect, fish, animal, mountain, and stream radiates his goodness. Go for a hike, take a walk through the woods, sit in a park, watch online videos, or read books. Do whatever invites you to marvel at God's wondrous creation. The magnificence of nature comforts, for it exudes God.

Deep calls to deep in the roar
of your waterfalls . . . and I am comforted.

[PSALM 42:7 NIV84]

Do what is right; then if men speak against you,
calling you evil names, they will become ashamed
of themselves for falsely accusing you
when you have only done what is good.

1 PETER 3:16 TLB

What about when we're in a good mood, then faced with someone acting sour?

Unfortunately, I'm good at catching others' bad moods. When I do, I need to remember who's delighted when I'm brought down. Yes, the devil himself. When we succumb to the lower level, instead of standing firm on the higher, we've focused on the situation rather than on God. That's what Satan wants. When we're disagreeable back, we're essentially saying, "You don't deserve my being good to you." That's a form of judgment, and we're not to judge (Matthew 7:1). Neither are we to repay evil for evil. "Don't snap back at those who say unkind things . . . Instead, pray for God's help for them" (1 Peter 3:9 TLB). When we—in prayer—turn the unpleasant person over to God, we're more likely to retain our cheerfulness.

If we say we're a follower of Christ, but don't act in goodness, what are we communicating about our faith? People notice our actions more than our words.

Lord, when those around me are bad-tempered,
may I turn them over to you in prayer
and respond with goodness.

They repay me evil for good and leave my soul forlorn.

PSALM 35:12 NIV84

When someone is hurtful toward me, I want them to know they've hurt me. I want to strike back. Where's the goodness in that?

God doesn't tell us to be good to others only as long as they're good to us. He says, "Do not be overcome by evil, but overcome evil with good" (Romans 12:21 NIV84). He holds us to an exceedingly high and difficult standard (see Matthew 5:38–41). Jesus is not asking of us anything he didn't do: Jesus modeled goodness in the face of rejection and mistreatment. When hurt, he didn't try to hurt back. That's asking a lot of us humans. We can't do it in our own power. We need "the strength and energy that God supplies" (1 Peter 4:11).

God doesn't view "They hurt me" as a valid excuse for refusing to live goodness. "Remember it is better to suffer for doing good . . . than to suffer for doing wrong" (1 Peter 3:17). God assures that even if we suffer for doing what's right, he will reward us for sticking with goodness (1 Peter 3:14). Our reward may not come in the here and now. But it will come.

Lord, you know it's hard to respond with goodness
when I've been hurt. When I want to strike back,
give me strength to offer your fruit of goodness instead.

Your kingdom come, your will be done.
MATTHEW 6:10 NIV84

When we choose Christ, we secure an eternity with God. And God promises an eternity of pure goodness. "Nothing impure will ever enter" the new heaven and new earth of time without end (Revelation 21:27 NIV84).

God's plan is to be forever united with us in absolute goodness. It is gifted to us through Christ.

> From the very beginning God decided that those who came to him—and all along he knew who would—should become like his Son. . . . And having chosen us, he called us to come to him; and when we came, he declared us "not guilty," filling us with Christ's goodness, gave us right standing with himself, and promised us his glory. (Romans 8:29–30 TLB)

We will not achieve perfection before we reach heaven. But every time we choose goodness, we'll be living a bit of heaven here on earth.

Thank you, God, that I can look forward to an eternal life of complete goodness and that you've equipped me to have some on earth as well.

*You can show others the goodness of God, for he called you
out of the darkness into his wonderful light.*

1 PETER 2:9

When our children were young, my husband and I had season theater tickets. They involved babysitters, a long drive, expense. But the plays were a treat we looked forward to. Once however, our preparation and anticipation had to be balanced against a performance that was, in our minds, evil. The play made us uncomfortable. In fact, it disgusted us. We left early on, disappointed, but glad we'd made the right choice.

1 Thessalonians 5:22 says "Stay away from every kind of evil." These days much so-called entertainment pollutes the mind, corrodes the soul, and tempts the heart. Evil parades in abundance, in movies, TV, songs, magazines, books, video games, and more. I'm no prude, but why use up any portion of my life ingesting garbage? Instead, I can turn off the TV, walk out of the theater, throw away the magazine, return the book, and switch the radio station. If a business has practices contrary to my beliefs, I can refuse to shop there. If people speak hurtfully about others, I can speak up or leave. I can support, encourage, and associate with those who stand up for Christian values.

Goodness is a choice God tells us to make (3 John 11 and Psalm 34:14). We're to "hate what is wrong, hold tightly to what is good" (Romans 12:9), and "take no part in the worthless deeds of evil and darkness; instead expose them" (Ephesians 5:11).

Lord, when I face a decision, help me choose the good.

Let's not get tired of doing what is good.
At just the right time we will reap
a harvest of blessing if we don't give up.

GALATIANS 6:9

Unfortunately, what's right and good isn't always what's easiest. Nor does it guarantee immediate reward. It may even seem that wrongdoers prosper. When I worked in the corporate world, I saw people who spent more time schmoozing than working, or who backstabbed or lied, get promotions faster than I did. Apparently, this observation is nothing new. The psalmist said:

> I envied the proud when I saw them prosper despite their wickedness. They seem to live such painless lives. . . . Did I keep my heart pure for nothing? Did I keep myself innocent for no reason? . . . I tried to understand why the wicked prosper. But what a difficult task it is! (Psalm 73:3–4, 13, 16)

Seeing unfairness can be discouraging. Yet, the Bible assures, "the prospect of the righteous is joy" (Proverbs 10:28 NIV84). Choosing good brings freedom from regret and the joy of knowing we're in God's will. We're told, "Do not set foot on the path of the wicked or walk in the way of evil men" (Proverbs 4:14). Instead, "always try to do good to each other and to all people" (1 Thessalonians 5:15). When the way seems arduous and the returns meager, we can draw on our fruit of patience, knowing we will be rewarded, if not on earth, then in eternity.

Lord, may I never tire of doing good.

I am fully convinced, my brothers and sisters,
that you are full of goodness.

ROMANS 15:14

One of my favorite childhood memories is hunting for four-leaf clovers with my grandmother. We spent hours competing for who could find the most. We both developed a good eye for spotting the few clovers with four leaves among the thousands with three.

I wish I were as able to spot the goodness in others, especially when that goodness is woven among traits that annoy me. Like hunting for four-leaf clovers, discovering the goodness in others can take time and effort. But we can always find it if we look hard enough. It's those four-leaf nuggets of goodness that God wants me to search for and focus on, not the three-leafed faults (Philippians 4:8).

I live in the country now. Instead of looking down for four-leaf clovers, I often look up and watch the swoops and soars of red-tailed hawks. What fun it would be to look down on the landscape with their bird's-eye view. God sees even more. He has a God's-eye view. He doesn't look at just the little piece of my situations I see. He observes every part of my life in the context of how it fits into others' lives, into his plan for mine, and his ultimate plan for mankind. Though I'll never have eyes like that, I can try to understand others' positions. I can strive to see at least some of what God sees.

Lord, help me look for and find the good in others.
Help me see beyond my limited perspective.

Don't copy the behavior and customs of this world,
but let God transform you into a new person
by changing the way you think.

ROMANS 12:2

I didn't used to say grace in restaurants or talk about my faith. I let the world impact my behavior. All because I cared what "they" thought. Now I care what God thinks. It's liberating. Now I can say with the apostle Paul, "We are not trying to please men but God. . . . We were not looking for praise from men" (1 Thessalonians 2:4, 6 NIV84).

It's said, "older and wiser." I'd change that to "closer and wiser." At every age, the closer we are to God, the wiser we become and the more we appreciate that "the wisdom of this world is foolishness to God" (1 Corinthians 3:19).

There's talk about peer pressure and kids today. We're quick to tell our children not to go along with the crowd or to care that "everybody's doing it." But do we take our own advice? For example, in church are we hesitant to raise our hands in praise for fear of what some may think? Which of our everyday actions are dictated not by what God thinks, but by what people think?

Remember, the joy of pleasing God is greater than the emptiness of seeking the approval of people.

Lord, may I always put pleasing you as my highest priority.

God showed his great love for us by sending Christ
to die for us while we were still sinners.

ROMANS 5:8

In *Saving Private Ryan*, Captain Miller leads eight D-day survivors on a mission to find Private Ryan. Because Ryan's three brothers were killed in action, it's been ordered he be located and returned safely home. Captain Miller and others save him but die doing so. Miller's last words to Ryan are "Earn this."

Years later, Ryan visits Miller's grave and says through tears, "I've tried to live my life the best I could. I hope that was enough. I hope that at least in your eyes I've earned what all of you have done for me." He then turns to his wife and says, "Tell me I have led a good life. Tell me I'm a good man." She replies, "You are."

Ryan's plea resides within each of us. We want those we love and care about to value us and tell us we've lived with purpose and integrity. Most of all, we want our Savior to know he didn't die for us in vain. "Tell me I have led a good life," we say in our heart. "Tell me I'm a good person." Christ replies, "You are."

We are good not because of anything we've done, but because Christ died for us. He never asks us to earn his sacrifice—we never could. It's a gift (Ephesians 2:8–9).

Lord, help me lead a good life; tell me I'm a good person . . .
all for and because of you.

For the happy heart, life is a continual feast.
PROVERBS 15:15

Sage and Montana, my two Australian Shepherds, love it when I bring them big, gnarly beef bones. Their eyes rivet on me as I hold up their treats. They dutifully sit, waiting for me to put one in each of their mouths. When I do, they run off with their prizes, find their favorite spots, and plop down to attack the bones.

Inevitably, each dog first goes to work sucking the soft, tasty marrow from the bone's center. That's not easy because that core is usually narrow. But my dogs don't give up. They suck and chew and suck and chew until every bit of marrow is gone. By the time they abandon them, the bones are just shells. Sage and Montana have sucked out all their goodness.

Life may seem tough, but there's plenty of goodness within it. We just need to go for it and suck out every bit we can. "Life is not a journey to the grave with the intention of arriving safely in a pretty and well-preserved body, but rather to skid in broadside, thoroughly used up, totally worn out, and loudly proclaiming, 'Wow! What a ride!!!'" (origin unknown).

In chewing on my life bone, Lord,
let me be sure to suck out all its marrow.

I will always remind you of these things, even though you know
them and are firmly established in the truth you now have.
I think it is right to refresh your memory.

2 PETER 1:12–13

Inspiration isn't my problem; remembering is. Try using these exercises to remind yourself of what you've learned, what you're striving for, and how blessed you are:

1. Create an acrostic. Take each letter of goodness (or any fruit of the Spirit) and use it as the first letter of what you want to remember. For example:

    Give everything to God
    Overcome my sinful nature
    Obey
    Don't give up
    No excuses
    Encourage others
    See the good in everyone
    Stand firm

2. Assign to each letter of the alphabet something or someone that points you to God's goodness. Apples, Babies, Clouds, Dimples, Easter, Friends, Grasshoppers, Ice cream, Jesus, Koalas . . . and so on. Then do the same with other fruit of the Spirit.

Lord, you know how easily I forget. Help me think of ways
to ensure I never lose sight of who you are,
what you've done, and who I want to be for you.

Give thanks to the Lord, for he is good!

PSALM 136:1

Over a year ago I sent a wedding gift to a friend's daughter. I chose it from her registry, and it wasn't inexpensive. She received it, but never mentioned it to me. I'm disappointed. It's not why I gave the gift, but a thank-you note would have been nice.

We're made in God's image. And I think that's one way we who are made in God's image reflect his character. We know from the psalms that he loves being thanked and hearing how much we're enjoying his gifts to us. That's not why he's good to us, but our thanks must make him feel really good. And isn't it exciting that we can make the God of the universe feel really good? We can make him smile!

How many of God's gifts of goodness do we neglect to thank him for? How many of his wonders do we take for granted? In his Gospel, Luke told of Jesus healing ten lepers. Only one thanked him. Jesus noticed and said, "Didn't I heal ten men? Where are the other nine?" (Luke 17:17).

When did you last thank God for sight, hearing, touch, taste, and smell? What about each day of health, each heartbeat, each hug? God shows us his goodness in countless ways. We can give him joy when we say, "Thank you, Father!"

Dear God, I will give thanks to you forever, for forever is how long it will take me to thank you for your goodness.

[PSALM 30:12]

Many . . . have done virtuously, nobly, and well,
with the strength of character that is steadfast
in goodness, but you excel them all.

PROVERBS 31:29 AMP

On a trip to Europe, I played darts with a group from Ireland. From them I learned that darts is more complicated than I'd thought. You don't just aim for the bull's-eye, but for many different spots depending on the game.

Proverbs 31 describes a "wife of noble character" and, in the process, gives us many things to aim for: trustworthiness . . . dedication . . . industry . . . focus . . . financial prudence . . . being on call 24/7 . . . emotional and spiritual strength . . . wisdom . . . kindness . . . ability to teach . . . taking good care of family . . . thinking of others . . . looking before leaping . . . planning and preparing for, and investing in the future . . . bringing good, not harm . . . taking good care of health and appearance . . . jumping in and getting things done . . . helping those in need . . . thinking ahead . . . acting with dignity . . . having a sense of humor. Just reading the list exhausts me. But unlike darts, we can win the game of life by targeting only the bull's-eye. Jesus is the bull's-eye. When we aim to please him in thought, word, and deed, we need aim nowhere else.

Lord, I want to live a life of noble character.
May I set my aim solely on pleasing you.

They will celebrate your abundant goodness.

PSALM 145:7 NIV84

Football season brings out the maniacal devotion of die-hard fans. I've been in stands where over one hundred thousand people are dressed in team colors, cheering, chanting, screaming, and dancing with glee. It's fun, but I can't help but think how amazing it would be if we celebrated God's goodness with the same fervor. Imagine if even a fraction of the energy at a packed sports stadium were put into a worship service, The Church would ignite, and the world could be set on fire with zeal and love for God.

God wants us to express delight in his goodness (Numbers 29:12; Psalm 135:3; 2 Chronicles 6:41; Psalm 145:7; Isaiah 63:7; Nehemiah 9:25). In fact, knowing his goodness, how can we keep silent? (Luke 19:40).

Given who God is and what he's done, you'd think every day would be like game day. We'd shout our praises loud and strong as in Nehemiah 8:12, when all the people celebrated "with great joy because they now understood" (NIV84) the scripture that was read to them.

If we claim to know God, let's not "deny him by the way [we] live" (Titus 1:16). I'm not expecting celebration of God with abandon every day. But wouldn't it be nice?

Lord, may I be at least as ready and eager
to celebrate the victory of your great goodness
as I am to celebrate the victory of my team.

Let your good deeds shine out for all to see,
so that everyone will praise your heavenly Father.
MATTHEW 5:16

I was feeling overwhelmed by negative, depressing world news, by stories of hatred, division, and discord. The spread of evil and the trampling of goodness were getting to me. But evil is nothing new. It made its entrance shortly after the world began, (see Genesis 3), and has permeated civilization since (see the rest of the Bible). God's word assures that he will be victorious and that we need not fear (Psalm 20:5; Psalm 23:4).

In the Gospel of Mark, Jesus explained his parable about a farmer sowing seed. The seed represents God's Word, and Jesus set out four possible responses to it:

1. Hear it, but allow Satan to immediately take it away.
2. Hear it and receive it, but with a shallow faith that allows worldly problems to distance us from God.
3. Hear it, but be so preoccupied with worldly worries and desires that God's Word is pushed aside.
4. Hear it, accept it, and live it.

Was I doing exactly what Jesus warned against? Was I allowing the cacophony of world events to drown out God's voice? Was I forgetting that he tells us over and over again not to be afraid? Was I allowing Satan a temporary victory? Was I forgetting to shine my light?

Lord, may I never allow the world's noise to drown out
your voice of reassurance and truth.

God saw all that he had made, and it was very good.

GENESIS 1:31 NIV84

In challenging, upsetting, or fear-filled times, it helps to have someone we trust say, "Everything's going to be okay." God gives us even greater assurance. During life's trials, troubles, and upheavals, he points us to the end of the story. He promises not just that everything will be okay, but that it will be good, very good. God's creation began with goodness, and it will end—and continue into eternity—with goodness.

> Then I saw a new heaven and a new earth, for the old heaven and the old earth had disappeared. . . . I heard a loud shout from the throne, saying, "God's home is now among his people . . . and there will be no more death or sorrow or crying or pain. All these things are gone forever." And the one sitting on the throne said, "Look, I am making everything new!" (Revelation 21:1, 3–5)

God reveals these truths as "an anchor for our soul, firm and secure" (Hebrews 6:19 NIV84). No matter what we experience, no matter how frightening, distressing, difficult, or painful our circumstances, in the end, everything will be good. In *Epic*, writer John Eldredge puts it this way: "[It will be] the return of the beauty, the intimacy, and the adventure we were created to enjoy and have longed for every day of our lives. And yet, *better*, for it is immortal. We can never lose it again. It cannot be taken away."

Thank you, God, for your assurance
that all will end in goodness.

Guard the good deposit that was entrusted to you—
guard it with the help of the Holy Spirit who lives in us.

2 TIMOTHY 1:14

When I was in school, though I'd studied the material throughout the semester, I needed to review it before test time, for I'd already forgotten much of what I'd learned.

In living the fruit of the Spirit, every day is a test. Even if you've faithfully read every page of this devotional, unless you (and I) review now and then, we'll likely forget things we learned and resolved to do. My bookcases are full of self-improvement books. With each, I've underlined, felt inspired, and been determined. Then, as days pass, I forget what I read. I need to go back occasionally, reread my underlining, and reresolve to put them into practice.

That's what I encourage you to do today—and periodically after that. Since goodness is essentially a combination of all the fruit of the Spirit, now's a good time to leaf back through this book, reread your underlinings, and remind yourself to put into practice those ideas meaningful to you. You can also ask yourself (and maybe someone close to you for feedback): "In which fruits have I made the most improvement and in what ways?" "In what areas do I still need more focus?" "What are some specific things I can do to improve?"

Lord, where would you like to see more improvement?
When have I made you smile? Thank you for this journey.
May I come ever nearer to my destination of living goodness.

PEACE

*The Lord bless you and keep you; the Lord make his face
shine upon you and be gracious to you.
The Lord turn his face toward you and give you peace.*

NUMBERS 6:24–26 NIV84

Dear Lord,

*Life is complicated. There's so much going on in my life, in the lives
of those I love and care about, and in the world. Sometimes it's
exhausting and scary. News headlines scream of crisis, tragedy, and
trials. Your creation struggles under the weight of evil. Yet I find
peace in knowing you will prevail.*

*Thank you for the certainty of you. Thank you for the knowl-
edge that regardless of what I face, you are with me. Not only are
you willing to handle all that comes my way, but you ask me to
bring it to you. You want to bear my burdens. I don't have to be
alone. That brings peace. In the midst of turmoil, may I look to
you, for when I feel your presence, I experience your peace. Knowing
your plan is for good and that you are in control brings calm.*

*In this moment, talking with you, I remember all these truths.
Yet when storms rage, it's easy to forget, to feel unsettled instead of
at peace. Help me to keep my hand in yours, and walk through
every storm, serene with confidence.*

*Your peace is a priceless gift. But a gift is something I must
receive to enjoy. Help me never forget to reach for you and accept
what only you offer—deep, true, and lasting peace, resting in your
embrace of assurance and love. Thank you, Lord, for your peace.*

Amen.

The Lord blesses his people with peace.
PSALM 29:11 NIV84

Close your eyes and think "peace."

What came to mind? Perhaps snow-capped mountain peaks reflected in a shimmering lake, swans gliding over glassy waters, a sleeping baby, a glorious sunset, or sipping a mug of cocoa by a crackling fire. Whatever you envision, peace feels good, doesn't it? There's nothing quite like it.

Peace is harmony, security, and safety. Webster's dictionary says *peace* is also "freedom from disquieting or oppressive thoughts or emotions, no war or fighting, a state of tranquility," and *tranquility* is "absence of agitation of mind or spirit, of disturbance or turmoil." When we have God's peace, we've no internal discord, no battle within our mind or spirit. We feel free from tension. Our soul is at rest.

I've felt that way when times are good. But what about when we're bombarded by the bad and nothing seems to go our way? Even then, we can feel God's peace, the only peace that doesn't depend on what's going on around us.

In the New Testament, *peace* is from the Hebrew *shalom* and Greek *eirene*, meaning "completeness" and "wholeness" (StudyLight.org). Though externally there may be turmoil, internally we have peace. Regardless of our circumstances, we have all we need. We are whole, complete . . . in the Lord.

Fill me with your peace, Lord.
When I think about peace, may I see you.

A wonderful future awaits those who love peace.

PSALM 37:37

F + SC + P + G + K + L + G = P. Modern math? No, age-old truth.

If we live faithfulness, self-control, patience, gentleness, kindness, love, and goodness, we'll have peace; if we have true peace, we'll live the other fruits. By answering "How peaceful am I?" it's a pretty sure thing we'll know how we're doing on the other fruits. Each fruit of God's Spirit is inextricably intertwined with the others.

The greater our faithfulness, the easier our self-control. The easier our self-control, the more certain our patience. The more certain our patience, the more effortless our gentleness. The more effortless our gentleness, the more frequent our kindness. The more frequent our kindness, the greater our love. The greater our love, the truer our goodness. The truer our goodness, the more solid our peace. The more solid our peace, the more radiant our joy. The Spirit's fruit all fit together. (If we put "the less" in each of those statements, they're all true as well.)

Some questions to consider:

1. Do I know true peace, or do I only feel peace when things are good? Why?
2. When do I feel most peaceful? Least peaceful? What do my answers tell me?

As we begin our focus on peace, it's a good time to reflect on our progress on the other fruits and to remember that, without God, quietness and stillness are just emptiness.

Thank you, God, for your plan. As always, it's perfect.

Every good and perfect gift is from above.
JAMES 1:17 NIV84

My *New Living Translation Bible Concordance* contains over two thousand scriptural references to the words *gift, give,* and their variants. My New Living Translation Bible contains fewer than fifteen hundred pages. On average, that's more than one reference to peace per page. God gives unrestrainedly, and he wants us to do the same. One gift God offers us is peace (John 14:27). Jesus doesn't give us just peace; he gives us *his* peace, the same peace he has. What an astounding gift.

The other fruits take effort. They're often difficult to live. But peace . . . aah . . . peace. God gives it when we follow him—those last four words are critical: *when we follow him.*

When we ask God for peace but feel we haven't received it, it's time to examine how obedient we're being. Am I seeking God and following his will? Am I submitting my life to him and surrendering my desires to his desires for me? Am I living according to his teachings and following his example? Am I trusting him? If the answer to any of those questions is no, am I coming to him with a repentant heart?

It's when we're able to answer those questions with *yes* that we receive God's gift of peace, his peace that passes all understanding (Philippians 4:7).

When I don't feel your peace, Lord, may it be a wake-up call that there's something in which I'm not following and trusting you. Please show me what that is.

Let the peace of Christ rule in your hearts.
Colossians 3:15 niv84

Jesus is God. He was also a man. He had emotions. He felt sadness (John 11:35), compassion (John 8:1–11), anger (John 2:13–17), even anguish (Matthew 26:36–46). Yet Jesus had peace. It permeated him and all he did. As God, this is understandable. But as man, how did he achieve immutable peace?

- *Jesus had an intimate relationship with God the Father:* "I am in the Father and the Father is in me." (John 14:11)
- *Jesus stayed in continual communication with God:* "Jesus went up on a mountain to pray, and he prayed to God all night." (Luke 6:12)
- *Whenever he felt overwhelmed, Jesus prayed, then continued on:* "Sit here while I go over there to pray. . . . Rise, let us go! Here comes my betrayer!" (Matthew 26:36, 46 niv84)
- *Jesus followed God completely:* "I do nothing on my own but say only what the Father taught me. . . . I always do what pleases him." (John 8:28–29)

Jesus was rejected, betrayed, hurt, insulted, derided. He "faced all of the same testings we do" (Hebrews 4:15). Yet he lived peace . . . through unrelenting prayer and a profound relationship with God. We can do the same.

---

*I come to you Lord, weary and burdened, knowing
you'll give me peace. I take your yoke upon me
and I learn from you, finding rest for my soul.*
[Matthew 11:28–29 niv84]

*Since we have been justified through faith,
we have peace with God through our Lord Jesus Christ.*

ROMANS 5:1–2 NIV84

The world can be frightening—wars, violence, disaster, disease, tragedy, corruption, hatred, terrorism. Hardly a recipe for peace. But as Christians, we hold the missing ingredients that make this turbulent concoction result in peace for us. We know the end of the story. Satan and evil are defeated. The Lord is victorious. We live with God for eternity (book of Revelation). We are saved (Romans 10:9). This knowledge brings peace in a world where peace would otherwise be unobtainable. As poet Charles W. Naylor (1874–1950) said in "I Know":

> I know on Whom my faith is fixed,
> I know in Whom I trust;
> I know that Christ abides in me,
> And all His ways are just. . . .
> Let scoffers scoff, let scorners sneer,
> My heart is full of peace;
> They cannot take the joy I feel,
> Nor make my hope to cease. . . .
> I know God is; I know His Word
> Unfailing meets each test;
> I calmly face a hostile world
> With soul and mind at rest

Thank you, Lord, for the knowing that brings peace.

I have told you these things so that
in me you may have peace.

JOHN 16:33 NIV84

Promise has been defined as "a statement . . . telling someone that you will definitely do something or that something will definitely happen" (American Sign Language). Humans make many promises but don't keep them all. God always keeps his promises (Psalm 145:13; Hebrews 10:23). He gives us the peace of certainty.

The Bible is filled with God's promises. Even when God doesn't use the word *promise*, we can rely on everything he says, for every word he speaks is true (Psalm 119:160; 1 Kings 8:56).

God didn't have to assure us. He didn't have to tell us anything. But he knows we're a fearful people who worry and get anxious. He wants us to have peace. So he chose to give us his promises. As the apostle Paul said, "No matter how many promises God has made, they are 'Yes' in Christ."

Thank you, Lord, for the peace of your promises
and for the assurance that you will keep every one.

God's gifts and his call are irrevocable.

ROMANS 11:29 NIV84

If you were offered a gift that would allow you to . . .

- think more clearly,
- understand more readily,
- reduce your stress,
- improve your health,
- clear your mind of worry,
- sharpen your focus,
- free up time to pursue interests,
- make it easier to live the fruit of God's Spirit,
- enjoy every day,
- improve your relationships . . .

would you accept and open that gift?

God offers that gift to each of us: it's the gift of his peace. Yet often we refuse to receive it. Instead we clutter our minds, tax our bodies, consume our hours, darken our days, and damage our relationships with anxiety, anger, irritation, and stress. And God's proffered gift of peace remains unopened. It's easy to get tangled up in the world, to try to handle every situation on our own, and to forget we don't have to (1 Peter 5:7; 2 Chronicles 20:15).

———————

Lord, please open my heart to your gift of peace.

Mightier than the thunder of the great waters,
mightier than the breakers of the sea—
the LORD on high is mighty.

PSALM 93:4 NIV84

During our cruise across the Pacific Ocean, the seas had been fairly calm. But one day large swells appeared, causing our ship to pitch and roll. The waters rose and fell like a vast bubbling cauldron. I stood on our stateroom balcony and watched, exhilarated by this glorious adventure. I felt no fear or even concern, only peace.

I wouldn't have felt that way had I been trying to navigate the ship myself. I'd have been terrified. The water surges that delighted me would have been threatening. I'd have become disoriented, lost. Had a storm hit, my attempts to steer would surely have spelled disaster. But because I was in the hands of a skillful captain who knew how to safely navigate the ocean, I felt peace.

Life is more complicated than the ocean. It contains more danger and requires greater navigational knowledge than the sea does. Yet how many times do I refuse to turn my journey over to God, my all-knowing, all-capable, wholly trustworthy Captain, and instead try to find my way alone?

Lord, even when my life pitches and rolls,
may I sit back and savor it,
knowing you are in control.

I have hidden your word in my heart.

PSALM 119:11 NIV84

One way we can receive God's gift of peace is by reading his Word. The Bible contains history but speaks to the present. Its truth can change paths, hearts, and lives. Countless times when I've been confused, frustrated, angry, afraid, worried, torn, in turmoil, or just plain lacking peace, I've opened my Bible. Without fail, reading it has brought me peace.

Have you ever had a Bible verse jump out and speak directly to you? Maybe you underlined it or marked it with the date. But when you read that same verse later, it doesn't impact you as it did earlier, or you can't even remember why you noted it. God's Word is living and active (Hebrews 4:1 NIV84): he uses it to respond to our needs. He hears our heart and connects with us through his Word: we read or hear a perfect verse exactly when we need it.

Other times I feel I should focus on a specific scripture, but I don't grasp right away how it applies to me. But, when I pray for insight, I inevitably receive it, either quickly, or after a period of time.

Experiences like these offer me evidence on a personal level that "all scripture is God-breathed" (2 Timothy 3:16 NIV84). As the Bible says, Jesus "came and preached peace to you who were far away and peace to those who were near" (Ephesians 2:17 NIV84).

Lord, help me remember that when I need peace,
I can find it in the pages and promises of your Word.

The Mighty One, God, the Lord, speaks
and summons the earth from the rising
of the sun to the place where it sets.

PSALM 50:1–2 NIV84

God begins and ends every day with his peace. Step outside as his world transitions from night to day or from day to night. Not *the* world; *his* world. Our circumstances and the man-made world may be brewing, buzzing, and blaring. Yet, at the cusp of both day and night, God's creation is inexorably permeated with his peace.

I'm blessed to live in Big Sky Country, graced most every morning and evening by a soul-stirring sunrise and breath-grabbing sunset. As I absorb their grandeur, my spirit joins in the words of David: "The heavens declare the glory of God; the skies proclaim the work of his hands" (Psalm 19:1 NIV84).

This morning our daughter texted a photo of the view from her train window as she traveled from Baltimore to New York City. It showed a delicately cloud-studded sky above a gold-edged sunrise reflected in serene water. Indeed, the message of peace God offers in his morning and evening skies goes "throughout the earth," its "words to all the world" (Psalm 19:4). "It is good to give thanks to the Lord, to sing praises to the Most High . . . to proclaim [his] unfailing love in the morning, [his] faithfulness in the evening" (Psalm 92:2).

Lord, what a perfect way to begin and end each day,
in the splendor of your beauty and blessed by your peace.
Thank you.

Be at rest once more, O my soul,
for the Lord has been good to you.

PSALM 116:7 NIV84

I love getting up before dawn—before others are up, before the world chimes in—to watch night's curtain lift and an untouched day commence. I've been delighting in a morning quiet time for over twenty years. Initially, I was working and raising three children, so quiet times were brief. Now I'm retired, our children are grown, and my quiet times have lengthened. Each morning my first thoughts are of God.

> Rising from sleep, I raise high the chalice of my life. Dressed in robes of joyful anticipation, I enter this day with an open heart. This is the awakening hour. This is the hour of praise. . . . The spark of light in my own soul is rekindled and I begin my day in glory. It is all about remembrance—remembrance of God and of good. (*Seven Sacred Pauses* by Macrina Wiederkehr)

Dawn embraces me with serenity. Its "silence is not empty, but brimming with God's presence" (Cameron Lawrence). Our house is hushed as I thank him for another day of life. I settle under soft blankets on my overstuffed chaise and continue my conversation with God. I read from the Bible and other books which teach and inspire. My soul is at peace.

Lord, thank you for the profound and abiding peace
that comes when I start the day with you.

I will lie down and sleep in peace, for you alone,
O Lord, make me dwell in safety.

PSALM 4:8 NIV84

One of my favorite cartoons is of Snoopy, of the classic *Peanuts*, lying atop his doghouse, saying, "When I think about something at two o'clock in the morning and again at noon the next day, I get two different answers." How true! And the answer at noon is always better. (I wish I could remember that at 2:00 a.m.)

I used to rehash concerns during the night and lose hours of sleep trying to solve problems. Now I'm learning to turn my cares over to God, who says, "Come to me, all you who are weary and burdened, and I will give you rest" (Matthew 11:28 NIV84). Both my soul and my body rest better when I relinquish my concerns to God. I then enjoy the peace that comes with remembering he watches over me (Psalm 121:3–4). His Word says, "When you lie down, you will not be afraid . . . your sleep will be sweet . . . for the Lord will be your confidence" (Proverbs 3:24 NIV84).

The Gospels tell of Jesus and his disciples in a boat on a lake. As a ferocious storm raged, Jesus slept. Panicking, his disciples woke him. Jesus calmed the storm and admonished them for their "little faith" (Matthew 8:23–26). Jesus's boundless faith allowed him to sleep while the tempests raged. That's the peace God wants us to have.

Lord, my mind and body need to sleep,
so I give all my cares to you.

Stop at the crossroads and look around.
Ask for the old, godly way, and walk in it.
Travel its path, and you will find rest for your souls.
JEREMIAH 6:16

Found on the internet: "I'm looking to hire a private guide to climb Mt. Rainier. Any suggestions?" Here's the response:

I recommend_____. I successfully summited Mt. Rainier with them. It was my first climb, my first 14er, my first alpine experience, my first everything! I felt very well taken care of and safe. The guides were very friendly and explained everything very well. I always knew what we were doing, where we were going, and what was expected of me. Go with them!

Our journey through life can be perilous, with myriad "firsts." I recommend Jesus, a Guide who has helped countless people summit life's mountains, traverse its valleys, maneuver through its jungles, and confidently face every "first." He, too, is friendly and explains everything well. With him, you'll know what you're doing, where you're going, and what's expected. There's no more perfect Guide. "He guides me along right paths. . . . Even when I walk through the darkest valley, I will not be afraid, for you are close beside me" (Psalm 23:3–4). About one hundred times the Bible says, "Do not be afraid." Following God, we can have peace no matter how treacherous the journey.

I will not be shaken, Lord, for you are right beside me.
[PSALM 16:8]

Times of refreshment will come from the presence of the Lord.

ACTS 3:20

In 1929 Coca-Cola initiated an advertising campaign which referred to drinking their soda as "the pause that refreshes." As Christians, we have access to a pause that refreshes better than anything else. We can take that pause anytime by temporarily stopping what we're doing and focusing on God. We can drink of his living water and never thirst again (John 4:7–14).

When we work out, pausing briefly between exercise sets can restore our strength and increase our efficiency in the next set. Likewise, pausing to focus on God renews our strength and increases our efficiency for what's next. His peace refreshes.

You may think, "My days are too hectic, too full, too busy, to pause. I don't have time!" Perhaps you don't have time *not* to pause.

A pause can be a simple "How am I doing, God?" or "Is there anything I should think about, notice, change?" We can mentally recite a verse like "Be still and know that I am God" (Psalm 46:10) or "In quietness and trust is my strength" (Isaiah 30:15 NIV84). We can offer a short prayer such as "Lord, please calm me down," or simply thank God for our blessings, be aware of his presence.

Our pauses can be as short, as long, as few, or as many as we choose. All will be time well spent, rewarded with God's peace.

As I go about my day, Lord, help me remember you're with me.
Remind me to pause for the refreshment
of peace that only you can give.

Those who live in the shelter of the Most High
will find rest in the shadow of the Almighty.

PSALM 91:1

In 2010 our son faced a medical crisis so devastatingly difficult, so crushing, I had trouble accepting its reality. I felt an oppression so great that at times I could hardly breathe. I turned to God. Our entire family did. We clung fiercely, unswervingly, unceasingly to him. God gave us a peace that truly passed all understanding. He was with us every excruciating step of the way. He also gave our son victory over cancer.

Clinging to God, crying out to him, loving him, trusting him, and praising him in every storm we face, no matter its magnitude, will bring us his peace. All of us will experience trying times, guaranteed. We need not praise God *for* those times, but *in* them. Life's squalls may roar and churn our lives in every direction. But when we hold fast to God, he gives us inner peace (Psalm 61:2–4). Early twentieth-century poet Jennie Mast said it well:

I cannot tell when the thunders peal,
How fiercely the storm may rage . . .
But I know, with my Savior always near . . .
The tempest will cease when His voice I hear,
And the darkest shadows flee.

You calmed the storm to a whisper and stilled the waves.
What a blessing was that stillness as you brought us
safely into harbor. I will praise you Lord, always and forever.

[PSALM 107:29–30]

We do not know what to do, but our eyes are upon you.

2 CHRONICLES 20:12 NIV84

There are at least two pieces of advice my children can count on me for: first, soaking in a hot bath works wonders; and second, don't make any significant decisions without prayer. The bath tip can be ignored without repercussions. Not so the decision advice.

When faced with a major decision, we often struggle, analyze alternatives, stress, lose sleep. We get caught up in our circumstances and forget we don't have to, that we can turn to God instead. Here's a five-step decision-making process that helps me:

1. Pray. Tell God in detail about the decision you must make. Talk to him as if you're talking to your best friend—because you are.
2. List the pros/cons, risks/benefits for each alternative, putting an importance rating on each (such as A–D or 1–4).
3. Pray again. Discuss your lists with God. Ask him what to do. Listen for his answer.
4. Make a decision. Do you still feel unsure, or do you feel peace?
5. If you don't feel peace, repeat steps 1–4 until you do. Don't implement any decision without that peace.

Lord, when I have an important decision to make, remind me to use these five steps to ensure my decision aligns with your will. (And thank you for hot baths!)

Don't worry about anything; instead pray about everything.
Then you will experience God's peace,
which exceeds anything we can understand.

PHILIPPIANS 4:6–7

Ours is a complex, confusing, fast-paced, sometimes frightening world. There's so much to learn, absorb, think about, remember, keep track of, and decide. Our minds are pandemonium-filled, cluttered, flitting, mega multitaskers. The result? Stress with a capital *S*. I've been there.

Envision a mind still filled with these complexities, but instead of chaos, there's order; instead of bedlam, composure; rather than worry, peace. Identical input, but a different mental environment, brings drastically different results. How to achieve this? With God. He "will keep in perfect peace all who trust in [him], all whose thoughts are fixed on [him]" (Isaiah 26:3).

Researchers estimate the average person has between twelve thousand and sixty thousand thoughts each day. Whatever the number, it's a lot. The Bible says to take each one captive "to make it obedient to Christ" (2 Corinthians 10:5). That takes effort and self-discipline, but the result is ordered thinking . . . and greater peace (Romans 8:5–6 NIV84).

Search me, O God, and know my heart; test me
and know my anxious thoughts.
Point out anything in me that offends you
and lead me along the path of everlasting life.

[PSALM 139:23–2]

God paid a high price for you.

1 CORINTHIANS 7:23

A man lamented, "I've prayed and prayed to win the lottery. Why haven't I won?" Immediately a voice from heaven said, "Try buying a ticket."

Here's the cost of a ticket for peace: believing and acknowledging out loud that Jesus is Lord (Romans 10:9; Hebrews 4:3), and walking with Jesus and following his way (Matthew 11:29).

Experiencing peace requires action in accordance with our belief. If we believe in exercise, but act like couch potatoes, we won't receive its benefits. We can believe in Jesus, but if we act like nonbelievers, we won't experience his peace. Jesus will "guide our feet into the path of peace" (Luke 1:79 NIV84) only if we follow him. "What good is it if you say you have faith but don't show it by your actions?" (James 2:14). What good is it if you say you believe in healthy eating yet fill yourself with junk food? Our actions either support or belie our professed beliefs. "Don't just listen to God's word. You must do what it says. Otherwise, you are only fooling yourselves" (James 1:22).

Lord, I want your peace. Help me remember to buy a ticket, and that for what I receive, the cost is infinitesimal.

PEACE

God is not a God of disorder but of peace.

1 CORINTHIANS 14:33

Leaving a store, I reached into my purse for my keys. My fingers felt for them through a morass of stuff. I removed objects for two minutes before finding those keys. When I got home, I turned my handbag upside down. Lipsticks, hand lotion, receipts, expired coupons, outdated lists, a hairbrush, an empty glasses case, even a pair of socks I'd stashed, all tumbled out. No wonder I had trouble locating my keys. I was hauling around a load of clutter I didn't need.

Have you emptied your purse lately? How about your car? Are they clean and lean, or do you mutter at their clutter? In your home is there a place for everything—and is everything in its place? How high are stacks of papers you'll get around to someday? Is your closet overflowing or color coded? And are your drawers stuffed or stellar? Do you have daily goals and a plan for achieving them, or are you winging it, bewildered by where the time goes? Look at where and with what you live your day. Is its essence order or disorder? Our answers to these questions make a difference in the amount and the quality of our peace. Disorder destroys peace.

Moving each superfluous purse item to its proper place in my house (in some cases the proper place was the trash) reminded me that when I simplify, organize, and clean, my days feel calmer; my peace is enhanced.

Lord, help me declutter so I can enjoy your peace.

Satan has asked to sift you as wheat.
But I have prayed for you . . .
that your faith may not fail.
LUKE 22:31 NIV84

We've talked about little enemies of peace. Now for our biggest adversary: Satan. He seeks to annihilate our peace by trying to separate us from God. While "nothing can ever separate us from God's love" (Romans 8:38), Satan wants us to abandon our relationship with God. The devil appeals to our sinful nature and encourages self-focus, doubt, fear, anxiety, anger, bitterness, unforgiveness, all the things God tells us to get rid of. Satan knows our vulnerable areas and aims at them. He dangles what ifs, whys, and why nots. He sends distractions that shift our focus from God to worldly things. He puts in our paths people who tempt and provoke.

How do we avoid this thief's deception? By being alert "so that Satan will not outsmart us. For we are familiar with his evil schemes" (2 Corinthians 2:11). When we're on the lookout, we can avoid or reject whatever Satan puts in our path, and "the God of peace will soon crush Satan under [our] feet" (Romans 16:20).

Keep me alert to the enemy and his often subtle tactics, Lord.
When my eyes are on you, nothing he tries
can take away my peace.

A peaceful heart leads to a healthy body.

Proverbs 14:30

Have your emotions ever made you feel ill? Mine have. It's not fun, it's pointless, and it's avoidable.

Research confirms that our thinking impacts our bodies. When we're stressed, angry, upset, anxious, or feeling any other nonpeaceful emotion, our blood pressure rises, our heart rate increases, our muscles tense, our stomach churns, our head throbs. Over time, this emotional stress takes its toll on our bodies. We've all seen people visibly age due to stress.

This stress-induced aging fuels the search for the proverbial fountain of youth. Antiaging products are a multibillion-dollar business. Sleep problems create a huge sleep-aid market. When stress results in poor eating habits, nicotine use, or excessive alcohol consumption, weight gain and ill health can result. What would people pay for a guaranteed antiaging, stress-eliminating, sleep-enhancing, weight-stabilizing, health-promoting remedy all rolled into one? It exists, and it's free for the asking. It's called the peace of God.

How much younger we'd look, how much less stressed, and more rested and healthier we'd be, if we lived the way the Bible says to—by giving our cares, disappointments, upsets, and stress to God and trusting him completely. What a burden would be lifted from our minds and consequently from our bodies. Instead of wasting money on expensive ways to look, sleep, and feel better, we can turn to the One who offers us the gift of peace. Our bodies will thank us.

*Lord, thank you for how my body responds
when I put my full trust in you.*

Peace be with you.
Luke 24:36

When I was recovering from a surgery, I found that fully focusing on God instead of on my body decreased my pain and brought me peace. When I concentrated on myself, my pain increased, my peace disappeared. Even in our daily lives, if we direct our thoughts to God and off our problems, our body reaps the rewards of peace.

Herbert Benson, author of *The Relaxation Response*, outlines a method for relaxing that lowers blood pressure, decreases heart rate, and causes other internal changes that counteract the harmful physical effects of stress. His approach involves sitting in a quiet place, breathing deeply and regularly, consciously relaxing your muscles, then focusing for ten to twenty minutes on a word or a prayer, passively allowing thoughts to come and go. Benson discovered that strong faith significantly increases the effectiveness of these actions.

I've often used Benson's method while mentally repeating a scripture. As I focus on its meaning and on God, I feel my mind and my body relax. The verses I've used most are "In quietness and trust is my strength" (Isaiah 30:15 NIV84) and "Be still and know that I am God" (Psalm 46:10 NIV84). There's no magic involved. It's merely making the effort to put our focus where it should be.

Lord, when I'm stressed, help me sit quietly, breathe deeply and slowly, and focus only on you and your Word.

The LORD is my shepherd; I have all that I need.

PSALM 23:1

Our society encourages acquisition, accumulation, and perpetual activity. We'd do well to remember Ben Franklin's words: "Content makes poor men rich; discontent makes rich men poor."

Activity-filled days may leave us more exhausted than exhilarated. I'm not suggesting a monastic existence. I'm as guilty as the next person of buying and doing. What I am suggesting is not overdoing it, and daily taking time to abide by Psalm 46:10: "Be still and know that I am God." My peace increases as I emphasize and contemplate it word by word:

BE still and know that I am God. *Focus on just being, breathing, sensing, experiencing.*

Be **STILL** and know that I am God. *Here,* still *has been translated "Enough! Stop!"*

Be still **AND** know that I am God. *Stopping is not enough. I need to focus on God.*

Be still and **KNOW** that I am God. *I can be certain, without doubt, that he is God.*

Be still and know that **I** am God. *I am not God. I am not in control. He is.*

Be still and know that I **AM** God. *He is the great I AM. He's with me right now.*

Be still and know that I am **GOD**. *With all that entails.*

Thank you, Lord, for the peace of knowing that with you, I have all that I need.

Make every effort to live in peace with all men.

HEBREWS 12:14 NIV84

Sometimes peacefulness takes effort. That's because there are people in this world besides ourselves. And not everyone has a peaceful impact. It can be quite the opposite. As the psalmist said, "I am a man of peace; but when I speak peace, they are for war" (Psalm 120:7 NIV84).

What does the Bible say to do when faced with those who upset, anger, and annoy us, who disrupt our peace, who "repay me evil for good and leave my soul forlorn" (Psalm 35:12 NIV84)? It says, "If it is possible, as far as it depends on you, live at peace with everyone" (Romans 12:18 NIV84). We're to focus, not on the other person's behavior, but on our own, leaving the rest to God (Psalm 35:1 NIV84). He will contend with those who contend with us (Isaiah 49:25).

God wants us to enjoy his peace. He knows we can be argumentative and antagonistic. That's why he reminds us, "Be at peace with each other" (Mark 9:50 NIV84).

Others can make it difficult, Lord.
Help me do what I can toward peace,
and to leave the rest to you.

*Those who are peacemakers will plant seeds of peace
and reap a harvest of righteousness.*

JAMES 3:18

God says, "Make every effort to do what leads to peace" (Romans 14:19 NIV84). We've asked ourselves how much peace we feel. Now we can ask how much peace we bring others.

- Do I make every reasonable effort to bring peace?
- When others provoke me, do I try to stay calm?
- Do I exhibit hot reactions or contagious peace?
- Do others see me as a peacemaker or a conflict-promoter?

"The wisdom that comes from heaven is first of all pure. . . . Then peace-loving and courteous. It allows discussion and is willing to yield to others" (James 3:17–18 TLB). We can ask God for wisdom to help us be peacemakers.

The apostle Paul instructed his protégé Timothy to "be an example to all believers in what you say, in the way you live" (1 Timothy 4:12). As aspiring peacemakers we, too, can be examples to believers as well as to any "who do not believe the word so they may be won over without words" by our behavior (1 Peter 3:1). We can exemplify the peace that following Jesus brings.

———————————

Holy Spirit, help me be a peacemaker.

He gathers the lambs in his arms
and carries them close to his heart.

ISAIAH 40:11 NIV84

Lonely New York City men and women are paying eighty dollars an hour to be cuddled. The cuddling service has a staff of forty professional cuddlers who offer nonsexual hugging (*The Week* magazine).

The very existence of such a business speaks to the power of a hug and the peace it can give. Hugs greet, calm, reassure, celebrate, communicate emotion, and convey compassion that words cannot. Hugs cannot coexist with animosity, anger, or aggression. Even if they're forced, hugs diminish negative emotions.

To live the fruit of peace, be generous with hugs. As long as we're not trying to hug a stranger, most people appreciate hugs, even those who aren't used to them or pretend not to want them. I can't imagine anyone who wouldn't benefit from a sincere hug. Those who resist may need a hug the most. But if they do stiffen up, move on and say a prayer for their peace.

It's great when we have someone to hug. But sometimes we crave a hug when no one's available. What to do? Ask God for a hug. He's always there with open arms. "He will quiet you with his love" (Zephaniah 3:17 NIV84).

On my desk is a statuette of Jesus hugging a child. I feel peaceful just looking at it, imagining I'm that child. In many ways, I am.

Thank you, God, for the gift of hugs.
We need each other, yes, but most of all, we need you.
Please hug me now.

My soul finds rest in God alone.
PSALM 62:1 NIV84

Fighting the facts takes energy—and it never does any good. The facts are the facts. Arguing will not change them. Feeling bad won't either. Playing the victim only makes things worse. Mentally wrestling with the facts will do nothing except wear us out and destroy our peace.

When we don't like what's happened, the fact remains, it happened. When someone believes something untrue about us or has said or done something that upset us, the facts are, they believed it, said it, did it. We can respond in one of two ways: (1) do what we can to make things the best they can be, given the current facts or (2) fight the facts and make things worse.

Getting upset over what is, doesn't change it. Telling someone they're wrong doesn't persuade them they are. To be convinced and change, they must come to that conclusion on their own. It's fine and even good to (peacefully) state our opinion. But then it's time to move on. Arguing, complaining, nagging, and criticizing only make others defend their position more adamantly.

The most important thing we can do is pray. God *is* able to change people and circumstances. He can also show us how to improve situations. Meanwhile, "Be willing to have it so . . . because acceptance of what has happened is the first step in overcoming the consequences of any misfortune" (William James).

Lord, give me the peace that comes with accepting the facts,
doing what I can, then leaving in your hands
whether they will change.

Catch for us the foxes, the little foxes that ruin the vineyards,
our vineyards that are in bloom.

Song of Songs 2:15 niv84

I'm agitated. I'm irritated. I'm irked. I do not feel peaceful.

Why? Our dog Sage enjoys refreshing herself in our pond. She's also figured out how to open our doors with her paw, and she has just trotted through four rooms leaving wet, slimy footprints.

Sure, they can be cleaned up. In fact, I just did. It wasn't difficult because the floors are hardwood. I could and should laugh this off. But just as soon as I put Sage back outside and cleaned up her mess she pranced in through another door. More dirty footprints. It would be funny if only I'd lighten up. So why is my mouth turned down, not up?

I let my happily panting dog outside once again. I look out a window at the sun-kissed land and thank God for our blessings. I apologize to him for being upset over something so small when I have such abundance. I thank him for health, family, friends, our beautiful life, and, yes, for Sage, who takes nothing too seriously. I ask God for peace. He gives it to me. He calms my soul, and I relax . . . just as Sage strolls in yet again. I reach for a towel. But this time I'm smiling.

Lord, help me notice when little things are getting to me.
Remind me that getting upset just isn't worth it.

In a desert land he found him, in a barren
and howling waste. He shielded him and cared for him;
he guarded him as the apple of his eye.

DEUTERONOMY 32:10 NIV84

When our son told us he was deploying to Afghanistan, I internally panicked. Every parent can understand my urge to plead "*Please* stay home." Every parent can understand that wasn't an option.

So I kept quiet, except for questions, most of which he couldn't—or wouldn't—answer. Questions like "How dangerous is it? How often can we talk to you? What will you be doing?" Our son was the one going into a high-risk situation, but I was the one at risk of falling apart. So I prayed long, fervently, and continually for his safety and for my (and our) peace. God answered my prayers.

Countless times during our son's deployment, people asked me questions like "Aren't you scared? How can you cope? Are you okay?" Amazingly, my honest answers were no, "with God's grace," and yes. The entire time our son was overseas, God granted me a peace that truly passed understanding. I wasn't worried.

I missed my son, of course. I checked the news each day, true. But I didn't feel anxiety. I knew only an inexplicable peace that could have come from nowhere and no one but God. My strength was, indeed, "in quietness and trust" (Isaiah 30:15).

Lord, I need you always, but during some seasons of life,
I see that truth more clearly. Thank you for bringing our son
safely home and for your peace while he was overseas.

Pour out your hearts like water to the Lord.
Lift up your hands to him in prayer.

LAMENTATIONS 2:19

Wouldn't it be wonderful to talk with someone who knows you completely, your every fear and desire, all your good, all your bad, every flaw and foible, all your victories and failures—yet loves you without condition or limit?

What it they also listened intently, wanted only the best for you, and possessed the wisdom to advise you perfectly toward that best? Oh, and they also had infinite ability and power. A tall order.

Yet, that is God, and we can converse with him instantly and constantly through prayer. If that knowledge doesn't bring peace, I don't know what will.

Trying to handle life on our own often results in turmoil, strife, and stress. But prayer brings peace, for our "soul finds rest in God alone" (Psalm 62:1 NIV84). Even when I've allowed myself to get so worked up I wasn't sure I could ever decompress, with prayer my tension eased and my tumult ceased.

Thank you, God, that I can talk with you anytime
and anywhere. Thank you for wisdom and understanding,
for their ways are pleasant and their paths are peace.

[PROVERBS 3:17]

You will keep in perfect peace all who trust in you,
all whose thoughts are fixed on you!

ISAIAH 26:3

As a child, I asked my parents to buy me a live chameleon vendors were selling at a circus. (They said no.) You could pin its little leash to your shirt, and the lizard would change color to match your outfit. That's what we humans are inclined to do. We blend into the habits and thinking of what and with whom we spend the most time. That's why the Bible counsels not to follow the wicked, stand with sinners, or join with mockers (Psalm 1:1–2). When we socialize most with those who love God, when we immerse ourselves in his Word, our character will become more like God's. If we spend the bulk of our time with nonbelievers whose greatest treasures are worldly, our character will become more worldly.

The same goes with our thoughts. We become like those thoughts we spend the most time with. If we nurse our hurts and negative thoughts, we'll likely become resentful and negative. If we cultivate God-pleasing, positive thoughts, we're on the path to being a godly, positive person.

We're also apt to find what we look for. In the cartoon *Dilbert*, by Scott Adams, Dilbert's coworker tells him about a new illness where a person feels great and then dies. Dilbert says with bewilderment, "I feel great. . . ." Look for problems and you'll find them. Look for Who brings true peace . . . you'll find him.

Lord, may I spend time with, look for, and focus on who
and what brings me peace, most especially, you.

The whole earth is full of his glory.
ISAIAH 6:3 NIV84

City living can be exhilarating, but not exceedingly peaceful. I smile when I see trees, bushes, and plants adorning high-rise patios and rooftops. Those tiny pockets of nature soften the harshness of concrete, steel, and glass. They bring their owners a measure of peace in a bustling city.

Yesterday, I picked up a dried caramel-colored leaf. An intricate capillary network embellished its underside in lacey, orderly beauty. That leaf, in its complex simplicity, uttered God's peace. Then I looked toward the mountains, the regal backdrop to my Colorado home. A gaze at them can pacify a raging spirit. Like generations before me, "I lift up my eyes to the hills—where does my help come from? My help comes from the Lord, the Maker of heaven and earth" (Psalm 121:1–2 NIV84). God placed us in a physical world that both exhilarates and calms. All nature bespeaks a power, a purpose, a plan. Nothing man crafts comes close to providing the kind of serenity that emanates from God's handiwork.

We humans crave that composure. Parks proliferate. Yards are landscaped. We put plants and flowers in our home. We travel to the world's natural wonders, marvel at photobooks that transport us to places we wouldn't otherwise see, and forward e-mails of scenic splendors. Whenever we need tranquility, we can turn to God's creation, where "he leads me beside quiet waters, [where] he restores my soul" (Psalm 23:2–3 NIV84).

Thank you, Creator God,
for all your wonders that speak peace.

Come to me, all you who are weary
and burdened, and I will give you rest.
MATTHEW 11:28–29 NIV84

When you feel weary and burdened, what little things refresh you and give you peace? What small indulgences help you relax? For me, its soaking in a hot bath, snuggling under a blanket with an absorbing book, savoring a massage, watching fireplace flames dance, listening to soothing music, or taking a walk. For others it may be playing with a pet, drinking hot chocolate, or tackling a sweat-inducing workout.

It's wonderful to have go-tos that help us unwind. I think God enjoys our taking pleasure in harmless and helpful idiosyncratic peace inducers.

Yet Jesus didn't say, "Pamper yourselves, all you who are weary and burdened, and that will give you rest." He reminds us that true peace comes only from him. He said, "The peace I give isn't fragile like the peace the world gives" (John 14:27 TLB).

No, I don't believe God is against our minor self-indulgences. He just wants to ensure they're not our only focus. Jesus teaches that, paradoxically, receiving his peace involves taking on a yoke. But because he carries it with us, it's easy and light (Matthew 11:30).

Lord, thank you for all my little enjoyments.
But let me never forget that lasting peace comes
not from coddling myself, but from following you.

O my Strength, to you I sing praises, for you, O God,
are my refuge, the God who shows me unfailing love.

PSALM 59:17

As I waited for medical test results for a family member, I had complete faith in God, but I wasn't feeling peace. So I thought about valleys God had brought us triumphantly through. I reviewed blessings he'd lavished on us. I reflected on his constant presence. I praised him for who he is, for his power, goodness, love, grace, and mercy, for all he's done, and for everything he will do. I praised him for being our King, Guide, Comforter, Refuge, Light in the darkness, Strength, Truth, Savior, Fortress, Healer, and Shield, the One who overcomes. I praised him for his patience, wisdom, magnificence, and glory. I focused all my being on God and his greatness. *Then* I found myself blanketed by his peace.

Praising God takes our attention off ourselves, our concerns, our worries, and our fears. It moves our thoughts to where they need to be—on God, for whom nothing is impossible

Thank you! Everything in me says "Thank you!" . . .
Thank you for your love, thank you for your faithfulness;
Most holy is your name, most holy is your Word.
The moment I called out, you stepped in.
You encourage me by giving me strength.
(Psalm 138:1, 3 MSG)

(And yes, the test results were excellent!)

————————————

I praise you, God, and thank you for the blessing of peace.

*If you, even you, had only known on this day
what would bring you peace.*

LUKE 19:42 NIV84

America lost another entertainer to suicide. This time it was a widely loved comedian, a man who brought laughter to other people's lives but couldn't bear his own life. Sadly, his story isn't unique.

Many in the entertainment business have turned to drugs, illicit sex, and material accumulation to fill their emptiness, and too many lives have been cut short by overdose or suicide. Those performers had fortune and fame. They could buy most everything . . . but peace. Many who are adulated because they appear to "have it all," are, in fact, lost, and empty. "They are headed for destruction. Their god is their appetite, they brag about shameful things, and they think only about this life here on earth" (Philippians 3:19).

Yet there is hope within their ranks. I saw it when Carrie Underwood and Vince Gill sang "How Great Thou Art" to a standing ovation. The duo clearly sang from their hearts of the God they know. Many in the audience were moved to tears.

God doesn't begrudge us fortune or fame as long as our hearts are with him (2 Chronicles 1:11–12).

---

*Lord, I pray that those who don't know you, find you . . .
and the peace that you alone give.*

If only you had paid attention to my commands,
your peace would have been like a river.

Isaiah 48:18 niv84

I love these peaceful words from the hymn "Dear Lord and Father of Mankind," based on a poem by John Greenleaf Whittier (1807–92):

> Breathe through the heats of our desire
> Thy coolness and Thy balm;
> Let sense be dumb, let flesh retire;
> Speak through the earthquake, wind, and fire,
>   O still, small voice of calm.
>
> Drop Thy still dews of quietness,
> Till all our strivings cease;
> Take from our souls the strain and stress,
> And let our ordered lives confess
>   The beauty of Thy peace.

In our frenzied, jam-packed, texting, beeping, honking, hectic days, we need to remember that "God is not a God of disorder, but of peace" (1 Corinthians 14:33 niv84). He can infuse the chaos of our lives with calm. We just need to pause, breathe deeply of his presence, and accept this gift.

———————————

Lord, please move me from disorder to order,
from commotion to peace.

Anyone who enters God's rest also rests
from his own work just as God did from his.

HEBREWS 4:10 NIV84

When she started her new job, our daughter was working seventy-plus hours each week. Initially, she thought the long hours were an anomaly. But her department's 200 percent turnover in fourteen months told her that extreme hours are the rule. She's stressed and exhausted. She needs rest and the peace it brings.

Aesop's fable tells of a goose that laid golden eggs. Eager to get those eggs, a farmer killed the goose to retrieve them. No more goose, no more golden eggs. "If you adopt a pattern of life that focuses on golden eggs and neglects the goose, you will soon be without the asset that produces golden eggs" (Stephen Covey, *The 7 Habits of Highly Effective People*).

God wants us to work, for "hard work brings rewards" (Proverbs 12:14). But God also knows the importance of rest (Genesis 2:1–3). When Jesus's "apostles returned from their ministry tour and told him all they had done," Jesus said, "Let's go off by ourselves to a quiet place and rest awhile" (Mark 6:30–31). Yes, we're to "work with enthusiasm, as though [we are] working for the Lord rather than for people" (Ephesians 6:7). But we also need to rest: we need to take care of the goose.

Lord, may those for whom we work recognize
the importance of our renewal through rest.

Pray for all people. Ask God to help them;
intercede on their behalf. . . . Pray this way
for kings and all who are in authority
so that we can live peaceful and quiet lives.

1 Timothy 2:1–2

It's almost a foregone conclusion (somewhat of a joke, actually) that any beauty pageant contestant will probably answer "world peace" when asked her greatest wish. Chuckle as we may, we all want world peace. Many countries are war-torn. America is blessed with peace within its borders. Sons and daughters have given their lives, so our peace will remain.

Yet threats of those who hate us loom. I've often felt there's nothing I can do—but there is. I can write a check or volunteer to work for causes and people I believe in. I can vote. I can communicate my views to representatives. Most important, I can pray. I can pray for leaders to seek and follow God's will and for desperate situations and broken lives around the world.

Author Phillip Yancey, in *Prayer*, shows that prayer can impact world events. He describes candlelight prayer that began in 1989 with small groups and grew to millions "until finally one night the Berlin Wall itself . . . yielded to a different kind of power and splintered into a million pieces."

The apostle James wrote, "The earnest prayer of a righteous person has great power and produces wonderful results" (James 5:16). And when one person's prayer joins that of another and then another and then another, unlimited power can be unleashed.

Lord, may I never doubt that my prayers can further peace.

*The past troubles will be forgotten
and hidden from my eyes.*
ISAIAH 65:16 NIV84

The present and future we can impact. The past we can't. That's why Satan has a field day taunting and haunting us with regrets and rehashing of hurts. He wants us to remember offenses even after we've forgiven them. When we replay past negatives, our peace is diminished, even destroyed. That makes Satan glad.

God blots out our transgressions and forgets our sins (Isaiah 43:25 NIV84). We're to cast all our cares upon him (1 Peter 5:7 KJV). Jesus came so we "may have life, and have it to the full" (John 10:10 NIV84). We can't have life to the full when we torment ourselves with memories that bring remorse or resentment.

God wants us to remember many things. Recollections that stir up guilt and bitterness aren't among them. In fact, he says to "forget the former things; do not dwell on the past" (Isaiah 43:18 NIV84). We're to learn from what's happened, grieve, and heal, but then move on in God's peace, "forgetting the past and looking forward to what lies ahead" (Philippians 3:13).

---

*God, keep me so busy enjoying life
that I take no time to brood over the past.*

[ECCLESIASTES 5:20]

*Letting the Spirit control your mind
leads to life and peace.*

ROMANS 8:6

I picked up my smartphone and pushed the button to light up its screen. The phone's face remained dark. The battery was dead. I plugged my phone into its charger. Its screen lit up.

A smartphone can do many things. But it can do none of those things if I forget to keep it charged. Knowing where the charger is, but not using it, does me no good. My phone needs daily recharging if I'm to continually enjoy its benefits.

If I "plug into" God and ask him for his peace, he'll give it to me. But I need to make that connection daily to retain that peace.

If I say that I trust in God, but try to go it alone, I won't find peace (Romans 15:13). Trusting means not just knowing God's there, but being connected to him through prayer and obedience. It means staying charged, not just an occasional reviving of our spirit. When we remain plugged into God, we'll travel the path of peace. Knowing where the path is, but not walking on it, is fruitless.

*Lord, when I start to lose my peace,
remind me to plug into you—and to live
with my battery fully charged.*

JOY

I am overwhelmed with joy in the Lord my God!
ISAIAH 61:10

Dear Lord,

I'm now on the last fruit of your Spirit. It's been quite a journey. Thank you for walking it with me. Thank you for the distance I've traveled, for the progress I've made. Thank you for picking me up when I've stumbled, pointing the way when I've forgotten it, and patiently bringing me here, to my journey's culmination, the fruit of joy.

Joy is the icing on the cake, Lord, a lavish dessert in the meal of life. But it's more than that because I don't just get it at the end. When I follow you and let your Spirit lead me, I can en-"joy" it every step of the way. That's so amazing—I can experience your joy even when I'm not happy, even when my days are rough, even when I'm barely holding on, as long as it's you I'm holding onto. What a gift Lord.

I want to open your gift of joy and keep it with me always. Remind me, Holy Spirit, as I walk this sometimes-jarring road of life, that I can carry your joy constantly, as long as I keep in step with you.

You've given me such joy—exuberant and overwhelming, profound and abiding. May I remain aware of all that I have in you, with you, and because of you. Thank you for the joy of knowing you, trusting you, and of the vast blessings which saturate me with joy. I love you . . . with all my heart, soul, mind, and strength.

AMEN!

I will go to the altar of God, to God—
the source of all my joy.

PSALM 43:4

It's a frequently repeated truth that there's a difference between happiness and joy. Webster's defines *happy* as "feeling pleasure and enjoyment because of your . . . situation" and *joy* as "a feeling of great happiness." Not much of a distinction there, but since we're talking about the fruit of God's Spirit, as always, there's so much more.

In the New Testament, the word *joy* is derived from the Greek *chara* meaning "gladness" and, more importantly, "the awareness of God's grace" (BibleHub.com). The fruit of joy comes when we see the big picture, knowing God is in control, has a plan, and loves and blesses us even though we don't deserve it. It's comprehending that God is with us no matter what, that we're forgiven, and will live with him for eternity. The fruit of joy is "God in the marrow of our bones" (Eugenia Price). It's not tied to any particular situation. We can possess and live this fruit even when we're not happy with our circumstances. When we let God's Spirit lead us, the result is joyful, pervading, and not destroyed by the vicissitudes of life.

———————

Lord, you've given me greater joy than those who have
abundant harvests of grain and new wine! Thank you.

[PSALM 4:7]

*Your eyes will shine and your heart
will thrill with joy.*

ISAIAH 60:5

I've felt my eyes shine and my heart thrill with joy. Oh, that I would live that way all the time. God has given me every reason to. Yet sometimes the light in my eyes dims and my heart becomes heavy. "Surely this is not right! Does a spring of water bubble out first with fresh water and then with bitter water? . . . If you are wise, live a life of steady goodness" (James 3:10–12 TLB).

Steady goodness. I like that thought. Looking back over the years, my living the fruit of God's Spirit looks like a stock market graph with its ups and downs, peaks and crashes. Yet, because of God's grace, my life graph shows an ongoing upward direction. And, the more I follow God's leading, the steadier my goodness, the less volatile my speech and actions, the more constant my joy.

The fruit of joy is not of this world. It's the outcome of opening our heart to God's Spirit. We can choose to let him lead us, or we can disregard him. But we can't have the fruit of joy and forget the other fruits. Joy is the result of living all of them. The more consistently we live the other fruits, the deeper and more unceasing will be our joy, regardless of life events. If our eyes aren't shining and our hearts aren't thrilling with joy, it's a good bet we're ignoring God's Holy Spirit.

---

*Lord, may I live in such a way that I fully experience
the wonder of your joy.*

Such knowledge is too wonderful for me,
too great for me to understand.

PSALM 139:6

Sometime after I began writing for *Daily Guideposts*, I sent a "Merry Christmas" e-mail to its editor. She replied quickly, wishing me the same. I was excited to think that the editor of *Daily Guideposts* knows my name. She recognized me.

Then it hit me. Yes, that's exciting, but what is absolutely thrilling is that the God of the universe knows my name! He recognizes me and answers quickly whenever I reach out to him. He says, "I knew you before I formed you in your mother's womb" (Jeremiah 1:5). Now *that* is mind-boggling and a reason to rejoice! Yet how often I've failed to recognize the joy and magnificence of that fact. Not only does God know each of our names, he knows everything about us (Psalm 139:1).

> O Lord . . . you know when I sit down or stand up. You
>   know my thoughts. . . .
> You see me when I travel and when I rest at home. You
>   know everything I do.
> You know what I am going to say even before I say it,
>   Lord. (Psalm 139:2–4)

And . . . God's Spirit lives in us (1 Corinthians 3:16). How amazing is that!

To think that you know who I am, call me by name,
know my every thought and action, and your Spirit lives in me,
makes me want to shout for joy before you Lord.

[PSALM 98:6 NIV84]

They were filled with joy when they saw the Lord!
JOHN 20:20

If ever there was an example of how the fruit of joy is unrelated to circumstances, Jesus is it. "He was despised and rejected—a man of sorrows, acquainted with deepest grief . . . it was our weaknesses he carried; it was our sorrow that weighed him down" (Isaiah 53:3–4). Jesus knew his mission and journey from day one. Yet he "was filled with the joy of the Holy Spirit" (Luke 10:21).

Jesus wants us to experience his deep, unconditional, and abiding joy. He said, "I have told you this so that my joy may be in you and that your joy may be complete" (John 15:11 NIV84). To ensure this, God gifted us with the Holy Spirit to teach us all things and to remind us of everything Jesus said (John 14:26 NIV84).

We love Jesus, though we've never seen him face to face. We trust him and "rejoice with a glorious, inexpressible joy" (1 Peter 1:8–9).

Thank you, Lord, that I don't have to let
circumstances rob me of my joy in you.
Holy Spirit, please remind me.

When I discovered your words, I devoured them.
They are my joy and my heart's delight.

JEREMIAH 15:16

I wanted to use the delay-start function on our oven so our meal would begin cooking while we weren't home. I stared at the oven panel, pushed some buttons, but couldn't get the oven to do what I wanted it to do. My husband located the instruction book. Surprise, surprise! With the help of its specific instructions, setting the oven for our outing was simple. Had we not read the manual and followed it, we wouldn't have been able to enjoy what our oven offered.

Thankfully, God gave us an instruction book for life: the Bible. If we don't read and follow it—if we just push buttons—we will miss out on much of what life offers. The Bible provides guidance on how to live an abundant and joyful life now and for eternity. As the psalmist said, "If your instructions hadn't sustained me with joy, I would have died in my misery" (Psalm 119:92).

The Bible is another manifestation of God with us always. It speaks so directly to my heart that often I feel as if it was written just for me. It was—for me, and for each and every one of us.

Your Word, God, is a lamp to guide my feet
and a light for my path.
Thank you for the joy it brings.

[PSALM 119:105]

With joy you will drink deeply
from the fountain of salvation!
ISAIAH 12:3

"It is sin to know what you ought to do and then not do it" (James 4:17). "The wages of sin is death" (Romans 6:23). The terror of those words is replaced by joy, for "God showed his great love for us by sending Christ to die for us while we were still sinners. And since we have been made right in God's sight by the blood of Christ, he will certainly save us from God's condemnation" (Romans 5:8–9).

What a relief! Christ paid for our sins, once and for all. "Therefore, there is now no condemnation for those who are in Christ Jesus because through Christ Jesus the law of the Spirit of life set me free from the law of sin and death" (Romans 8:1–2 NIV84). Hallelujah! Joy everlasting (Isaiah 61:7)!

Our forgiveness brings joy to us and to God. "There is joy in the presence of God's angels when even one sinner repents" (Luke 15:10). We can give God even more joy by leading others to him. Jesus said, "The fruit they harvest is people brought to eternal life. What joy awaits both the planter and the harvester alike!" (John 4:36).

Lord, thank you for the unending joy of our salvation.
May I share that joy with others in the hope
they will give you joy by being "brought to eternal life."

I take joy in doing your will, my God,
for your instructions are written on my heart.

PSALM 40:8

If I knew I was about to die, I would so carefully choose the words I wanted to say to those I love. I'd want to be certain to say what mattered most. I feel sure we all would. I believe Jesus did too.

Jesus knew his crucifixion was imminent. Just before his arrest, he said to his disciples (John 14):

- Obey my commandments.
- Remain in me.
- I will send the Holy Spirit to help you do these things.

Why did Jesus see these things as crucial? In his words, "I have told you this so that my joy may be in you and that your joy may be complete" (John 15:11 NIV84). He knows the only way to have this comprehensive joy is to abide in him and do what he's instructed. He realizes we need help, so he sent his Holy Spirit.

Children think they know what will make them happy. Wise parents recognize what will create the best life. They tell their children to obey, not to make their lives harder, but better. We think we know what will make us happy. Jesus knows what will bring us joy: "Yes, joyful are those who live like this! Joyful indeed are those whose God is the LORD" (Psalm 144:15).

Lord, may I remember your words,
that obedience to you is to bring me joy.

What joy for those who trust in you.

PSALM 84:12

My husband is an excellent driver. No matter the weather or road conditions, he remains unflustered. I'm fine driving—as long as the air is still, the sky is clear, and the roads are flat, straight, and dry.

On some road trips we've taken, I've been driving when conditions turn. Wind buffets, rain comes down in sheets—and of course this is the point when the road becomes circuitous, steep, or under construction. And I'm sure the rain will suddenly turn to snow, and ice will immediately cover the roads. At those times I'm quick to turn the car over to my husband. It's a relief when I do. I trust his driving and can relax and enjoy our adventure instead of fearfully clenching the wheel. It's a joy to have him take over.

The Bible says, "Those who trust the Lord will be joyful" (Proverbs 16:20). Webster's defines *trust* as "assured reliance"; *assured* means "sure or certain"; and *reliance* is "the act or state of depending on." When we turn a situation over to God, certain he'll handle it best, that brings joy—gladness unaffected by circumstance. It's a relief to know our lives are in his capable hands. "Those who look to him for help will be radiant with joy" (Psalm 34:5).

In everyone's life, storms rage, obstacles appear, the road becomes precipitous, darkness descends. When we turn the wheel over to God, we need not fear (Romans 15:13).

*Thank you, Lord, for the joy that comes
from turning it over and trusting you.*

I am with you always.

MATTHEW 28:20

There's a lot of criticism—valid and otherwise—about social media. Electronic communication has exploded. One reason it's so popular is that God designed us as relational beings. He says it's not good for us "to be alone" (Genesis 2:18.) So he created an earth that teems with relationships: family, friends, companions, colleagues, neighbors, acquaintances, even pets. Social media is one way we communicate. (Well, maybe not with pets . . . yet!)

But God has also guaranteed that no matter how numerous or few our earthly relationships, none of us, not one, will ever be alone. God is with us, as Father, Son, and Holy Spirit. That will not, cannot, change (Malachi 3:6). Furthermore, he has "made us glad with the joy of his presence" (Psalm 21:6 NIV84). And Jesus has assured us, "I am with you always, even to the end of the age" (Matthew 28:20). He even sent "another Counselor to be with us forever, the Holy Spirit" (John 14:16 NIV84).

We need each other. And it's fun to communicate through social media . . . as long as we don't overdo it. Most important is that we never let anything overshadow our relationship with God, who promises that, even without social media, we're never alone . . . and never will be.

Thank you, God, for the joy of connection
and of knowing you are with me always and forever.

*I will make you beautiful forever,
a joy to all generations.*

ISAIAH 60:15

Joy feels good. It feels so good, I can't imagine anyone turning it down. The Bible tells us how to have it:

- "Joyful are those who obey his laws and search for him with all their hearts." (Psalm 119:2)
- "How joyful are those who fear the LORD—all who follow his ways!" (Psalm 128:1)
- "You love righteousness and hate wickedness; therefore God has set you above your companions by anointing you with the oil of joy." (Psalm 45:7 NIV84)
- "All who seek the LORD will praise him. Their hearts will rejoice with everlasting joy." (Psalm 22:26)

We experience joy when we wholeheartedly seek and follow God, when we reverence and praise him, and when we love what is right. When we feel joy, we radiate beauty (Psalm 34:4–5; Isaiah 60:5). Joy can even bolster our health (Proverbs 17:22).

With joy we feel better, act better, look better, and live better. Why would we choose anything else?

Thank you, God, for the joy of joy.

Sing joyfully to the Lord.
PSALM 33:1 NIV84

Psalms is one of the most expressive, emotional books of the Bible. Each psalm was written as a song. "Music is what feelings sound like" (anonymous). The Psalms contain a spectrum of heartfelt feelings from utter anguish to pure joy.

Have you ever been so joyful you felt like singing? Singing is a natural expression of joy. Even God sings with joy: "The Lord your God . . . will rejoice over you with singing" (Zephaniah 3:17 NIV84). The birth of Jesus brought so much joy, the angels sang: "Suddenly the angel was joined by a vast host of others—the armies of heaven—praising God. 'Glory to God in the highest heaven,' they sang" (Luke 2:8–14 TLB). Joy can be so intense it's impossible to keep inside: "The Lord is my strength and my shield. I trust him with all my heart. He helps me, and my heart is filled with joy. I burst out in songs of thanksgiving" (Psalm 28:7).

The impulse to sing with the joy of the Lord is nothing new (see Psalm 63:5; 71:23; 84:4; 98:4). Singing provides a release that blesses both singer and listener. One psalmist had a great way to begin the day: "As for me, I will sing about your power. Each morning I will sing with joy about your unfailing love" (Psalm 59:16–17).

Lord, when I'm bursting with joy,
let me sing to you with all my heart.

May you be filled with joy, always thanking the Father.
COLOSSIANS 1:11–12

In my predawn quiet time, nestled in my comfy chair, the only light the moon and flickering flames in my fireplace, I snuggled under blankets and hugged my coffee mug. My two dogs snoozed. Outside, bare cottonwood branches were silhouetted against a steel-gray sky.

I usually start these special times with prayer. But that day I felt like just sitting in soundless, wordless worship. In the quiet, I surrendered all I am to the Creator of all things. I felt peaceful, wrapped in God's presence. I felt consuming love from him and for him, and intense gratitude for all he is and all he's done. I felt comforting trust, secure in his wisdom and plan. I felt . . . joy.

I've sometimes felt guilty for not continuously singing, skipping, dancing, or laughing out loud with delight. If I'm not wearing a perpetual grin, perhaps I'm not showing sufficient appreciation for my blessings. After all, isn't such an overflowing what joy means?

Sometimes it does. But as I sat silent and still that morning, I understood that joy doesn't have to be rollicking. Joy is profound. It's soul-touching awareness of God's grace, goodness, and love. It's peace coursing through our veins. It's being awed by God's magnificence.

It's wonderful when joy erupts into smiles, laughter, dancing, and song. But it's glorious when joy simply permeates our being, reassuring us that all is well . . . all is well.

Thank you, Lord, for allowing me to experience your incomparable joy.

*Surely you all know that my joy
comes from your being joyful.*

2 CORINTHIANS 2:3

I'll never forget the radiant faces of my husband and our daughter Lauren when they walked down the aisle toward her future husband. The reason for Lauren's joy was clear. She was about to embark on a lifetime with the man of her dreams. My husband, however, was handing over a portion of his heart. Why was he beaming? Because Lauren's joy brought him joy.

Letting go of our children is difficult, even painful. Yet it's also filled with joy. When our children are joyful, so are we. I believe our heavenly Father feels the same way about us.

As parents, we want our children to obey us as they grow up. We believe that obedience will bring them the best life possible. Similarly, God our Father knows obedience to his Word is the only way his children will experience true joy. As parents, we also feel joy when our children trust us, turn to us, seek our guidance, and love us. I'm sure God feels the same.

God said of Jesus, "This is my dearly loved Son, who brings me great joy" (Matthew 3:17). As God's child, I want to bring him great joy as well. I can do this by having joy; I can have joy by loving God, turning to him, and living what he's taught. What a perfect plan.

May my life, Father God, be one that brings you great joy.

May all who seek you rejoice and be glad in you.
PSALM 40:16 NIV84

Think of your best friend, someone you can always count on, turn to, and share your innermost thoughts with. Think of how good it is when you're together.

Whether you think you have such a friend or not, you do. His name is God. You can turn to him anytime, anyplace, and share your thoughts, from the lightest and most casual to the deepest and most private.

This ability to talk with God—to pray—is cause for joy. How distressing life would be if we had to wait for an appointment to speak with God or, worse, if he were never available, or too preoccupied, or considered us unworthy. That won't happen. The gift of communicating with him is a constant.

Prayer acknowledges God's presence and power. When we pray, we talk to GOD. When we listen, GOD talks to us. GOD wants us to come to him. Don't rush over these realities. Let them sink in. Absorb their enormity. Feel their joy.

Thank you, Lord, for being my very best friend.

The grasslands of the wilderness become a lush pasture,
and the hillsides blossom with joy. The meadows are clothed
with flocks of sheep, and the valleys are carpeted with grain.
They all shout and sing for joy!

PSALM 65:12–13

The book of Job may seem a strange place to find joy, but it's there. In Job 38 and 39, God describes a tiny fraction of all he has made. "The wings of the ostrich flap joyfully, but they cannot compare with the pinions and feathers of the stork. . . . Do you give the horse his strength or clothe his neck with a flowing mane? Do you make him leap like a locust?" (39:13, 19–20). God's sampling hints at the infinite diversity and intricacy of all his creation and reveals a God who designs with joy and for joy.

Some humans overflow with creativity; others, not so much. Regardless, we all take pride in and receive joy from whatever we create, and we want our creation to give joy to others. When it does, we feel joy. Place those realties as a grain of sand on the endless beach of God's might. What indescribable creativity! What incalculable joy! "Sing, O heavens, for the Lord has done this wondrous thing. Shout for joy, O depths of the earth! Break into song, O mountains and forests and every tree!" (Isaiah 44:23).

You created the kitten and the blue whale,
the starfish and the solar system. I praise you,
Creator God, as I find joy in your creation!

Let all that I am praise the Lord.

PSALM 103:1

After his God-empowered victories over the Philistines, King David of Israel was jubilant over the magnitude of what God had done for his people. "David danced before the Lord with all his might. . . . David and all the people of Israel brought up the Ark of the Lord with shouts of joy" (2 Samuel 6:14–15). David's wife Michal watched. "When she saw King David leaping and dancing before the Lord, she was filled with contempt. . . . 'How distinguished the king of Israel looked today,'" she mocked (2 Samuel 6:16, 20). David didn't care whether his worship appeared unkinglike. All that mattered to him was praising God—and praise he did.

Webster's defines *praise* as "spoken or written words about . . . good qualities . . . an expression of approval . . . of thanks to or love and respect for God." It is total focus on the positives. Sometimes I say, "I praise you, God!" That's fine. It's good. But what honors God even more is when we, like David, articulate the particular things we're thankful for.

Psalms 103–107 are excellent examples of praise. They're filled with joy and specificity: "You send rain on the mountains. . . . You fill the earth with the fruit of your labor. You cause grass to grow for the livestock and plants for people to use" (Psalm 104:13–14). Wholehearted praise with detailed gratitude expresses our joy and brings even more joy to God.

I will praise you Lord, with all my heart;
I will tell of all the marvelous things you have done.
I will be filled with joy because of you.

[PSALM 9:1–2]

What joy for those whose disobedience is forgiven,
whose sin is put out of sight.

PSALM 32:1

Imagine a world with no forgiveness. People would carry hurt and bitterness forever, a permanent "you owe me" attitude. Unforgiveness would accumulate across the globe like a boundless trash heap, polluting all lives with its devastation.

Because we're human, unforgiveness does exist. But, thanks to God, so does forgiveness. Forgiveness releases both giver and recipient from the pain prison of unforgiveness. What joy to be forgiven. What anguish not to be. What freedom and relief to forgive. What misery not to. "Purify me from my sins, and I will be clean; wash me and I will be whiter than snow. Oh, give me back my joy again" (Psalm 51:7–8).

Forgiveness is God's eraser on life's blackboard. While humans may refuse to use it, God always will. All we need do is ask. "Forgive me . . . O God who saves; then I will joyfully sing of your forgiveness" (Psalm 51:14).

A woman wanted to divorce her husband because he had kept a notebook listing every offense, small to large, she'd ever committed in their life together. That sounds awful, yet, isn't it what many of us do in our minds? Hardly conducive to joy.

Love keeps no record of wrongs (1 Corinthians 13:5). God says, "Love each other in the same way I have loved you" (John 15:12). That includes the joy of forgiveness.

Because of you, Lord, I'll never have to experience
the distress of living in a world that knows
no forgiveness. Thank you.

Joy and gladness will be found.
Isaiah 51:3

Every parent wants their children to have joy. God is no exception. Part of Jesus's earthly mission was to bring us "the full measure" of his joy (John 17:13 NIV84). The Bible tells us how to experience it:

- *Avoid conflict:* "There is . . . joy for those who promote peace." (Proverbs 12:20 NIV84)
- *Don't consider ourselves better than others:* "The humble will be filled with fresh joy from the Lord." (Isaiah 29:19)
- *Shun the world's evil:* "O the joys of those who do not follow the advice of the wicked." (Psalm 1:1)
- *Turn to God as our protection and strength:* "O the joys of those who take refuge in him!" (Psalm 34:8)
- *Trust God completely:* "O the joys of those who trust the Lord." (Psalm 40:4)
- *Be compassionate:* "O the joys of those who are kind to the poor!" (Psalm 41:1)
- *Know Jesus:* "I will see you again and you will rejoice, and no one will take away your joy." (John 16:22 NIV84)
- *Pray to God in the name of Jesus:* "Ask, using my name, and you will receive, and you will have abundant joy." (John 16:24)

---

*Thank you, Lord, for showing me
how to experience your joy.*

This is the day the LORD has made;
let us rejoice and be glad in it.

PSALM 118:24 NIV84

Maybe you've seen it on YouTube: a five-year-old climbs atop a bathroom sink. In front of a mirror, she pumps her arms and effuses:

> I can do anything good; I like my school; I like anything; I like my dad; I like my cousins; I like my aunt; I like my Alison; I like my mom; I like my sister; I like my hair; I like my haircut; I like my pajamas; I like my room; I like my whole house. My whole house is great! I can do anything good! Yeah, yeah, yeah. I can do anything good, better than anyone! (Jessica's Daily Affirmation video)

While you and I may forgo standing on our sinks, what if we—like Jessica—were to begin our days with a joyful enumeration of our blessings?

I begin my days with quiet time. I thank God for my blessings, then we talk, and I absorb his love. The psalmist's words could be mine: "Satisfy us in the morning with your unfailing love, that we may sing for joy and be glad all our days" (Psalm 90:14 NIV84). My quiet time adds joy-fuel to my day.

Now I just need to add proclaiming out loud "I love my house, I love my husband, I love my kids, I love my dogs, I can do anything!" I may even stand in front of a mirror.

Let me never begin a day Lord, without the joy
of counting my blessings with you.

You thrill me, Lord, with all you have done for me!
I sing for joy because of what you have done.

PSALM 92:4

A relaxation technique I use always surprises me. . . .

The method is simple. I begin with the top of my head and, moving down through my body, I consciously relax each muscle along the way. The surprise is how tense my muscles are and how much relaxing there is to do. What a difference this deliberate release of stress makes.

We can use the same technique with our brains: relax our mental "muscles" and release the thoughts we're mentally clenching. Let go of each frustration, worry, and attempt to control the beyond-our-control. Turn over to God each cerebral tension and free our minds to experience the fruit of joy.

The Bible says, "always be joyful" (1 Thessalonians 5:1) and to "give all your worries and cares to God" (1 Peter 5:7). Those two instructions are related. When we clutch our tense thoughts, we squeeze out joy. When we release them, joy is freed to flow. We can also read Philippians 4:8 and heed its instruction to focus on the good.

Our daughter did this when our son and his family planned a cabin weekend in the woods. When I bemoaned the 100 percent chance of rain, she said, "That'll be so much fun! What an adventure! It'll get really muddy, and the kids will love it. Then they'll go inside and be all cozy together!" A good lesson in opening the floodgates of joy.

Lord, help me mentally and physically relax,
let go, and welcome your joy.

All his days his work is pain and grief;
even at night his mind does not rest.

ECCLESIASTES 2:23 NIV84

Many work hard and joylessly, then remain entangled in their rush and fluster, neglecting to open their eyes and hearts to the evening's glory. What a relief it can be to deliberately shed the day's cares as the sun goes into hiding for the night.

If it's been a day well lived, we can savor its memory. If it's been less than stellar, we can look forward to a fresh start tomorrow. Either way, evening offers an opportunity to turn to God with gratitude, to "take a created day and slip it into the archive of life" (Jacob Glatstein in Macrina Wiederkehr's *Seven Sacred Pauses*). While our responsibilities might not end at sunset, even a few moments' reflection on the good can refresh our joy.

For those with a job outside the home, it's been suggested that when arriving home in the evening, before even getting out of the car, we take a deep breath and make a conscious decision (perhaps after a quick prayer), to leave all the day's issues and concerns in the car, where they can be picked up the next morning, if we so choose.

Whatever method we use, what joy we forfeit when, as day's curtain descends, we ignore its offer of decreasing pace, designed to usher us into rest.

Be at rest once more, O my soul, for you, Lord,
have been good to me.

[PSALM 116:7]

What has happened to all your joy?
GALATIANS 4:15 NIV84

All this talk about joy. What if we're just not feeling it, find it elusive, or think it's left us completely? When that's the case, the Bible shows we're not alone:

- "Joy has left our hearts." (Lamentations 5:15)
- "Gone now is the gladness, gone the joy of the harvest." (Isaiah 16:10)
- "Joy has turned to gloom." (Isaiah 24:11)
- "There is shouting yes, but not of joy." (Jeremiah 48:33)
- "Oh, give me back my joy again." (Psalm 51:8)
- "Give us back the joys we once had!" (Lamentations 5:21)

When we're wandering through a joyless dessert, we can learn from these scriptures. What had happened to cause the feelings expressed in those verses? What events preceded them? Where were these people in their walk and relationship with God?

God knows we may have times when our joy runs dry (Deuteronomy 32:10 NIV84). When joy wanes, God is ready to lead us "through the vast and dreadful desert land" (Deuteronomy 8:17 NIV84). When we take his hand, though his living water may at first sputter within us, it will inevitably gush into a flood of joy.

When we find ourselves more joyless than joyful, we can say with the psalmist: "Why are you downcast, O my soul? Why so disturbed within me? Put your hope in God, for I will yet praise him, my Savior and my God" (Psalm 42:4–5).

Lord, I take your hand. Lead me to an oasis of joy.

They are being tested by many troubles. . . .
But they are also filled with abundant joy.

2 CORINTHIANS 8:2

Bad things happen. Horrible, tragic, excruciatingly painful things happen. When they do, how can we possibly feel joy?

Joy is knowing that no matter what, God is with us, loves us, has a perfect plan, and is in control. "He is my fortress, I will not be shaken" (Psalm 62:6 NIV84). Nehemiah 8:10 says, "The joy of the Lord is your strength." Similarly, the strength of the Lord is our joy. The prophet Jeremiah reassures:

> [God says], "I know the plans I have for you . . . plans to prosper you and not to harm you, plans to give you hope and a future. Then you will call on me and come and pray to me, and I will listen to you. You will seek me and find me when you seek me with all your heart. I will be found by you," declares the Lord, "and will bring you back from captivity." (Jeremiah 29:11–14 NIV84)

As believers, "we have this hope as an anchor for the soul, firm and secure" (Hebrews 6:19). Knowing God will release us from pain's captivity brings joy. We don't have to "grieve like people who have no hope" (1 Thessalonians 4:13).

Paul wrote to the Philippians from prison, where he was in chains for his testimony. Yet in its four chapters, he uses the word *joy* (or a variant of it) sixteen times. Despite his troubles, Paul rejoiced in the Lord. We can too.

Whatever happens, may I always rejoice in you, Lord.

[PHILIPPIANS 3:1]

Now we see but a poor reflection as in a mirror;
then we shall see face to face.
Now I know in part; then I shall know fully.
1 CORINTHIANS 13:12 NIV84

I studied the black and white image. Another grandchild, another miracle, partially revealed in this ultrasound. I could certainly see a head. Maybe ears. And was that a leg? I attempted to inventory the parts, but most of the time I could only guess. Still, what a privilege and thrill to see even a hazy reflection of what was to come.

Later, when I held our newborn granddaughter in my arms, I stared in awe at her perfection. The once-so-important ultrasound image no longer mattered: I was seeing her face to face. The photo had intrigued me; seeing her in person was overwhelming. I now grasped fully marvel the ultrasound had allowed me only to imagine.

Is this how I'll feel when I meet Jesus? God's Word gives a glimpse of what it will be like. This life allows a hint of its joy. But as with our granddaughter's ultrasound, it's only a peek at, merely a taste of, the splendor that's to come. The Bible says no eye has seen nor mind conceived what "God has prepared for those who love him" (1 Corinthians 2:9 NIV84). Cuddling his masterpiece—our granddaughter, reminds me those words are true.

Lord, it amazes me that all the grandeur you've provided
on this earth is only a hazy indication of what eternity
with you will be like. I can only imagine.

—— JOY ——

We were filled with laughter, and we sang for joy.
Psalm 126:2

In *The Healing Power of Humor*, Allen Klein tells this story. . . .

Once upon a time there was a grumpy husband. Nothing his wife did made him happy. If she served him juice, he wanted prunes. If toast was buttered, he wanted it plain. If eggs were fried, he wanted them poached. Once, to stop the complaints, his wife fried one egg and poached the other. Looking at the plate, her husband grumbled, "You fried the wrong one."

I'm sometimes like that grumpy husband, finding fault with pretty much everything, determined not to smile or laugh. How ridiculous. What a waste. Joy and laughter are mine for the taking. Yet at times, for no good reason, I restrain myself. I don't know why. It's like choosing rotten apples instead of fresh.

How many times a day do you laugh? Not just smiles but let-loose laughter. My guess is the answer for all of us is . . . not enough.

King David, a man after God's own heart, wasn't afraid to laugh (1 Chronicles 15:29). Do we, like him, freely express those impulses, or wear an emotional corset? Why do we contain our laughter when there's no good reason to?

Being joyful and contagious with laughter is a way of thanking God for all he's done, for I'm sure that when we laugh, it brings him joy.

Lord, may my joy spread freely through laughter.

Though seeing, they do not see.

MATTHEW 13:13 NIV84

There's a game I play with my husband, David. He doesn't like it, but it makes a point—we can look, but not really see. My game is this: making sure I'm out of David's sight, I ask him what I'm wearing. Occasionally he gets it right. Sometimes he comes close. Usually he has no idea, even though he's been "seeing" me all day. I admit, knowing he'll immediately ask me the same question, I don't start the game until I first make sure I know what he's wearing, for often I don't really see him either.

There's a small, totally-white ceramic plaque on my study wall. Squiggly raised designs cover it. In its center is the word *JOY*. With the squiggles, *JOY* doesn't jump out. I have to look for it. Sometimes life is like that.

Look around your home. Focus on your favorite things and think about why you like them. Visualize one by one some of the blessings in your life. Outside, study a tree, look closely at a flower, absorb the sky's beauty. Pay attention to what you normally don't think about, like the ability to walk, see, taste, hear, touch, smell. Wiggle your fingers and toes. Take a deep breath and thank God for your lungs. Feel the joy of all that you too often take for granted. Open your eyes and heart. Look for and *see* the joy.

Open my eyes, Lord, that I may truly see.

*I am going to keep on being glad, for I know
that as you pray for me, and as the Holy Spirit helps me,
this is all going to turn out for my good.*

PHILIPPIANS 1:19 TLB

Over a hundred years ago, the book *Pollyanna* was published. It's the story of an eleven-year-old orphan who lives with her bitter, stern aunt. Pollyanna's optimistic attitude changes not only her aunt's life, but the lives of the townspeople. Her approach to living centers on what she calls the "Glad Game." Pollyanna and her father had received a missionary barrel in which she'd hoped to find a doll but found only a pair of crutches. Her father told her to be glad she didn't need them, and the Glad Game was invented. The game is: try to find, in everything, something to be glad about.

Actually, the Glad Game was born about 1,850 years earlier. The apostle Paul told the Philippians, in essence, if there is *anything* to be glad about, that is what they should fix their thoughts on (Philippians 4:8). When things look bleak, or struggles come, we can nonetheless look for and discover something to be glad about. No matter what, because God is with us, we can always be glad. As David said, "I have set the Lord always before me. Because he is at my right hand, I will not be shaken. Therefore, my heart is glad" (Psalm 16:8–9 NIV84).

I will be glad, Lord, and rejoice in you.

[PSALM 9:2 NIV84]

A glad heart makes a happy face.

PROVERBS 15:13

My mother gave me a book called *14,000 Things to Be Happy About* by Barbara Ann Kipfir. While 14,000 seems like a lot, I'd bet that, if we took the time, each of us could come up with an even greater number of things that have made and do make us happy.

What would be on your list of life's little joys? Mine would include coffee mugs, house turrets, columns on buildings, a juicy peach, fluffy clouds, the taste toothpaste leaves, sherbet-colored crayons, squirting pressurized whipped cream, watching my kids (and now my grandkids) eat their first ice cream cone, and the look on someone's face when they open a gift from me and it really is what they wanted.

Mentally listing my joys brought two observations. First: it was hard to stop. Second: it made me smile. (I could become addicted to joys-listing!)

It's fun and fascinating to see what comes to the forefront when I let my mind meander through life's little joys: the glitter of untouched snow in moonlight, salt-laden soft pretzels, phone calls from our kids, Handel's "Hallelujah" chorus. . . .

Driving, waiting in line, making dinner, bedtime—those times and many others, are all great times to inventory the joys God lavishes on us.

*Bountiful God, may I never stop counting
all you have given to be joyful about!*

Look! Here he comes, leaping across the mountains,
bounding over the hills.

SONG OF SONGS 2:8

I want to live with dog joy. . . .

We live on land that allows our Australian Shepherds, Sage and Montana, to run free. Each morning they quiver with anticipation. When I let them out, it's as if they've been shot out of a cannon. They tear headlong across the field, their joy obvious.

Another burst of joy comes when they hear "Let's go for a walk!" Sage stands wiggling by the door. Montana, despite his sixty pounds, jumps on my lap as I put on my shoes. Cuddling and shaking with delight, he can't contain his elation. If I take too long, he yelps his joyful anticipation. Outside, both dogs prance circles around me, zigging and zagging, streaking off periodically, then return, panting. "Let's go for a ride" initiates another eruption of joy as they run to the car and leap into the back seat.

It's not our dogs' energy level I envy—although I'd love to have that too. What I truly want is their unleashed joy at small pleasures. If we displayed that joy level, I'd bet God would wear a big smile.

Lord, may I not hesitate to let go and let loose with joy!
P.S. Thank you for my dogs and all they teach me!

> *The Lord is the Spirit, and wherever*
> *the Spirit of the Lord is, there is freedom.*
>
> 2 CORINTHIANS 3:17

Freedom. What a joyful word. Is there anyone who doesn't want to be free to live as they choose?

God put the love of freedom into human hearts. The psalmist felt it: "I prayed to the Lord, and the Lord answered me and set me free" (Psalm 118:5). God gifts us freedom to accept or reject him, to follow him or do as we please. Our choices have consequences, some major and eternal. If we use our freedom to choose God, he wants more than our obedience, and he despises empty religious rituals. God desires our hearts, voluntarily given. Forced love is no love at all.

America has long been known as the land of the free. In our founding freedom, we chose God, and labeled ourselves "one nation under God." The Bible says, "What joy for the nation whose God is the Lord" (Psalm 33:12). Now, many Americans use their freedom to reject or ignore God. Not coincidentally, the level of joy in our country has decreased dramatically.

I think God would agree with this statement from an unknown source: "If you love someone, you must let them go free. If they return to you, they are yours forever. If they don't, they never were."

> *Lord, I choose you. I pray that our nation*
> *and our world choose you as well.*

Joyful is the person who finds wisdom,
the one who gains understanding.

PROVERBS 2:13

Life teems with variety and complexity. It's a kaleidoscope of change requiring continual decision-making and navigation of twists, turns, obstacles, and surprises. From birth we learn what works and what doesn't, what hurts and what heals, what creates and what destroys. It's a slow and oftentimes painful process. Wisdom helps smooth the way. "If you need wisdom, ask our generous God, and he will give it to you" (James 1:5).

The Bible offers wisdom throughout, and the Old Testament book of Proverbs contains practical and wise observations about daily living. Its chapters 1–4, 8, and 9 extol the benefits of seeking and following godly wisdom: "Wisdom will enter your heart and knowledge will fill you with joy"; "I guide you in the way of wisdom and lead you along straight paths. . . . Hold on to instruction, do not let it go; guard it well, for it is your life" (Proverbs 2:10; 4:11, 13 NIV84).

Wisdom brings joy because it points us to the best choices for earthly life and for eternal life: "All who follow my [wisdom's] ways are joyful. . . . Joyful are those who listen to me. . . . For whoever finds me finds life" (Proverbs 8:32, 34–35).

Thank you, God, for the joy of knowing you'll show me the way.
Help me remember to ask for wisdom.

Give and you will receive.
LUKE 6:38

When our daughter Rachel was in high school, she volunteered with the organization Extra Hands for ALS. This group helps families dealing with amyotrophic lateral sclerosis, a progressive neurodegenerative disease. There is currently no cure.

At first Rachel was hesitant about volunteering. She wanted to spend her time with friends and sports, but college applications were looming. She knew that community service would bolster her resume, so she said yes.

Once she met Lisa, a mother with ALS, and her seven children, Rachel's reluctance to give any time turned into a desire to give more. For two years she spent four hours a week with them. She developed a deep respect and admiration for Lisa, a woman of faith Rachel describes as "the most phenomenal person I've ever met." Here are more thoughts from Rachel:

> It was crazy because Lisa knew she was dying, yet seemed happier than I often did with all my high school drama. . . . Being with her and her children taught me that giving isn't about material things; it's being there for each other, spending time together. Giving them joy gave me joy, as well as forever memories. We never know when we have just one day left. Lisa, who had every reason to be sad, was always laughing and giggling. She inspired me to emulate her uplifting spirit.

Thank you, Lord, for blessing us when we give to others.

He sets the prisoners free and gives them joy.
PSALM 68:6

Charles Dickens's *A Christmas Carol* never grows old. In it we see Ebenezer Scrooge, a cantankerous old man, locked in bitterness and greed, become a joyful, generous, congenial fellow. At the start, Scrooge was far from overflowing with the fruit of God's Spirit. His "bah humbug" ways blinded him to how foul he appeared and how unimportant his existence was to others.

But then Scrooge was visited by three spirits—Christmas Past, Christmas Present, and Christmas Yet to Come—and a transformation occurred. By letting Scrooge watch himself and other people's reactions to him, the spirits opened his eyes and heart to his need to change. And change he did. His joyful delight when he realized on Christmas that it wasn't too late to celebrate resonates in readers' hearts long after the story ends.

Like Scrooge, many people wander in a joyless land of their own making. Their gloom is habit, lack of awareness, and, most impactful, not making God their top priority. The joyous news is that with God, transformation can occur. "Whenever someone turns to the Lord, the veil is taken away. . . . So all of us who have had that veil removed can see and reflect the glory of the Lord" (2 Corinthians 3:16, 18). Bah humbug is no fun for the humbugger or the humbugees. Bah humbug is a joyless prison. On Christmas Day Jesus entered this world "to proclaim freedom for the prisoners and recovery of sight for the blind" (Luke 4:18 NIV84). God blessed us, every one.

---

*Thank you, Lord, for opening my eyes
and heart and setting me free.*

A cheerful look brings joy to the heart.

PROVERBS 15:30

I laughed when I saw my friend's Christmas pin.

"Had a tough week?" I asked. She looked puzzled.

"Your pin." I pointed to the red and green rhinestone piece that read "OH OH OH."

"Oh goodness," she said, unfastening the clasp and turning the jewelry to read "HO HO HO." "I didn't realize I was wearing it upside down!"

How many times have I felt "ho ho ho," but my face read "oh oh oh"? It's easy to let my face go limp even when I'm feeling joyful. So now, when I catch myself wearing a sullen expression, I make it a point to smile. (I also wonder whether others feel as glum as they look.) When we have the fruit of joy, it's a good thing to notify our face. We don't have to laugh out loud or do a jig. Simply turning the drooping corners of our mouth upward can make a difference in how we and those who see us feel.

I read about a woman who, for forty years, has intentionally not smiled or laughed . . . so she doesn't get wrinkles! She said that even when she feels happy, there's no need to display it. I disagree. Bring on the wrinkles, for when I consider the magnitude of joy God has allotted me, I've resolved to—as often as I can remember—show it on my face. If someone asks me why I'm smiling, I can tell them. It's joy.

Lord, I've been given so much ho ho ho,
let me not project oh oh oh.

For to us a child is born, to us a son is given,
and the government will be on his shoulders.
And he will be called Wonderful Counselor, Mighty God,
Everlasting Father, Prince of Peace.

ISAIAH 9:6 NIV84

"Silent night, holy night, all is calm, all is bright." Candle by candle, the sanctuary crescendoed with the light of Jesus on Christmas Eve. I looked down the row at each of my family's faces and joy flooded my soul. "Thank you, Lord," I whispered. "Thank you for the gift of your Son and of my precious family. Thank you, Jesus, for coming to earth to give us this joy."

Christmas Eve is a time of quiet and expectant joy as we anticipate Christmas Day, the celebration of Jesus's birth, and seeing our loved ones' faces as they open their gifts. I try to imagine what God must have felt on the threshold of his Son's birth. Here was the Gift to surpass all gifts, the One that would offer his children joy unimaginable. Its time had finally come.

What excitement and anticipation God must have felt. His joy was about to become our joy. This is the holy and magnificent anticipation of Christmas Eve.

———

Merry Christmas, God. Happy Birthday Jesus.
May the gifts we open on Christmas Day remind us
of your greatest gift of all.

Suddenly the angel was joined by a vast host of others—
the armies of heaven—praising God:
"Glory to God in the highest heaven," they sang,
"and peace on earth for all those pleasing him."

LUKE 2:13–14 TLB

A YouTube video brought me joyful tears: it was a flash mob at a shopping mall at Christmastime singing Handel's "Hallelujah" chorus.

As the video began, the camera panned normal holiday crowds. Suddenly one person stood and began to sing. They were soon joined by others in the planned choir that gradually became quite large. As beautiful as their singing was, most stirring was the crowd's reaction. Some people grinned. Others stared in wonder, stood at attention, knelt, took pictures, or joined in the singing. There was a palpable joy, a pause in the pandemonium, when awe and praise temporarily replaced hubbub. In this hectic, self-focused world, I found it heartwarming and reassuring to see a crowd stop its busyness and unite in singing "And he shall reign forever and ever, King of kings and Lord of lords!"

How wondrous that night-interrupted-by-singing over two thousand years ago must have been. Unsuspecting shepherds saw a lone angel appear and begin to sing. The angel was soon joined by the armies of heaven in soul-stirring praise to God. It must have been the flash mob to beat all flash mobs. Like today, the singing stopped the nearby humans in their tracks and filled their spirits with the joyous message, "Glory to God in the highest, and on earth peace, good will toward men" (Luke 2:14 KJV).

Lord, this Christmas season, may we frequently stop
whatever we're doing to rejoice in the birth of your Son.

You have made known to me the path of life;
you will fill me with joy in your presence.

PSALM 16:11

God led his chosen people from bondage in Egypt toward freedom in the Promised Land. Despite his faithful provision and protection, they grumbled and complained and were afraid to enter Canaan. Because they hadn't trusted him, God kept them wandering forty years. The forty years wasn't random: that length of time assured that none who had complained would enter that rest (Deuteronomy 1:26–40).

When the new generation was on the verge of entering the Promised Land, they had the same choice their parents had: they could choose life, or they could choose death. If the children of Israel returned to God and obeyed him with all their heart and soul, he would bless them. If they did not, they would bring curses upon themselves. God was clear: "I have set before you life and death, blessings and curses. Now choose life" (Deuteronomy 30:19 NIV84).

God's reference to life and death does not just mean literal living or dying, but to fullness of life and experiencing all the good he has planned for those who choose him: "If you keep the commands of the Lord your God and walk in obedience to him . . . the Lord will open the heavens, the storehouse of his bounty" (Deuteronomy 28:9, 12 NIV84). The choice remains for us today.

May I always choose life, Lord, in all its fullness and joy.

I want all of you to share that joy.
Yes, you should rejoice, and I will share your joy.

A plaque in my study reads, "Don't Forget to Be Awesome." Those words remind me that I want to give God my best. Just being "nice" isn't sufficient. Good isn't good enough. Pleasant isn't either. Fine is fine, but that's about it. I want to be awesome for God, for awesome is what he is for me.

Today, due to overuse, the word *awesome* is on the brink of losing much of its weighty meaning. Actually, it's already fallen over that brink. Yet, I still love the word. Awesomeness is contagious. It can change lives. It contains energy. It is thoroughly positive. It exudes joy. So despite the word's excessive use, I still want to be awesome—make that extra effort, go that additional mile, give that added push to everything I do—and not just accept "good enough." To be awesome, I need the constant help of our Awesome God.

I enjoy phoning my friend Karen, for one reason because I love to hear her say, "Bye-bye." She always sounds joyful. Perhaps I should consider a connection between her saying good-bye to me and her joy, but her conversations are upbeat from start to finish. And the happy lilt with which she concludes our talks sticks with me. It makes an impact. It's a form of awesomeness.

Actions speak louder than words. I don't want my actions to suggest I'm repressed, oppressed, or hard-pressed. I want them to be joyful, smile-full, life-full, spreading God's joy . . . awesomely.

Lord, help me be awesome—for you.

O Lord, you are my God; I will exalt you
and praise your name, for in perfect faithfulness you have done
marvelous things, things planned long ago.

ISAIAH 25:1 NIV84

As I sang in church today, the magnitude of God's love and perfect plan coursed through me. When I think of his creation, his blessings, answers to prayer, guidance, presence, plan, of all he is, has done, and will do, I'm overwhelmed. I'm amazed. And that's what we sang with these words from Charles H. Gabriel's "I Stand Amazed in the Presence":

> I stand amazed in the presence
> Of Jesus the Nazarene,
> And wonder how he could love me,
> A sinner, condemned, unclean.
>
> O how marvelous! O how wonderful!
> And my song shall ever be:
> O how marvelous! O how wonderful!
> Is my Savior's love for me!

Yet I've experienced only a single ray of the glorious sun of his wonders and power, only a taste of the magnificence to come. Jesus said, "I still have many things to say to you, but you are not able to bear them or to take them upon you or to grasp them" (John 16:12 AMP). Oh, how marvelous all that we know. How much greater the joy to come.

Joy upon joy my God. I sing, humbled with heartfelt praise.

*Now all glory to God, who is able to keep you from
falling away and will bring you with great joy
into his glorious presence without a single fault.*

JUDE 1:24

Revelation, the Bible's final book, sets forth the vision of end
times and eternity that Jesus revealed to the apostle John. Here
is part of it: "I heard what sounded like a great multitude, like
the roar of rushing waters and like loud peals of thunder, shouting: 'Hallelujah! For our Lord God Almighty reigns. Let us
rejoice and be glad and give him glory!'" (Revelation 19:6–7
NIV84). Heaven will include glorifying God forever.

Think back over your lifetime. Focus on moments that
were the most beautiful, on times when you felt like crying out,
"This is glorious!" Your times may be anything from delectable
meals, stirring symphonies, radiant sunrises, and breathtaking
mountain vistas, to profound love, the miracle of birth, the bliss
of a wedding, or gratitude for blessings. Reflect on whatever has
made your soul sing,

How did you feel at those moments? Pretty tremendous?
Now multiply those feelings by a number vast beyond measure.
That will give you an inkling of what it will feel like to glorify
God without end. It will feel indescribably grand, continually
and forever.

When we meet God face to face, we'll experience such
intensity of joy that we won't be able to keep ourselves from
shouting, "Hallelujah! For our Lord God Almighty reigns!" It
will be for his glory . . . from and to our joy.

---

*Lord, there's no greater joy than being so overwhelmed
by your magnificence that we want to glorify you forever.*

We will no longer be infants. . . .
We will in all things grow up into him
who is the Head, that is, Christ.
EPHESIANS 4:14–15 NIV84

Years ago, as I sat down to nurse our first child, he looked up and said, "I want a Coke."

My jaw dropped. I suddenly saw him with new eyes. He was two years old. No longer an infant. But because I was with him every day and growth is gradual, I hadn't realized how big he'd gotten. (I never nursed him again.)

We've all said or heard, "My, how you've grown!" When we don't see a child for a long time, we're often amazed at how much they've matured. Yet a parent, living with them daily, may still see them as younger.

We're at the end of our year's focus on living God's fruit. Over the course of this year, we've grown. Yet because our growth has been gradual, we may not have realized it. It's time to compare our present character and actions with those of a year ago and celebrate the growth that God and others undoubtedly see. But remember, when we choose photos to put in an album, we pick the best, not the worst. Assemble a mental album of your victories. Forget your slipups and backsliding. And, "thank God for all of this! It is he who makes us victorious!" (1 Corinthians 15:57 TLB).

Lord, when I'm tempted to focus on mistakes,
open my eyes with a "My, how you've grown!"

*I keep working toward that day when I will finally be
all that Christ saved me for and wants me to be.
Forgetting the past and looking forward to what lies ahead.*

PHILIPPIANS 3:12–13 TLB

Growing up, my sister and I played a walking game. We'd put our arms around each other's waist and walk side by side. One of us would be the leader, and the other would try to match their quickly changing steps. The challenge was to keep in step with the leader. It required constant focus, for the minute we didn't pay attention, our feet would no longer be in sync.

In the book of Galatians, after Paul lists the fruit of the Spirit, he says: "Since we live by the Spirit, let us keep in step with the Spirit" (Galatians 5:25 NIV84).

That's something to remember as we continue our journey to truly live these fruits every day we have left on this earth. To keep in step with the Spirit, we need to walk side by side with him, arms around each other, focusing intently on the Spirit's steps, carefully matching ours to his.

———————————————

*Thank you, God, for this year where I've learned so much
and come so far. I know the journey's not over.
Thank you that you'll walk with me every step of the way.*

THE JOURNEY CONTINUES . . .

I press on to take hold of that for which
Christ Jesus took hold of me.
PHILIPPIANS 3:12 NIV84

Lord God,
A year has passed since we embarked on this journey. You've been with me through it all. I've stumbled, I've fallen, I've gotten up again. I've kept on, steadied by your hand and embraced by your love.

I took this journey for me, yes, but more important, I took it for you. I want the abundant life you offer, but most of all, I want to give you the gift of me, of my loving you with all my heart, soul, mind, and strength. And that means sticking with you no matter life's circumstances, putting you first always, and obeying you in all that I do. Because I am human, that is a journey, one that will never end.

I celebrate that having focused on the fruit of your Spirit for a year, I'm further along on that journey than I've ever been. Ensure I never grow complacent or think I've arrived. I can always do better and more, and that is the gift I offer you. I will never stop trying to live as you've taught, my heart forever with you. Help me to never get tired of doing what is good, for I trust that at just the right time I will reap a harvest of blessing if I don't give up (Galatians 6:9).

I pray that I have made you smile, and that I will continue to make you smile throughout eternity.

Amen.

ABOUT THE AUTHOR

Kim Henry has been studying the Bible for more than twenty-five years and for two years taught a private Bible study on the fruit of the Spirit. She has also served as a Stephen Minister.

Since 2015 Kim has been a regular contributor to *Daily Guideposts*, an annual devotional book with a readership of over five hundred thousand each year.

She spent seventeen years as a corporate defense litigation attorney and eight years as vice-president of human resources for two major corporations, where her work involved extensive writing and speaking. Kim has an analytical mind tempered by humor and empathy, fired by a deep love for the Lord. She has a passion for self-improvement, a dogged determination, and a heart that seeks to understand.

Kim has three grown children and five grandchildren and lives with her husband in Colorado. She loves to spend time with family and friends, hike, take walks, work out, and lead a healthy lifestyle. Her travels to over seventy countries in the last several years have broadened her perspective and deepened her insight.

For more information, visit:
KimTaylorHenry.com

IF YOU ENJOYED THIS BOOK, WILL YOU CONSIDER SHARING THE MESSAGE WITH OTHERS?

Mention the book in a blog post or through Facebook, Twitter, Pinterest, or upload a picture through Instagram.

Recommend this book to those in your small group, book club, workplace, and classes.

Head over to facebook.com/worthypublishing, "LIKE" the page, and post a comment as to what you enjoyed the most.

Post a picture of the book on Instagram with the caption: "I recommend reading #MakingGodSmile by Kim Henry // @worthypub"

Pick up a copy for someone you know who would be challenged and encouraged by this message.

Write a book review online.

WORTHY®
PUBLISHING

Visit us at worthypublishing.com

twitter.com/worthypub

instagram.com/worthypub

facebook.com/worthypublishing

youtube.com/worthypublishing